THE SHAPE OF WINE

Grape wine has been produced for at least 4,000 years, having been aged, stored and transported in every conceivable type of vessel. Its seductiveness has been enhanced by this packaging: primarily three strikingly different containers – amphorae, wooden barrels and glass bottles.

Henry H. Work brings extensive wine experience as a cooper, working with wine barrels and living in California's Napa Valley to provide a richly detailed and vivid account of wine containers through the ages. This book delves into the history, evolution and present use of containers, vessels and stoppers; from animal skin sacks to barrels, from glass bottles to upstart packaging such as wine casks, and even aluminium cans. It considers the advantages and weaknesses of their construction, designs and labels, methods of shipment and storage, as well as their impact on marketing wine to customers.

This is an enlightening and innovative read which draws on the most current archaeological research, scientific data and wine business trends. It is richly peppered throughout with the author's own visits to many of the locations explored in the book, bringing history to life. This book will appeal to individuals within the wine industry as well as undergraduates in the fields of history, archaeology, food and hospitality, as well as all people interested in wine.

Henry H. Work has been involved in the wine industry for over 40 years. He has previously published *Wood, Whiskey and Wine: A History of Barrels* (2014) which explored his profession and passion for the wine industry. His research interests are in amphorae, wooden barrels, glass bottles and the world of wine.

ROUTLEDGE STUDIES OF GASTRONOMY, FOOD AND DRINK

Series Editor: C. Michael Hall, University of Canterbury, New Zealand

This groundbreaking series focuses on cutting edge research on key topics and contemporary issues in the area of gastronomy, food and drink to reflect the growing interest in these as academic disciplines as well as food movements as part of economic and social development. The books in the series are interdisciplinary and international in scope, considering not only culture and history but also contemporary issues facing the food industry, such as security of supply chains. By doing so the series will appeal to researchers, academics and practitioners in the fields of gastronomy and food studies, as well as related disciplines such as tourism, hospitality, leisure, hotel management, cultural studies, anthropology, geography and marketing.

Food Tourism and Regional Development
Edited by C. Michael Hall and Stephan Gössling

Food, Wine and China
A Tourism Perspective
Edited by Christof Pforr and Ian Phau

The Shape of Wine
Its Packaging Evolution
Henry H. Work

For more information about this series, please visit: https://www.routledge.com/Routledge-Studies-of-Gastronomy-Food-and-Drink/book-series/RSGFD

THE SHAPE OF WINE

Its Packaging Evolution

Henry H. Work

Routledge
Taylor & Francis Group

LONDON AND NEW YORK

First published 2019
by Routledge
2 Park Square, Milton Park, Abingdon, Oxon OX14 4RN

and by Routledge
711 Third Avenue, New York, NY 10017

Routledge is an imprint of the Taylor & Francis Group, an informa business

British Library Cataloguing-in-Publication Data
A catalogue record for this book is available from the British Library

Library of Congress Cataloging-in-Publication Data
A catalog record has been requested for this book

ISBN: 978-1-138-30086-6 (hbk)
ISBN: 978-1-138-30126-9 (pbk)
ISBN: 978-0-203-73263-2 (ebk)

Typeset in Bembo
by Taylor & Francis Books

Dedicated to the memory of Anne Marie Grosjean

CONTENTS

FIGURES

TABLES

EXPLORATIONS

ACKNOWLEDGEMENTS

For continued support, encouragement and listening to my complaints, I want to thank my wife, Karen Work. For their excellent assistance in editing and organizing the book, I thank my Taylor & Francis editors, Faye Leerink and Ruth Anderson. And for their warm and generous hospitality I thank Paul and Anne Marie Grosjean. It was from their Bordeaux-area home that Karen and I made many interesting forays to learn about the historic and current vessels used to shape wine.

INTRODUCTION

Over the past 8,000 years, wine has been packaged in three strikingly different containers – amphorae, wooden barrels and glass bottles. The amphorae and barrels have been used to make, store, age and ship wine; whilst the glass bottles have been primarily in use for aging and transportation. The story of these vessels, and their related containers, is intricately intertwined with the long history of wine; the amphorae in regular use for some 6,000 years, barrels for 2,000, and now glass is going on 300 years.

By the first millennium BCE, the amphora had become the container of choice for wine because of its ability to seal out oxygen and nest tightly in ships while being transported. These attributes also made it an ideal vessel to ship olive oil, grains and garum (the fermented, salty brines of small sea fish).

Barrels, too, have been used to store and transport numerous other products ranging from beer to whiskey, animal hides to tobacco, and cheese rennet to whale oil. They kept the wine or the other contents safe from the environment, the predations of rats and insects, and unscrupulous workers. Additionally, compared to the dense ceramic amphorae, their capacity is far greater for the weight of the container. Yet, despite the heaviness of some of their products, such as wine or water, barrels can be easily moved simply by rolling.

For glass bottles, wine of course is just one of the many liquids (liquors, juices, yogurts, medicines and spices, etc.) and foods (apple and tomato sauces, pickles, peanut butter, and preserves) which are transported, sold or stored in glass.

The point of mentioning these traits and other products is that the manufacturing capabilities and limitations, the designs and labels, the methods of shipment and storage, the intended usage for individuals or groups of people, and the marketing aspects for their individual products have all influenced how these containers have been transported, bought and sold. This has been true for wine as well as for the other commodities. As often as not, an important aspect for one industry has had carry over into another.

Today's wine no longer moves in amphorae or wooden barrels, but usually in glass bottles enclosed in cardboard cases. Often these are shipped on trucks for regional distribution, or in metal containers, stacked upon ships, for intercontinental delivery. Among the hundreds of complex trading routes, wine will go from New Zealand and Australia to the United Kingdom, from Chile, Argentina or South Africa to the United States, or from the US, France and Italy to the rest of the world.

Some 2,000 years ago, the network for shipping wine was just as complicated, although the distances were not as great. Then, traders were shipping wine across the Mediterranean and into Europe and to a lesser degree throughout the Middle East and Asia. In this large arena and for thousands of years, the amphora was the 'container' of choice. During the era of the Roman Empire there was a slow shift to barrels. Only within the last several hundred years have we seen barrels replaced largely by glass bottles.

While wine seems to have been a driving force for how the containers were utilized, this cannot be assumed. The wine, like the olive oil and garum, needed an air tight container which the amphora provided. But which came first? Did the amphorae evolve out of the generic need for a ceramic container which could keep out oxygen? Or did the ancient traders and the vintners, garum and olive oil producers all find that the amphorae best fitted their unique and separate shipping container requirements?

For barrels, it seems logical that they were developed to more easily transport larger quantities of wine. But equally, could they have been built primarily for beer or to keep rodents out of grains or flour storage?

And the history of glass dates to well before the technology was available to construct bottles, either by moulds or by blowing. Yet the routine shipping of wine in bottles was an afterthought only once the ability to make the vessels large and strong enough evolved in the eighteenth century.

My interest in these containers started first with the barrels. I was a cooper, a barrel maker, by trade; working with wine barrels, and to a lesser extent the barrels destined for bourbon and whiskey and whisky. My wife, Karen, was in the hospitality business as a caterer and chef. Later, she grew grapes; making and marketed her resulting wine. Living in California's Napa Valley, these professions naturally involved us in the world of wine.

Our travels, both for business and pleasure, have taken us to many of the world's wine regions. Those journeys, to Europe in particular, have introduced us to the history of wine's culture, and by extension, its packaging throughout the ages. A number of specific visits are included in the 'Explorations', to add a personal dimension to the vessel's narratives.

We commence by examining the earliest evidence of wine and the vessels used to contain and package it. The investigation then shifts to the amphorae as they came into prominence, the barrel as it rolled into the first millennium of the current era, and the factors which made the wine bottle the container of the moment. Additionally, we will explore some of the newer materials now packaging wine, as well as the various large bulk wine containers. Finally, we look at some of the peripheral materials and the issues involved in packaging wine.

Additionally, metric measures are denoted, unless a specific regional unit is more appropriate, and years are delineated as BCE – Before the Common Era, the equivalent of BC; and CE – the Common Era, the equivalent of AD.

1

ANIMAL HIDE SACKS AND EARLY CERAMIC POTS AND JUGS

Wild grapes

Our Neolithic hunter–gatherer predecessors roamed far and wide for their next meal. Recent archaeological studies have found that these peoples' understandings of the flora and fauna of their environment has been under-appreciated (McGovern, 2009). More specifically, the evidence of their wine making skills is being pushed back further and further into the past. Let us start by looking at what kinds of vessels our winemaking forebears might have used.

What to put it in?

Wine takes its place on the altar of those few precious items that undergo long journeys in order for people, far and wide, to enjoy them. To this end, the story of the vessels used for wine is intertwined with the methods to first make the wine, and then to transport to it to the next town, across the Mediterranean, or around the world.

Before ceramic containers were invented, the Neolithic hunter–gatherer peoples must have sought natural receptacles to store and transport a variety of liquids (McGovern, 2009). Most probably the earliest need for those containers was to carry water in dry locations. Later they would need vessels for wine, and once they started domesticating animals, containers would have been required for milk and yogurt. Before the invention of ceramic pots, these containers were most likely a piece of wood with a natural depression, a gourd or large nut, a sea shell, or even a piece of animal gut or hide. Later, perhaps, fibre baskets would be added to their list of possible containers. All would have worked relatively well, and be, to one degree or another, adaptable to the nomadic lifestyle.

Nevertheless, all those vessels had shortcomings. The wood, the nut and the shell would have been difficult to close to keep the liquid from sloshing out if it was being transported. The animal skin might have impacted the flavour, as could have the gourd. Thus, one can imagine that those early people were constantly seeking other alternatives and materials which had all the attributes they required for their liquid and particular travel or storage situation.

Pottery did not appear to be one of these vessels until relatively recently. Evidence that people started moulding clay and then firing it, or at least baking it in the hot sun, suggests it started about 25,000 years ago (Cooper, 2000). Clear archaeological conformation of man making pots and bowls, however, does not appear until the Jomon culture of Japan, dated to about 12,000 years ago. By about 9,000 years ago pottery started showing up in the Middle Nile Valley (Cooper, 2000).

Related to the vessels used for wine, at some point our forebears realized that prolonged exposure to oxygen was detrimental. Or at least they recognized that wine left in an open bowl or pot turns bad. Eventually they must have made the connection that putting wine in ceramic pots and jars, those made with small openings which could then be sealed, remained drinkable longer.

As the working with pottery evolved, before glazes were developed, the insides would have been smoothed with stones to minimize the porosity (Cooper, 2000). Later, the interior was glazed, or coated with resins or pitches to reduce seepage or the contact with air, and to minimize any negative tastes. Until the pots and jars evolved to the long, thin, amphorae shape, transporting the bulbous styles would not have been easy.

The initial pots and jars would have been small. Slowly, as ceramic technology improved, their size was increased to hold more and more wine or other liquids. The majority of the archaeological remains indicate that, as the wine making evolved, some of these large earthenware jars were partially or fully buried in the ground to keep the contents cool, as well as to reduce the evaporation. It is likely then that the wine would have been dipped or ladled out into smaller jars or into animal skin sacs for transporting further afield.

During the past century of archaeological digs and finds, many of the ceramic pots and jars dated to well before the current era (before Christ) have been assumed to contain wine, or wine-like liquids. The key word, however, is 'assumed', as no actual wine has been found; an occasional residue yes, but their original organic contents dried up and decomposed hundreds or thousands of years ago.

How do we know those jars contained wine? Until recently, it was at best educated speculation: was there a red residue inside the jars; have grapes pips been found in or near the jars; was there a hieroglyph or stamp on the container which indicated wine contents; or were the jars or pots in an area where native wild grapes grew?

In an age of more rigorous science, however, that secondary evidence is not quite good enough. We now realize that there were many other possibilities for fruit concoctions which the ancient peoples could have been making (McGovern, 2009). In the past 20 years the archaeological inquiry into what vessels actually held wine has evolved from speculation to fact. Science now has the ability to examine the portions of residue, detailing the contents of those vessels with far greater accuracy.

One man who has pioneered these investigations is Dr Patrick E. McGovern.[1] Skilfully combining his biochemical competence and his passion to unravel some of the ancient mysteries of wine and beer, he has travelled the world to provide rigorous scientific testing of the oldest vessels believed to contain wine and other alcoholic beverages (Penn Museum, 2018).

McGovern suggests that the first alcoholic beverage was honey and rain water naturally fermented in a notch of a tree, hundreds of thousands of years ago (McGovern, 2009). Fast forward to our hunter–gatherer forebears living in Africa, then migrating on to Europe and into Asia. Whether they collected this concoction, or even whether they were able to duplicate it in a vessel, is unknown. At this point there is no evidence, at least none has been found; whatever vessels were potentially used have likely long since rotted away.

McGovern theorizes these ancient peoples might have made wine, initially perhaps accidently, later with some understanding of what they were doing. In the greater Middle East and China, the Eurasian variety (*Vitis vinifera* sp. *sylvestris*) of wild grapes was available (McGovern, 2009). Those vines have been around at least for 50 million years (Lukacs, 2012). As hunter–gatherer tribes moved through the river valleys during the late summer and early fall, they gathered the wild grapes. If, instead of eating them right off the vine, they placed them in vessels – wooden bowls, gourds, or an animal sack – some juice would have seeped from the grapes to the bottom of the vessel (McGovern, 2009). The juice may have tasted as good as eating the grapes.

Further, if perhaps some juice was left in the gourds or wooden vessels, it would have fermented naturally. "Owing to natural yeast on the skins, it gradually ferments [the grapes] into a low-alcohol wine", McGovern suggests, "a kind of Stone Age Beaujolais Nouveau" (2009). Upon tasting of the juice, the ancient peoples would have noticed the 'sugariness' of the grape had been replaced by a 'sweetness' from the alcohol, along with a complexity of flavours and aromas. Left too long, of course, eventually they would have detected a tart, sour flavour, that which we now associate with vinegar – the oxidation by bacteria of the alcohol in the wine into acetic acid and ethyl acetate.

A few opportunities of 'hitting the booze' at the right time – just after fermentation and before the vinegar set in – and some of these peoples probably thought this was pretty good stuff. Perhaps they even thought of it as a 'nectar from the gods' (Suckling, 2007), although that phrase did not come about until government leaders saw the advantage of controlling the use of wine or priests started utilizing it in their services, and the poets wrote about it, these lines from John Milton being some of the most famous:

> Though in Heaven the trees
>
> Of life ambrosial fruitage bear, and vines
>
> Yield nectar …
> *(Masson, 1890: 293)*

Eventually, the early people figured out the ideal time to pick the grapes, which containers facilitated fermenting the juice, and when best to drink it. Along with using materials for the vessels that did not impact the flavour of the wine, the ability to close or cap the container would have been one of the most important early milestones in winemaking technology (McGovern, 2009). Ceramic bowls and pots became key containers, although precisely how or when has yet to be discovered.

Further on, early 'vintners' must have experimented with adding flavourings to the wines. At some point, they learned that various additives – such as terebinth, a resin from a pistachio tree – preserved the juice. Other additives were used to change or enhance the wine flavours such as pine and cedar resins, frankincense and myrrh (McGovern, 2009). Lacking other forms of sugar, honey was a common addition to sweeten tart or sour wines.

Archaeologists suggest that many peoples could have discovered the enjoyment of fermented grapes, or other fruits such as figs, baobab fruit, or sweet gourds, at various times and in various places. For the nomadic tribes, thousands of years of exploring the flora of Africa, Europe and Asia must have resulted in numerous experiences with fermented fruit. The evolutionary changes of the flora, the people's understandings of them, along with vessels to collect and store the resulting harvest, can only suggest that over time, the ideal fruits and the methods to process them, became standardized for each group of people.

Making wine in a clay jar

If some of the first vessels used to contain fermented wine were wooden, the early wine makers may have realized that they were not ideal. Wine in a shallow wooden bowl, with its large surface exposed to the air, would have quickly turned to vinegar. Nor, until barrels and enclosed tanks were developed in the last millennium BCE, could a wooden container have been large enough to hold any significant volume of juice. A vessel in the shape of a hollow tube of some sort – say bamboo or the like – might have been better at minimizing the oxygen contact, especially if it could have been stoppered. It may, however, have also introduced off-flavours into the wine.

Another problem with utilizing wooden containers occurs during re-use. Over time, microorganisms hide and accumulate in the pores and crevasses of the wood. While some of these, like yeasts, are helpful, others are not. They create moulds which impact the wine's flavours. Even today's wine barrels are not immune. Despite rigorous cleaning, overtime the bacteria build up. Most wineries do not keep their barrels used to make table wines much longer than ten or 15 years.

The first hints that pottery was used for wine-type liquids was during the Neolithic period in China, roughly 7000 to 5600 BCE. McGovern and his Chinese colleagues have found traces of wine residue in ceramic jars dating from that period at the Jiahu site in Henn Province, south of Beijing and west of Shanghai. From several of the jars the scientific team was able to extract a residue. Using high-tech equipment – "liquid chromatography-mass spectrometry, carbon and nitrogen isotope analysis, and infrared spectrometry" (McGovern, 2009) – they were able to determine that the contents were a fermented beverage made from either grapes or hawthorn fruit (both of which grew wild in the area), with honey and rice added.

The jars they were examining were the shape of a bulbous amphora; two handles with a narrow opening at the top, and capacities of between 15 to 30 litres. The shape would have been a reasonable size for pottery – large enough to store a significant quantity of liquid though still smallish and not too heavy in order to move them about if necessary.

If the liquid did contain the grapes, as opposed to the hawthorn fruit, it was probably the world's first documented grape 'wine' (McGovern, 2009). But McGovern wonders why, with the apparent migration of man out of Africa, passing through the Middle East before eventually reaching China, wine was not made there first. Perhaps it was, but archaeologists have yet to find that early evidence. Or the earliest possible vintners in the Middle East had yet to discover how to make clay bowls and jars. If they were using wood or animal skin sacks, most likely those types of containers would have long since decomposed, lost as clues or evidence to their efforts.

Middle Eastern wine

To examine the next oldest archaeological evidence of wine we jump to the Middle East. For a number of years, excavations of historic sites have taken place in the mountainous area between the Black and Caspian Seas. This is now the region encompassing eastern Turkey, northern Iran and Iraq, Georgia, Armenia and Azerbaijan. It is known to have the wild Eurasian grape (*Vitis vinifera* sp. *sylvestris*). As the scientists prowl among the ruins, they uncover older and older evidence of winemaking.

Recently, two sites have shown evidence of winemaking, going back to 6000 to 5800 BCE; about 8,000 years ago. Working in Georgia, an international group of archaeologists have been excavating the ruins of two small villages, Shulaveris Gora and Gadachrili Gora, located about 50 kilometres south of the present-day capital of Tbilisi (McGovern et. al., 2017). Among the uncovered relics have been the sherds of large pots. Some of these sherds are definitely the bases, or portions of the base, of these containers. It was these pieces which were chosen to be tested, as they were the most likely to yield any wine residue. The results of the chemical analysis showed positive for tartaric acid, a clear indicator of wine. The plant and animal remains' in the soil next to the sherds provided accurate dating of the pots and wine.

The next oldest site, relative to finds of winemaking equipment, is to the south, found in a Neolithic village, Hajji Firuz Tepe. McGovern and his colleagues (2009) discovered ceramic containers there which are 7,000 years old, dated from 5400 to 5000 BCE. The site is located in the northern Zagros Mountains in what is now Iran.

Arranged next to a wall in what is believed to be a kitchen of one of the village houses were six ceramic jars set into the floor. Each of these were of about nine litres capacity, and had narrow openings. Clay stoppers were also found at the site. McGovern (2009) subjected scrapings from the jars to his rigorous chemical analysis. Some were found to contain the tartaric acid; another contained resins, which were added to wines as preservatives.

The start of commercial winemaking

Eventually winemaking was taken to a larger scale. A cave, designated Areni-1, in the rugged mountains of Armenia, the general area of the two historic sites noted above, appears to be the site of the world's oldest 'winery' (Owen, 2011). Or at least it is a location where quantities appear to have been made for more than just a few people. The site is about 70

FIGURE 1.1 Underground in the Areni-1 cave complex
Smithsonian Institution, by Sossi Madzounian

kilometres south of Yerevan, Armenia's capital, and 50 kilometres east of the historic Mount Ararat (which is now in Turkish territory).

After people started using the cave, at some point a portion of the roof collapsed, sealing in the secrets of the winery and its artefacts. There they lay until 2006, when a team of archaeologists from UCLA and Ireland began a dig within the cave. After several years of excavation, they uncovered a 60-centimetre deep ceramic vat, of about 55 litres capacity. This large clay jar was positioned beneath a shallow, 1 metre long basin, also made with hardened clay (Owen, 2011). Similar arrangements of a grape stomping trough placed above a large pot remained into Egyptian and Roman times, as murals and the finds in those eras attest (Caillaud, 2014).

At Areni-1, the grapes would have been placed in this shallow trough to be trodden by foot. The juice from the stomping then flowed by gravity into the vat where it was left for fermentation. Other ceramic jars, some set into the cave's floor to keep them cool, have been found, suggesting further storage and aging. These artefacts date back over six thousand years, to 4100 BCE in what has been termed the Copper Age, and the capacity of the vat and jars suggest winemaking on a large scale.

The archaeologists examined the insides of the jars with the same industriousness as McGovern and discovered malvidin, which is one of the pigments responsible for wine's red colour. As *Vitis vinifera* is one source of the chemical, this is a good indicator for wine. McGovern, however, while applauding the find of the trough and jars also suggested that instead of wine, the malvidin could have come from other fruits, such as the pomegranate (Owen, 2011). If it turns out that the source of the malvidin was wine grapes, then a large winemaking facility, such as found in the Areni-1 cave, indicates that grapes probably had been domesticated by about 4500 BCE.

At the cave, the archaeologists also uncovered 20 burials. Some of these had drinking cups laid in with the bodies. As the site is in a remote area, if the wine was not traded, it possibly suggests that the drinking of wine was part of the funeral ceremony (Owen, 2011). While we do not yet know the entire rational for the burials alongside the winemaking equipment, the age, style and materials of the winemaking equipment are nonetheless important notes in wine's expanding history.

Wine: a growing industry

Although not nearly as old, further evidence has been found of another Middle Eastern commercial winemaking facility. This was from a site dated at between 3500 to 3100 BCE (McGovern, 2009). The site is Godin Tepe, also in the Zagros Mountains of western Iran. Despite an elevation of 1500 metres, this ancient village was on a trade route that extended east from at least Afghanistan, and west to the Mesopotamia plains of now Iraq. It is entirely possible that the wine was one of the traded items (McGovern, 2009).

Here again, ceramic vessels had been in use, probably to make the wine, but not transport it. At Godin Tepe, the jars had bulbous bodies, with some of the attributes of the later amphora style – long necks (to facilitate pouring) and a small opening that could have been stoppered (McGovern, 2009). On the exterior of the jar's head and foot, rope-like designs had been embossed, with their purpose unclear. Several archaeologists suggest that ropes could have been used to hold the jars on their sides (McGovern, 2009; Morris, 2013). The reason, they propose, would have been to keep the clay stoppers moist; the same rational for positioning wine bottles with cork stoppers horizontally. This method of keeping the seals tight reduces the possibility of oxygen entering to spoil the wine. Additional support for the theory that the large jars were placed on their sides was the discovery of 'red deposits' on just one side of the jar's interior, where the lees would accumulate. McGovern's testing confirmed that these deposits were indeed wine.

McGovern and his archaeological team also encountered an unusual method for removing the seals from the jars; unusual at least in the sense of what we would consider either intuitive or practical. When the wine was ready to be removed, the jars were apparently turned upright. Instead of unseating the clay plug, the whole of the top appeared to have been sliced off (McGovern, 2009), much like the dramatic opening of a champagne bottle with a sabre. McGovern suggests this was to keep the debris from the stopper from falling into the wine whilst being removed. He further notes that this hacking-the-top-off method was used as well for amphorae in Egypt's New Kingdom, some 1,500 years later (McGovern, 2009).

This is puzzling; why would the jars have been purposely destroyed, at least for further use for wine storage? Especially so if the potters had taken the time and effort to emboss the ropes on the clay. Were the jars so easy to make that even 3,000 years ago they were 'throw-away' items? How could portions of the clay stopper impact the wine if the wine had been in contact with it while the jar was laying on its side? Did bacterial contamination overcome those ceramic jars as it does with wood? Additionally, was the wine to be poured into smaller containers or was it to be drunk at that time;

perhaps through straws? These are additional questions for the archae-ologist's research.[2]

Further examination of the jars revealed another method of removing the wine, or at least a portion of the wine. Drilled through the sidewall of the jars was a small hole. It was high enough above the bottom of the jar to avoid getting any sediment or residue (McGovern, 2009). At about ten centimetres off the bottom, could it have been to empty the contents? It would have been a slow process. Or was it simply for sampling the wine? A hole to extract wine for sampling is not so unusual. Some wine barrels have a small hole in which a wooden spile or spike is utilized to release a flow of wine into a glass or beaker for testing. Additionally, wooden wine vats and stainless-steel tanks have spigots for sampling the wine.

Investigations in a subsequent room yielded a number of large jars of about 60 litres. This was probably a room where the wine was fermented, or at least stored. Perhaps the wine was ladled out of these jars into the smaller ones or animal skins for transporting. While no ladles were found, a large funnel was (McGovern, 2009), supporting the theory. Funnels have been found in numerous sites – both those from the Iron Age to more recent excavations in Turkey and Syria (McGovern, 2009).

Winemaking around the Mediterranean

By the fourth to third millennium BCE, grape growing and winemaking had spread around the north-eastern end of the Mediterranean. In 2015, a team of archaeologists discovered remnants of wine in ceramic jars hidden deep within some volcanic caves on the southwestern end of Sicily (Tanasi, 2018). Analysis of 100 milligram samples scraped from a collection of these pots revealed that wine was one of the food stuffs contained within them. Since these containers were found well into the cave, it is believed that they were associated with offerings for gods and/or food for the afterlife of the people who were laid to rest in that site.

Related to this finding of wine in that region, some copper tools and utensils also have been discovered in and near the caves. Interestingly, Sicily has no ores from which to make the copper pieces. Tanasi (2018) believes that to obtain the copper items, or the raw ore with which to smelt them, the wine was currency of trade with the Peloponnesian peoples of Greece for these commodities.

The wine culture was spreading; we move next to Greece. Most probably, the viticulture and winemaking in any given locale was more widespread than the spotlight on these isolated sites indicate. Additionally, it may have been accelerated in any given region by new ideas passed along with the trade between the communities. Our time line of the locations is irregular as these are the only sites where wine residues and equipment have been found.

In northern Greece, the site of Dikili Tash yielded grape pips as well as two handled mugs, typical of wine drinking, and very possibly indicating a wine culture dating back to about 4200 BCE (Valamoti et al., 2007).

Because of the heat, wild grapes did not grow in Egypt (McGovern et. al., 2009). Nonetheless, once the early rulers of Dynasties 1 and 2, roughly 3000 to 2700 BCE, developed a taste for imported wine, they decided to grow their own, domesticated grapes. McGovern believes that their imported wine was coming from near the Jordan Valley; present-day Palestine. It has been suggested that they sourced that same area to import grape vines, along with viticultural specialists to plant, set up irrigation and grow the vines, and winemakers to make the wine (McGovern et. al., 2009).

Some of this history is known through written reports and hieroglyphics. To test that wine definitely was what the written narratives and images were referring to, McGovern and colleagues decided to examine several Egyptian containers purported to hold wine (McGovern et. al., 2009).

The team chose vessels from two different sites and 3,500 years apart. One sample for testing was from a ceramic jar found in a tomb at Abydos on the middle Nile River in Upper Egypt, dated to about 3150 BCE. A second sample was from an amphora dated from 400 to 600 CE, found in a tomb at Gebel Adda, in Lower Nubia in southern Egypt. This later period represented the final phase of Egyptian winemaking before the Islamic conquest in about 600 CE.

The initial jar was one of about 700 in the tomb, and is believed to have come from the Levant, perhaps used to transport the wine. Its residue showed traces of tartrates, again a clear indicator that at one point, wine had been stored in the vessel.

The amphora for the second sample was identified, by an inscription on the shoulder, as a type of ceramic vessel typically used to transport wine. The sample from this amphora also indicated tartrates (McGovern et. al., 2009).

What is interesting for our discussion is the switch from a bulbous jar to a sleek amphora. The jar was certainly suitable to store wine if it had a good closure, but inefficient to transport it. The amphora was excellent for shipping wine, as well as a sealed storage container. However, as the large numbers indicate, many must have been used to contain a significant quantity of wine.

FIGURE 1.2 Egyptian amphora wine-jar of Nedjmet, circa 1340–1300 BCE
Trustees of the British Museum

FIGURE 1.3 Early Crete unglazed amphora, 2050 to 1550 BCE, Middle Minoan
period
Trustees of the British Museum

Back to the Middle East

To gain some understanding of the wine culture – amounts being made and
consumed – around the Middle East in the first millennium BCE, we turn to a
recorded historical event. In about 870 BCE, the Mesopotamian people had
completed a new capital city, Nimrod, a site north of present-day Bagdad. As a
celebration, King Ashurnasirpal II put on a grand feast for some 70,000 of his
subjects. Massive amounts of food were served, and the guests washed it all

down with 10,000 skins each of beer and wine. Most of the diners would have been impressed to be served the wine. Having been imported from vineyards in the distant hills to the northwest, the transportation added significantly to the price; it cost ten times that of the locally made beer (Standage, 2005). This huge amount of wine indicates that the Assyrians had developed an elaborate culture of drinking wine. Along with its associated rituals, "Wine and drinking paraphernalia", as British science and technology writer Tom Standage suggests, had "became emblems of power, prosperity and privilege" (2005).

When Nimrod was excavated in the early twentieth century, one stone relief showed King Ashurnasirpal II sitting on a throne, holding what is probably a shallow, gold bowl of wine (Standage, 2005). Sadly, it is believed that this relief has recently been destroyed by ISIS (Arraf, 2015).

By 785 BCE, cuneiform tablets of the Assyrian Nimrod people indicate that each of some 6,000 people in the royal household was receiving a daily ration of wine. Most of the people received one *qa* (the equivalent of about 1 litre), divided up among 10 people, while skilled workers got one *qa* per six (Standage, 2005).

The records indicate the use of animal skin sacs and ceramic jars, but the use of amphorae to ship the wine appears be more of a Mediterranean tradition. Wine was shipped down the Tigris and Euphrates rivers, as noted by Greek historian Herodotus in 430 BCE that in their boats "their chief freight is wine" (Standage, 2005). However, the boats were made of pulpy wood or reed, which lasted just the down-river trip. That type of construction of the boats suggests that they may have been too flimsy to carry a load of wine in amphorae, with the additional weight of the ceramics. If amphorae were not in use, most likely larger ceramic vessels were used in the 'wineries', and wine was, at least in this region and period, transported in animal hide or gut sacks.

By the seventh century BCE, wine growing had pushed westward with the Greeks producing wine on a large commercial scale, growing grapes in Arcadia and Sparta on the Peloponnese peninsula, then spreading eastward to Attica and Athens (Standage, 2005).

By the first millennium BCE, around the Mediterranean the ceramic amphora became the wine container of choice for shipping and some storage of wine. However, before we move on to explore these containers in Chapter Two, if you have a chance to visit Bordeaux's newest shrine to wine, La Cité du Vin, do so. There, in a stunning complex, the entire history of wine is wonderfully encapsulated, including details on the amphorae.

FIGURE 1.4 La Cité du Vin, Bordeaux
Karen Work

EXPLORATIONS 1.1
LA CITÉ DU VIN IN BORDEAUX, THE WINE TRADING CAPITAL

Open to the public in 2016, *La Cité du Vin*'s uniquely designed building rises out of the rusting industrial landscape north of the Chartrons, Bordeaux's historic wine trade district. The main building resembles an oblong torus, encased in glistening stainless steel. At one end is an eight-story wing, with a tasting room at the top. Skyward-stretching glass panels twist about this tower, offering an impression of a giant swirl of wine gushing out of a glass.

An edifice this striking and devoted entirely to the history of wine is fitting for Bordeaux. For this is a city which has one of the longest and most continuous associations with growing, making and selling wine.

For our visit to La Cité du Vin educational museum, my wife and I took one of the cities' modern trams; just five stops from Bordeaux's centre. Alighting from the tram gave us our first close look at the building. The initial impression was of a building with a uniquely different shape. It is totally un-classic – so radically dissimilar to Bordeaux's lovely limestone edifices – making a preliminary appreciation difficult. Once inside, however, any disparagement was quickly cast aside.

The main exhibition hall in La Cité du Vin contains its extensive permanent displays. These arrays of mostly hands-on stations do a superb job covering all facets of wine – the long history of grape growing and winemaking, the selling and trade in wine, world-wide regional differences, as well as the etiquette of serving wine. In the course of these presentations, all the vessels of wine – the amphorae, barrels, and bottles – as well as the accoutrements of wine service – glasses, decanters, labels, etc. – are examined and explained.

The many presentations are accomplished with an amazing array of high-tech gadgets and multimedia displays. Take, for example, the pairing of wine with food: As a visitor to La Cité du Vin, you sit at a simulated restaurant table while virtual plates and glasses of wine are offered. On the backs of facing chairs, the real-life images of a chef, a wine writer and a sommelier are projected. Over the course of a 'meal', these virtual people discuss the pairing of the wines with different foods as if they were sitting right across the table from you.

Further in the museum, workshops, specific tours, sensory tastings, and extensive wine libraries – ones both for books and another of wine – along with a gift shop and restaurant, complement the total presentation.

Most tours end up in the tasting room, located in the building's top floor. With a panoramic view of the Bordeaux landscape, and a wonderful clear wine bottle chandelier-cum-art-sculpture sparkling overhead, the visitor is able to taste a variety of wines from producers and regions from around the world; a fitting way to end a 'tour' of the world of wine.

La Cité du Vin is undoubtedly the most extensive presentation on the total world of wine I have ever experienced. Like La Cité du Vin, Bordeaux is certainly unique. Mention Bordeaux almost anywhere in the world, and the majority of people will either recognize it as the French city of wine fame, or at least a wine region. Either way, it is a well-known entity having marketed itself successfully for over the past 2,000 years; for well before the Romans took over Gaul, Bordeaux was transshipping wine in amphorae.

Thus, as we explore all the containers and vessels utilized for wine, it is fitting to incorporate Bordeaux – and the Chartrons specifically – as the pivot, a home base if you will. Through it we can view the various vessels which have been used to store, age, and package and transport wine. While Bordeaux was not where the first commercial wines were made – China, Egypt and the Middle East holding that distinction – it has certainly played a major role. Along Bordeaux's river banks, amphorae were lugged by slaves off boats, the staves for the wooden barrels arrived to make the casks which were subsequently used to store and ship the wine, and by the eighteenth century a glass factory had been built to produce wine bottles.

Conclusion

The earliest wines were made in natural containers – wood, shells, gourds, animal skins. Ceramic vessels start showing up around 12,000 years ago, gradually getting larger as wine making shifted from making it for just a family or village to making it on a commercial scale. However, until the shape which we associate with amphorae – long, narrow – evolved, most likely wine was transported in animal hide sacks.

Notes

1 As of this writing, Dr Patrick E. McGovern is the Scientific Director of the Biomolecular Archaeology Project for Cuisine, Fermented Beverages, and Health at the University of Pennsylvania Museum in Philadelphia, and an Adjunct Professor of Anthropology.
2 See McGovern, 2009; Morris, 2013: pp. 70–9; and Dietrich et al., 2012: pp. 674–95.

References

Arraf, J. (2015). ISIL fighters bulldoze ancient Assyrian Palace in Iraq. *Aljazeera News*, [online] 6 March 2015.

Caillaud, C. (2014). Les céramiques et le vin: élaboration, stockage, commerce, de l'Antiquité à l'époque moderne, de l'amphore aux tinajas. In: *1er Colloque International, La terra cotta e il vino*. Imprunta, Italy: Artenova, [online] pp. 4–89.

Cooper, E. (2000). *Ten Thousand Years of Pottery*. Philadelphia, PA: University of Pennsylvania Press.

Dietrich, O., Heun, M., Notroff, J., Schmidt, K. and Zarnkow, M. (2012, September). The role of cult and feasting in the emergence of neolithic communities.

New evidence from Göbekli Tepe, South-eastern Turkey. *Antiquity*, 86(333), pp. 674–695.

Lukacs, P. (2012). *Inventing Wine: A New History of One of the World's Most Ancient Pleasures.* New York: W. W. Norton & Co.

Masson, D. (1890). *The Poetical Works of John Milton.* Vol. II. London: Macmillan and Co.

McGovern, P. E. (2009). *Uncorking the Past: The Quest for Wine, Beer, and Other Alcoholic Beverages.* Berkeley: University of California Press.

McGovern, P. E., Mirzoian, A., Hall, G. R., and Bar-Yosef, O. (2009). Ancient Egyptian herbal wines. *Proceedings of the National Academy of Sciences of the United States of America*, 106(18), pp. 7361–7366.

McGovern, P., Jalabadze, M., Batiuk, S., Callahan, M. P., Smith, K. E., Hall, G. R., Kvavadze, E., Maghradze, D., Rusishvili, N., Bouby, L., Failla, O., Cola, G., Mariani, L., Boaretto, E., Bacilieri, R., This, P., Wales, N. and Lordkipanidze, D. (2017). Early neolithic wine of Georgia in the South Caucasus. *Proceedings of the National Academy of Sciences of the United States of America*, [online] 13 November 2017.

Morris, S. P. (2013). From clay to milk in Mediterranean prehistory: tracking a special vessel. *Backdirt: Annual Review of the Cotsen Institute of Archaeology at UCLA*, [online] pp. 70–79.

Owen, J. (2011). Earliest known winery found in Armenian cave. *National Geographic News*, [online] 12 January 2011.

Standage, T. (2005). *A History of the World in Six Glasses.* New York: Walker and Co.

Tanasi, D. (2018). Prehistoric wine discovered in inaccessible caves forces a rethink of ancient Sicilian culture. *The Conversation*, [online] 13 February 2018.

Valamoti, S.M., Mangafa, M., Koukouli-Chrysanthaki, C., Malamidou, D. (2007). Grape-pressings from Northern Greece: the earliest wine in the Aegean? *Antiquity*, 81, pp. 54–61.

Website

Penn Museum (2018). Patrick E. McGovern, Biomolecular Archaeology Project. www.penn.museum.com

Blog

Suckling, J. (2007). Nectar of the Gods. James Suckling uncorked. *Wine Spectator*, 5 November 2007.

2

AMPHORAE

That woman could put on a grand party

Towards the middle of the final millennium BCE, the amphora was the primary vessel in which wine was being transported from Italy, and to a lesser extent from Greece and Spain, to the Celtic leaders throughout northern Europe. In return, the Gauls sent tin, cattle and slaves south. Eventually, as the Romans invaded and placed their administrators and soldiers in strongholds throughout Europe, they too requested the elixir of the grape. Again, it came initially in amphorae.

EXPLORATIONS 2.1
THE LADY OF VIX AND AMPHORAE

Throughout central and southern France, museums, *oppida* – the Celtic forts – and the remains of Roman villas, all tell a story of a vast trading network in which wine was one of the main commodities. Recent visits to a number of these note that up until the beginning of the first millennium CE, the wine was shipped in amphorae. Those historical sites showed that during the Celtic era there was lot of wine sloshing around the countryside.

The wine-containing amphorae followed several primary routes into what is now Europe; generally, in boats and barges along the main rivers. To the west of the Alps, wine was either shipped to Marseille to go north by barge up the Rhône, or to Narbonne to be hauled across the Entre-deux-Mers towards Bordeaux where it was transferred to ships to be transported up the Atlantic coast. East of the Alps, it would generally travel up the Danube.

The Côte d'Or, now famous for its Burgundian wines, was on one of the extended paths of the northern Rhône route. Not so long ago, archaeologists found what appeared to be an ancient, undisturbed tomb. This was a spectacular find. Even in 1953 it was especially rare, as most of the significant graves have, over the years, been robbed of anything of apparent value. This particular tomb was in central France, about 200 kilometres southeast of Paris. It turned out to be the grave of a Celtic woman of significant means; perhaps a noble lady. She died in about 480 BCE. Once her tomb and the unique accoutrements accompanying her to the afterlife became publicized, she was described as the *Lady of Vix*, a reference to her stature and to the small, Seine River village nearby to where she was found.[1]

Her remains were discovered in a *tumulus*, or burial mound. Below the heaped-up earth was a pit, about as large as the average bed room. Its walls were lined with logs. As the archaeologists who uncovered her grave surmise, once her body had been placed in this room, the roof too was covered with wooden beams, and atop them, soil to a thickness of several metres. At some point during the 2,500 years since she was entombed, the logs rotted and the roof collapsed. This was actually fortunate; it helped to preserve her and her belongings from the decaying effects of oxygen, as well as to keep them safe from grave robbers.

The archaeologists found her remains lying in an elaborately decorated wooden wagon; its four wheels neatly stacked against one wall. Around her neck was an exquisite gold torc, adorned with two tiny winged horses at the bulbous ends. Torcs were worn by the Celtic warriors. The fact that she had one may have indicated her fighting prowess. Several bronze brooches, intended to retain her toga-like garments, also were discovered with the body. These pins were inlayed with coral and amber; neither are native to the area and would have been imported to this middle-of-France region.

What does this have to do with amphorae and wine? Certainly, the finding of an intact tomb, and especially one of a noble woman from 2,500 years ago, was incredible in and of itself. Among her other treasures were a bronze *oenochoe* (wine pitcher), a two-handled wine drinking cup from Greece, and, most spectacularly, an elegant bronze *krater*. Kraters are bowls or basins which were typically used by the Greek, Roman and Celtic elite to mix water with their wine prior to serving. The mixing was intended to dilute a very heavy, heady wine or make the precious liquid go further.

The krater found in the grave of the Lady of Vix is unique not only for its size – at about 1100 litres, the largest ever unearthed – but also because of its Grecian design. It has two elaborate handles sporting the heads of Gorgons adorned with tiny lions. Encircling the upper edge of the krater is a richly detailed frieze displaying a procession of Greek soldiers, some on foot and others in chariots.

France and wine; what could be more natural? Except that during the era of the Lady of Vix, there were no domesticated wine grapes being grown in that part of France. What was she doing with such a large container, one which could theoretically hold enough wine for several hundred people?

Although possibly they picked wild grapes to eat, it is not believed that the Celtic tribes living 2,500 years ago in what is now France were growing grapes for wine. The best evidence indicates that wine grape growing and wine making only first appeared in the Languedoc and Roussillon – southern regions of France – from about 150 to 100 BCE some 300 years *after* the Lady of Vix died. By 50 BCE, the planting of vineyards is thought to have expanded to the west towards Bordeaux and north towards Lyon (Loughton, 2014). Yet, apparently the Celtic nobility loved wine – and 1100 litres will treat a lot of quests. How did this krater get to this part of France? Its story is tied to how wine – apparently copious amounts of it – was transported to France in the first millennium BCE.

The majority of wine being shipped to the north came from Italy, from numerous vineyards, in amphorae made by its regional potters. Additionally, there is increasing evidence that some of the wine was originating in Spain and southern France in amphorae made in those areas as well. A portion of the wine was also shipped across the Mediterranean from the Greek isles. It was trans-shipped through Marseille, as at that time the city was run by the Greeks and known as Marsala

(Loughton, 2014). This may account for the Grecian design on the krater which was found with the Lady of Vix.

Although, of course, we cannot assume the krater was actually utilized for wine. It could have been just a symbol of her stature or wealth; set out to impress people but never filled. The residue in the vessel was not tested. In the 1950s when it was discovered, it was decided that such a unique find could not be displayed in a small, isolated village; it needed to go to Paris. It was most likely cleaned of any residue prior to being transported to the capital city. Additionally, the instruments available to accurately test a residue for wine were not in existence, and that era's archivists, knowing it was a krater, would have just naturally made the assumption of its use.

Historian Robert Wernick (2005) suggests that the krater might have been a part of a legend; a gift of the Spartans to the Greek King Croesus, described by Herodotus. According to this myth, it was then stolen by the Samians. Conjecture beyond that is that it became part of probably more than a few spectacular items which were traded around the Mediterranean; status symbols of precious and rare art used as political bribes or to make a few merchants wealthy. Others believe that it was fabricated in Italy by Greek craftsmen, thus the style. Either way, somehow it ended up with this Celtic noblewoman.

Ancient trade routes

How wine in amphorae, the krater and the other magnificent wine-serving paraphernalia found their way to what was a rather remote place is still somewhat of a mystery. One explanation lies in the fact that the village of Vix is near the highest navigable point on the Seine River. It is thought that the Celtic chieftains controlled such trading avenues – the river reaches and the overland passes. In return for passage though these territories, the rulers received gifts – Greek ceramics and other finished pieces in bronze (Chaume, 2013). It was the traders who were transporting, among other items, the wine in amphorae.

Tin was one of the important items the traders took south. It would have been in the form of *blooms*, or raw, manageable chunks of ore. It was being shipped from the mines in Cornwall. From those pits, it was sailed across

FIGURE 2.1 Lady of Vix krater
Musée du Pays Châillonnais – Trésor de Vix by Mathieu Rabaud

the Channel and paddled, poled or hauled in boats and barges up the Seine eventually to be delivered to the smiths in southern France and Italy. Before iron smelting became established in Europe, lumps of tin were added to copper to make bronze, making it a significantly harder, stronger metal. Bronze was prized and utilized for implements like swords and tools for the Roman soldiers, craftsmen and farmers, or the incredible art objects like the Vix krater. These tin ore blooms could have also been being transported to

Celtic bronze workshops, such as the ones in Bibracte, the capital of another Celtic tribe, the Aedui, located a short distance to the south. The small community of Vix is about six kilometres north and downstream from the larger town of Châtillon-sur-Seine. Vix sits at the base of a steep, flat-toped hill. Atop that hill, the remains of a Celtic oppidum – a fortified town – have been discovered. It was at the base of the hill that the grave of the Lady of Vix was uncovered in a necropolis, an area of tombs. Most probably, she was associated with the tribe who inhabited the oppidum, or used it in times of war. It has also been suggested that she was the head of the tribe, as men and women in the Celtic tribes were often considered equal (Knüsel, 2002). At the very least she must have been associated with the nobility of the tribe to warrant such an elaborate, treasure-filled tomb.

Above the town of Vix, the Seine River becomes too shallow for the movement of boats and barges. The traders would have off-loaded their goods for the 100-kilometre overland trip, southeast via Dijon, to the Saône River, the northern extension of the Rhône River. Traders going south to Lyon and then on down the Rhône to Marseilles, or heading north to Paris and on to Britain, would have only this short overland stretch in which to carry their wares by donkey with pack saddles, or in horse or oxen-drawn carts.

Otherwise the entire trip would have utilized the rivers which afforded far easier and more efficient means to transport goods, especially the heavy amphorae, in the days before substantial, all-weather roads. Additionally, as this Cote-d'Or region consists of mostly rolling hills with low passes, they would have been easily negotiated, even with pack animals heavily loaded with amphorae or blooms of tin.

Also found with the krater in the grave of the Lady of Vix was a Grecian bronze pitcher for wine and in a similar-era grave in Lavau, an Etruscan ceramic pitcher – red background with black figures (Urbanus, 2015). These items, in both graves, indicate a strong wine culture existing 2500 years ago in the Celtic tribes, and an active trading network which could transport many litres of wine in the amphorae, as well as the various wine paraphernalia.

The amphorae

Early twentieth-century archaeologists were dazzled by the spectacular finds of glazed pots and bowls, ceramic figures and funerary urns. These, mostly men, thoroughly described their finds, but largely failed to analyse how these items were enmeshed in the cultures in which they were found. Or as Greek archaeologist Mimika Giannopoulou put it in discussing *pithoi* – large ceramic jars – how "very important [these items were] for the study of the economy, domestic and public, particularly for the prehistoric period, for which there is no other evidence except material remains" (2010).

Today's scientists are very much concerned about how any and all finds relate to their historical period. They recognize that while some types of ceramic bowls or pots were used to contain the earliest wines, those with the shape which we now recognize as amphorae most likely only evolved in a) settled areas where there were grapes to make the wine or olives to make oil, and b) where there was a need to transport these two liquids (Cooper, 2000). For wine, these criteria limited the development of its growing and making to the mid-latitudes where the Eurasian grape (*Vitis vinifera* sp. *sylvestris*) grew, such as around the greater Mediterranean – Portugal in the west, Germany in the north, Iran to the east, and Morocco to the south, and particularly the Caucasus where the first evidence of wine making began so long ago (McGovern, 2009). Iran was on east–west trade routes, and did have large earthen jars for storing wine, but with fewer rivers, the idea of using amphorae on donkeys or camels does not seem practical, at least as a starting point. Moving wine in skin sacs appears more logical (Cooper, 2000).

Lukacs (2012) believes that the narrow amphora style was developed first in Egypt. Its slender shape would have enhanced the shipping of amphorae full of wine in boats on the Nile River as well as across the Mediterranean and Red seas. The Egyptian royalty, like the Celtic royalty, fell in love with wine, but as they had no native species, they had to import it, in amphorae. The Egyptian/eastern Mediterranean style of amphorae, with its pointed tip, would have facilitated setting them in the sandy river banks while loading or unloading ships.

However, since the Egyptians initially imported wine, most likely from the Levant, until they could develop their own vineyards (McGovern et. al., 2009), it is possible that they only developed the narrow-style for the amphorae as a more efficient way to bring wine to their shores. Nevertheless, it seems more reasonable that this pointed style was developed in locations which would be closer to the vineyards – in or near the ports on the Black, Caspian or eastern Mediterranean seas – in order for the vintners and traders to utilize the amphorae on the ships which transported their finished wine to other markets.

Regardless of where the amphorae were first developed, it still begs the question; were the first narrow-styled amphorae created for wine or olive oil? And this is a question yet to be answered.

Mass produced – amphorae details

The amphorae made during the second and first millennium before the Common Era came in an enormous variety of shapes, sizes and styles. Amphorae capacities ranged from 7 to 80 litres, with the wine amphorae typically within the 20 to 30 litres sizes (Twede, 2002). They were being made, probably a better term would be mass produced, in every major community around the Mediterranean, and to a lesser extent at sites along the major river ways flowing into that sea (Quercia et al., 2011).

The word amphora (plural amphorae) is Latin, from the Greek word *amphoreus*, but the shape – long and slender, with two handles – seemed to have evolved in numerous styles and in many locales. The evolution of these various permutations is obscure, as are the factors which influenced the potters who made the amphorae, the merchants who employed them and the traders who transported them. While the generalities about the trade routes have long been known, actual information about the products and the traders themselves is only now being understood as terrestrial archaeologists continue to delve into the remains of the Eurasian trading sites, and marine archaeologists dive the wrecks of trading ships.

Most probably the reasons for crafting amphorae one way or another melded together. Likely it was a question of push and pull: the potters attempting to make a saleable product quickly and inexpensively; the vintners and olive oil producers wanting the most efficient vessels for storing and transporting their wine and oil; and the traders wanting a reliable vessel for the commodities they were attempting to move, in keeping with the methods they were utilizing for their journeys.

For the potter, the size and shape of the opening would have been determined by what type of seal or cover was to be utilized. Stretching animal hide across the opening would have required a rim to facilitate tying on the skin with a cord to keep it in place during a long, rough journey. If a clay plug was used, it would have required an evenly rounded, V-shaped opening into which it could be tightly seated. Even with a bit of wax, reed, or a clay slip to use as a gasket, to tightly seat a clay plug, an accurate circular opening would have been required. Wooden or cork bungs are more forgiving of irregularities. However, they too were often overlaid with a clay seal (Twede, 2002).

For wine, and a few other liquids such as olive oil and garum, minimizing the exposure to air was a critical requirement. Thus, the historic ceramic vessels for transporting and aging wine, other than the kraters for mixing the wine, all have openings with small diameters, whether they were used for transportation or not.

Most amphorae have longish necks. Besides facilitating the sealing, this would have assisted in emptying the amphorae by controlling the volume of liquid being poured out. Because the amphorae with its liquid content was heavy, it would have been back-breaking to cradle the amphora in order to discharge the contents. They could have been set upon the lip of a large pot if that is what they were being poured into. Otherwise, it would seem practical to set the amphora upon some kind of sawbuck (sawhorse) or bar which was utilized as a fulcrum to aid in emptying the wine out slowly. The larger ceramic jars, such as those found in the Areni-1 cave or at the Godin Tepe site, were too large to pour. As many have been found set halfway into the ground, a scoop or ladle of some sort must have been utilized.

Handling and lifting the containers were other requirements. Thus, a long, thin vessel with handles came into being. For the workers who had to haul the amphorae, a narrow vessel would have been easier than a bulbous one, either to carry along one's side or to sling over one's shoulder. Numerous reliefs and murals depict men hauling an amphora upon their shoulders. The handles first appeared in about 1500 BCE with the Canaanites, on the Syrian-Lebanese coast (Twede, 2002). They would have facilitated lifting, as well as tying on to a pole slung between the shoulders of two workers. The narrow base would have allowed the amphora to be rolled in a vertical position, with the handles assisting in controlling it (Twede, 2002; Gallimore, 2010).

However, moving loaded amphorae around must not have been easy. I have lifted a few; even when empty they are heavy and bulky. With amphorae in use for well over two millennia, obviously the traders, or at least their slaves, adapted.

Here, perhaps, the design flaw, or the limitation of the amphorae if you will, is exposed. The amphora may have been the ideal container for the time, but it is not a particularly efficient vessel. It was ideal in several ways. Making ceramic vessels in the Middle East was practical; clay was a cheap and widely available resource, and a warm, dry climate in which to dry the products was the norm; whereas the extensive forests of straight-grained wood, such as needed to construct barrels, were not. Working all but the softer woods would have been difficult with bronze tools. The harder woods, such as oak, could only have been reasonably worked by iron tools, which did not come into general use until about 1200 BCE (Tylecote, 1976), several thousand years after amphorae first started being utilized. The ceramics of an amphora could cool liquids by evaporation if it was porous, or could keep liquids relatively stable, fresh, and odour-free if it had a smoothed, glazed or pitched interior.

Most likely the long, thin shape evolved as the amphorae's role for transporting liquids become increasingly important. That shape might have been adapted equally well to carrying on pack animals, such as camels or donkeys, and nesting in the holds of boats and barges. The major disadvantage, however, was that the long, thin shape reduced the capacity of the amphorae, providing significant weight for a limited capacity.

Further, a pointed bottom did assist in keeping the amphorae steadier in a ship facing rolling seas. Although, over the years, the hard tips of these amphorae probably did no good to the interior of a ship, grinding away at the relatively soft wood if any movement was allowed as the ship rocked and swayed with the waves. In museums today, we see re-creations of amphorae stacked in the ship's holds. Often, they are placed in a lattice network of wood with the amphorae nested in the gaps. Besides helping to stabilize the load, perhaps a secondary purpose of these lattice of poles or boards was to keep the tips of the amphorae from scraping the bottom of the boat. These lattice frameworks were easily replaceable, a ship's interior bottom only with great difficulty.

Finally, with the amphorae remaining as the primary container for transporting liquids in the Mediterranean for several thousand years, there was an element of tradition. Because their father or mother did it a certain way, subsequent generations of potters kept making the same thing over and over, for hundreds, if not thousands of years. Only serious disruptions can overcome the resistance to change.

**EXPLORATIONS 2.2
VISITS TO OTHER FORMER CELTIC STRONGHOLDS:
CHÂTEAUMEILLANT – A TREASURE TROVE OF
AMPHORAE**

Besides being transported along the river ways, amphorae were occasionally moved into the Gaul countryside. Throughout the centre of France, the remains of Roman walls and bits of pottery abound; the

French have long been aware of their Celtic ancestors and the Roman incursions into their regions. To find out more about this, my wife and I visited the village of Châteaumeillant, south of the large central French city of Bourges. (Bourges was called *Avaricon* by the Celts, and *Avaricum* by the Romans.) I had read of the small town of Châteaumeillant in which some 600 Gallo-Roman amphorae had been found in various caches throughout the village. Thinking that perhaps it might yield further information, I booked a room at the local hotel and drove northeast from Bordeaux. Serendipitously, we hit pay dirt.

For the village of Châteaumeillant, the real finds of the amphorae only started in 1956. The story goes that a local man was visiting a friend's garden. As they admired the vegetables and flowers, in one section the ground gave way and the visitor fell into an old pit. Unhurt, but realizing he may have stumbled upon more than just a pit, he asked if he could start digging. Sharing the enthusiasm of his friend, the gardener agreed. While they did not find any great bronze or gold treasure, they hit upon a goldmine of amphorae, mostly empty, but also mostly intact (Stillwell et al., 1976).

Word of the trove of amphorae was hard to keep secret. As the gossip spread, everyone in the village started to look more seriously in their wells and old outhouses, and at the odd depressions in the ground. Other caches of amphorae began showing up. At one site, some 60 amphorae were found. Then the questions started: What were all these amphorae doing in this middle of France location, a village seemingly far from the river trading routes? (At this time in 1956, the artefacts associated with the Lady of Vix were still being analysed, with their implications yet to be fully understood.) Why and when were the amphorae hidden? Most were empty, but some still had their seals still intact, although the liquid was long since gone. What had they contained?

The townspeople, as well as scholars, suggested numerous answers. One thought was that the town was a distribution centre for wine, olive oil and garum imported and transported up the rivers and then overland, from Italy and Spain, prior to Caesar's invasions of Gaul. Others thought that these caches were the storage places for some Celtic nobility who hid the amphorae from the invading Romans. If the amphorae had held wine, perhaps these were the remains of one fantastically great party. Initially, most of these theories were possible. More importantly, these questions prompted a broader examination of the area's history.

One major discovery was that the town was actually sitting upon an ancient Celtic oppidum. Another one, as it turns out, as subsequent archaeological research has identified some 200 of these fortified hill-tops. They were built in the second and first centuries BCE by the 29 Celtic tribes, spread from Germany to Spain (Casey, 2013). Deciphering part of Caesar's *Commentarii de Bello Gallico* – his descriptions of attacking and occupying France – it is believed that this particular oppidum was the one he called *Mediolanum*. However, by the time he and his legionnaires got to it, it had been burned. This destruction was part of a defensive, scorched-earth policy, dictated by the local Celtic leader Vercingetorix, when, in 52 BCE, the Roman legionnaires were making their final invasion (Stillwell et al., 1976; McDevitte et al., 1869).

In Châteaumeillant, serious archaeological digs, aimed at understanding the nature of the oppidum and its people, commenced in 2001 under the supervision of Professor Sophie Krausz, of Bordeaux's Montaigne University. Over the next several summers, she and her excavation teams of tanned and mud-covered diggers started making some significant finds, as well as developing the chronology and interpreting the data related to the amphorae. Many of the artefacts and much of the detailed interpretation of the finds have been subsequently displayed in the town's Musée archéologique Émile Chénon. This museum is small, but well organized, with a wealth of information about the amphorae and the Mediolanum oppidum.

Professor Krausz' research enabled her to date the oppidum; construction commenced in about 200 BCE and was fortified in about 100 BCE (Krausz, 2007). This is a similar time-line for many of Europe's oppida. Having sacked Rome in 390 BCE, the Celtic tribes must have thereafter realized that Rome had them in its retaliatory sights. However, after Caesar's invasions and once Gaul was under Roman control, this now Gallo-Roman village rose from the ashes and lasted from about 50 BCE to 476 CE (Krausz, 2007).

Krausz and her colleagues also found that some of the Gauls in Châteaumeillant were seriously interested in wine. It seems the town was a commercial centre, and centre for several Roman roads (Krausz, 2007). Most probably it was the nobility and/or the increasingly prosperous merchants and craftspeople who were able to afford this luxury. These were the people who were making the money from the escalating trade with Rome – slaves, tin (for bronze), cattle and perhaps grains and cheeses sent south, which in turn brought wine, fancy vases and urns, and jewellery and other luxury items.

Obviously, this trade was well established and had been going on for a long time, as the finds in the Lady of Vix's tomb attest. Unlike the village of Vix, which was on a major river trade route, towns like Châteaumeillant were not fully involved into the wine trade until after the Romans came and the road system became more fully developed (Krausz, 2007).

In their search for the history of the oppidum, Krausz and her team located a number of ancient wells. Digging down in these has shown they held some exceptional artefacts. In 2012, a small bronze lion weighing 3.6kg was found and dated to about the second or third century CE (Krausz, 2007). Was this possibly another gift of a trader like the krater to the Lady of Vix? Or was it just a beautiful object that a person of wealth in the town could afford? At this point it is uncertain how the lion got to Châteaumeillant and who might have owned it.

In another well, a horsehead spout, perhaps used to empty the wine from a grape stomping trough, and a beautiful bronze oenochoe, thought to have been imported from Pompeii, were extracted from the muck and rubble dumped into these wells over the past 2,000 years. These items indicate a culture in which wine was part of the everyday life.

Of the numerous amphorae which have been found throughout the town, the oldest has been dated to about 200–150 BCE. They were of a Greek-Italian style, and it has been determined that they contained wine. Interestingly, while the amphora style changed somewhere between 135 and 50 BCE to an Italian-made type, the wine appears to have still been obtained from the same Italian vineyards. This was probably due to a shift at the vineyard; from purchasing foreign amphorae to ship their wine towards purchasing them from a local ceramic factory or making their own (Krausz, 2007).

By 50 BCE, Gaul was under Roman control. Research about the amphorae indicates that after 50 BCE the wine was being shipped from Italy, northern Spain and southern Gaul; the olive oil from southern Spain and Portugal; and the *saumures* (fish sauce) was Lyonnaise, although perhaps the fish were caught in the Mediterranean and then processed or re-packaged in Lyon. Then from 27 to 14 BCE the amphorae style changed again, now coming from the western Mediterranean. These amphorae had contained both foods (olive oil and fish sauce) and liquids. There was another change after the second century CE (Krausz, 2007).

This large number of amphorae and luxury goods in a small village far from the major rivers indicates a complex trade network extending throughout the northern European countryside. Taken together, this system and the products it transported, reinforce the idea that wine, along with magnificent vessels, such as the Vix krater, or smaller but exquisite items such as the Châteaumeillant lion, could have made their way into the centre of France. Before the Roman invasions, the Celtic towns and villages processed and produced products – grains, perhaps minerals or clays, meat, cheeses, etc. – which Romans and others wanted. There must have been numerous itinerant traders moving these commodities by cart, donkey, and where possible boat and barge. In turn, the prosperity created from this trade – making money from the selling of products or charging taxes on the movement of goods – allowed the nobility, and the craftsmen and farmers, to get their wine, and occasionally unique pieces of statuary or jewellery.

[Additionally, the hotel in Châteaumeillant turned out to be a gem; a wonderful host, a comfortable room, tasty and properly portioned meals, and of course good local Meneton-Selon (Haute-Loire region) wine.]

EXPLORATIONS 2.3
VISIT TO ANOTHER CELTIC STRONGHOLD – THE OPPIDUM OF BIBRACTE

The Celtic oppidum of Bibracte sits atop the 800 metre Mont Beuvray. Bibracte is 140 kilometres east of Châteaumeillant and 120 kilometres south of Vix. It has steep sides, but rather than peaked, its summit stretches out over several hundred hectares of gently sloping fields and forests. Lower down, on a saddle of the mountain, there is now an excellent museum. Despite being a formidable hill, it was another fortress that faced, and subsequently fell, to Caesar's legionnaires. Additionally, despite the elevation, thousands of wine amphorae – broken shards and intact vessels – have been found in the archaeological digs atop the mountain. Over the years of its habitation, a huge amount of wine was hauled, by hand or with animals, up to that Celtic encampment.

The displays in the Bibracte museum offer the visitor a thorough insight into understanding of the historical importance of the Bibracte site. A small restaurant nearby even offers a Celtic-style meal – consisting mostly of legumes and pork – but no Roman wine to accompany the repast. To view the ruins atop the hill, a mini bus will take the visitors up the steep hillside. I chose to walk. I wanted to experience what it might have been like for its inhabitants, those of the Celtic Aeduni tribe, as they climbed the hill to their homes at the end of the day. For me, it was just past noon and I was still relatively fresh. They, on the other hand, making the climb at dusk might have been tired from tending their crops or watching their herds and flocks on the lower slopes. Additionally, they might have had to haul up the wood for their night's cooking fires. Or they might have had the extra burden of lugging an amphora of wine or a bag of salt to their abodes. I also wanted to feel the breathlessness the Roman legionnaires might have experienced after advancing rapidly up through the lower forests and pastures to raid the oppidum, and who then had to repel the spears and arrows from the Celtic defenders to surmount the bulwarks.

The walking track takes one up through a forest of mature oak, chestnut and beech. Opening into a meadow near the top, the breathless visitor is confronted by the tall *murus gallicus* – the oppidum's surrounding protective walls built in a distinctive Celtic style. The original walls have long since been destroyed or fallen apart. This one, the *Porte du Rebout*, at an original gate site, has had two sections re-constructed to serve as examples of those historic ramparts. Looking up at the steep rock-covered walls topped by vertical timbers, I felt dwarfed as I entered between them. Once within these oppidum 'walls', I climbed the ramparts and looked down. Despite their substantial appearance, I could feel a bit of the fear the defenders must have felt while watching hordes of shielded and battle-hardened Roman legionnaires march up the slopes.

This oppidum site, like so many other Celtic forts, was strategically chosen. Sitting atop Mount Beuvray, the large expanse of relatively flat hilltop had several springs. Except where the gate was, the sides of the mountain fall away abruptly, providing the Celtic lookouts views of all the surrounding valleys below. From where I looked down, it was easy to see east into the Arroux River valley, the main artery along which any marching army might approach.

Stretched along the top of the hill are a number of ruins; houses, farms and workshops. More than a few of the latter were used by blacksmiths for bronze and iron work, indicating that Bibracte was an important centre for metal products. In another area stands the rocky outline of a Greek-style villa which was built after the Romans took over. It is reported that this was where Julius Caesar stayed to write his memoirs (Caesar, 1869).

While people probably lived on and about the hill prior to it becoming an oppidum, it really was not developed defensively until about 150 BCE. Aerial photographs have picked out two defensive walls – one about 5 kilometres in circumference and the other of some 7 kilometres. Both enclose a huge area, enough to protect perhaps several thousand inhabitants in times of war.

Over the years, the various archaeological digs – and there were at least three ongoing under tented roofs when I visited – have extracted thousands of amphorae shards, and numerous whole amphorae. The researchers surmise that these containers brought enough Italian wine, and possibly wine from the new vineyards in southern France, such that the consumption of wine filtered down through every layer of the population. It should be remembered that vineyards in France were only just starting to be planted around 150 BCE along the Mediterranean coasts (Loughton, 2014; Anonymous, 2013) and plantings not yet reached Lyon on the Rhine by the time of the Bibracte settlement.

Again, the evidence from these amphorae indicates a far-reaching and complex trading network. As the crow flies, Bibracte is only about 60 kilometres from the Saône River, the northern extension of the Rhône, whereas Châteaumeillant is some 100 kilometres. Items could be barged up or down the Saône, but anything coming or going to these and other oppida to the Saône's ports had to go overland.

There is emerging evidence that the Celts had built substantial, all-weather roads (Salač, 2010). We have seen that the Lady of Vix was laid in an elaborate wooden cart. While hers may have been purely ceremonial, it was most likely designed on existing models and technology. The methods and issues of transportation of wine – on land and at sea – will be discussed in greater detail in Chapter 10.

Amphorae production

As the amphorae were increasingly demanded in the greater Mediterranean trading system, not only for wine, but also for other liquids and occasionally grains and small fish, this must have pushed the potters into making them more and more efficiently, on a commercial scale. The fabrication process evolved from initially hand coiling the pots to throwing them on a foot-powered potter's wheel. Due to their size, it was usually a multistep process, with time allowed for intermittent drying, as well as building sections of the amphorae then combining the body, base and neck at the ends, along with adding the handles. There is also some evidence that moulds were utilized by various ceramic factories (Twede, 2002).

Archaeologists, by combing the multitude of ancient records, are now beginning to compile more detailed information about the ceramic factories, and how exactly the potters made the amphorae for storing and shipping wine.

Obtaining the clay was paramount, and fortunately relatively plentiful all around the Mediterranean. The potters, like the later barrel coopers obtaining timber, would have sourced it from as close by and convenient a spot as possible. The grades of clay must have produced variations in the quality of the amphorae; one of the reasons some may have been recyclable. To extract the clay from the pits and river banks, wooden and bone tools would have been used initially, shifting to bronze and iron as those metals became available (Gallimore, 2010).

We get some idea of the size of the workshops – numbers of workers, kilns, etc. – from the records of one Roman era factory which note that it was contracted to produce 15,300 amphorae per year (Gallimore, 2010). This works out to about 50 per day, accounting for some non-productive days, for a group of workers each making several per day and engaged all year round.

The amphorae required for wine would have been primarily needed in the late fall or winter; shortly after fermentation to primarily ship the wines, and to store the better ones. Depending upon the ultimate use of the amphorae, building the vessels may have been seasonal; allowing the workers to engage in other activities – such as tending crops or crafting other products – throughout the year (Gallimore, 2010).

After forming the vessels on the wheels and assembling all the parts, loading the kilns and firing would have been the next critical step. There is little written evidence of what actual fuel was used, but most likely it was wood. Someone, the workshop owner or the potter, would have had to pay for it, or at least paid for the labour to gather it. Building up the heat in the kiln, and then cooling the pots would have taken four, five or more days. Records indicate kilns capable of holding 200 to 800 amphorae existed (Gallimore, 2010).

One account notes a defect rate of 5% to 10% due to serious cracks, breakage or other flaws. These numbers make me wonder why, with all these efforts and costs associated with making the amphorae, the vintners in Godin Tepe, the archaeologic dig in northern Iran, would have sliced off the tops of their aging vessels?

Gallimore (2010) notes that most, if not all amphorae, destined to contain wine had their interiors coated with pitch to minimize intrusion by oxygen and seepage of the wine through the relatively porous ceramic walls. Besides the need to help preserve the wine by the addition of spices, sea water, terebinth, etc., and to sweeten wine by the addition of honey, some of these additives probably ameliorated the bitter or very piney taste of the resins used to coat the interiors of the amphorae.

Given the numbers of amphorae produced, numerous people in the hills where the pine and other resinous timber existed must have been engaged in obtaining the sticky liquid. Where there were pine forests, Italy for example, pitch was exported. It was sent to other areas, such as Egypt, where it was not plentiful. There were some factories specifically set up to apply the pitch coating, as the rough chunks and blocks obtained in the forests would had to have been heated in order to allow the substance to coat the insides (Gallimore, 2010). The hot pitch was poured into the amphorae and then they were rolled on the ground – presumably on straw or other soft material to minimize breakage – to ensure complete coverage of the interior.

A mountain of discarded amphorae

One of Rome's hidden treasures, at least for archaeologists, has been Mont Testaccio. It is not rock and soil. This is actually a man-made mountain; a colossal pile of discarded amphorae, started over 2,000 years ago.

Mont Testaccio is where the first really serious examination of amphorae started. In the 1870s, as German archaeologist Heinrich Dressel (1845–1920) excavated into Mont Testaccio; he found numerous different amphorae styles and patterns in the shards. He soon realized that there were some common configurations. This prompted him to commence a formal catalogue of the types he encountered.

Monte Testaccio is an enormous pile of ancient amphorae located near Rome's former port. 'Enormous' may not be an adequate word to describe that literal mass of amphorae. It is some 40 metres high and covering 22,000 square metres (about 2.2 hectares). If you do not stop at one of the bars which have sprung up around its base, it takes about 20 minutes to completely circle on foot. The pile is largely the remains of the amphorae used in the olive oil trade.

During the Roman Empire era, oil was being shipped into the city from other Italian regions, and as far afield at Spain and Tunisia. Upon arrival at the port, the amphorae were emptied, either into other containers for distribution throughout the city, or as the final containers for that delivery. However, as the importation of the oil continued, and with the amphorae piling up all over the town, the Roman administrators realized that they needed an organized method to dispose of the thousands of empty vessels. Some types and styles could be recycled; the ends cut off to become pipes, or cut in half to become roof tiles. But many could not, those originating in Spain and from sites along the southern Mediterranean in particular.

The officials decided on a radical course of action. They directed that the discarded amphorae would be broken into smaller pieces, which were then piled up at one site. To reduce the odour and to secure them into position as the mound rose higher and higher, the pieces were sprinkled with lime, which had the effect of cementing them together. Slowly, over the years, this mountain grew from the disposed thousands, and then what was to become millions, of used amphorae.

As Dressel dug into the hill and studied the broken pieces, he observed significant differences between the amphorae. He began to identify unique styles of rims, handles, necks and bases, as well as the common dimensions of their lengths and bellies. Cataloguing these characteristics, their stories began to emerge; where and when they were made, the producer of the amphorae, and often even indications of the specific oil product contained within. Many of the amphorae had unique 'stamps' upon them. These were where the potter had impressed an initial or symbol into the clay of the amphorae's shoulder or handle. These stamps indicated the vessel's producer or the intended contents.

Besides helping Dressel catalogue the amphorae, the markings had a more important purpose. It is believed that they identified the oils and wines for the labourers, mostly slaves, who moved the amphorae around the docks, warehouses and distributed them within the city. Many, or probably most, of these people could not read, so these various markings helped them to correctly identify and organize the amphorae when offloading upon arrival in the city or readying for trans-shipment (Twede, 2005).

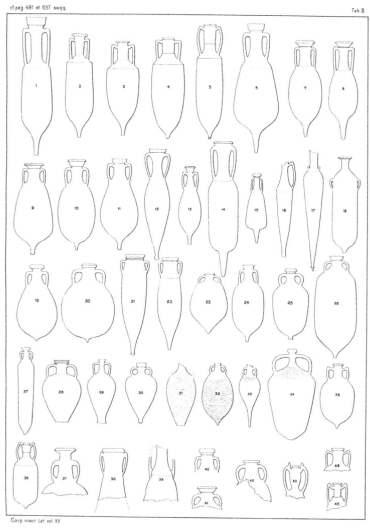

Tab. II.

Corp. inscr. Lat. vol. XV.

AMPHORARVM FORMAE

FIGURE 2.2 Dressel's drawing of the types of amphorae he found in Rome's Mount Testaccio. Types 1 to 6 were Roman amphorae used for wine (Kauffman, 2010)
H. Dressel's Plate II, published in: CIL XV 2.1 post p. 996. Courtesy of Corpus Inscriptionum Latinarum, Berlin-Brandenburgische Akademie der Wissenschaften

What Dressel, and the other archaeologists who have succeeded him, have found is that there are almost as many 'types' or 'styles' of amphorae as there were workshops which produced them. British archaeologist and historian Mathew Loughton, in reviewing the sources of amphorae which were shipped to just a small region in southern France, has identified and mapped the location of hundreds of the kiln sites. They are spread along the coasts of Spain and Italy, as well as elsewhere around the Mediterranean (Loughton, 2014).

Using Dressel's initial lists, archaeologists have continued to identify and define the styles. The primary types of amphorae have come to be known as: Dressel, Greco-Italian, Republican (Roman), Spanish, and Phoenician. Each of these, however, has numerous sub-styles, delineated by numbers and/or letters. Almost all these amphorae types have, at one time or another, been containers for wine.

By starting to identify these differences, Dressel and subsequent archaeologists and historians have been able to trace the lineage of many of the amphorae. From this accumulated data they have developed a more detailed understanding of the trading routes and the products that were shipped throughout the Mediterranean and Europe for the past 5,000 years (Bevan, 2014). However, we as will see, amphorae were phased out by the seventh century CE, being replaced largely by the wooden barrels and other containers.

Wine for Romans and others

The Romans, having conquered the Greeks in the second century BCE, and having subsequently incorporated those people and their values into their own society, became enamoured with much of their culture (Grout, 2015). Besides beginning to enjoy wine, the wealth obtained by making and selling wine must have certainly been part of the appeal.

Initially the Romans imported some of the Grecian varieties, such as wines from the Greek islands of Chios and Cos, a sea-water flavoured wine. Meanwhile, the Roman farmers were domesticating their own native grape species.

The majority of the Italian grapes were grown on large estates, utilizing slave labour (Grout, 2015). Owned by wealthy Romans, the wine was made for both the Romans, as well as to export to the Celts to the north. Wine demand also increased domestically. By the first century BCE, the city had approximately one million inhabitants. To meet this demand, more and more acreage was expropriated by the estates for planting grapes. Ironically,

FIGURE 2.3 Amphorae stacked in ship's hold
Courtesy of Mark Cartwright of *Ancient History Encylopedia* (www.ancient.eu)

it was the displaced rural population who were filling Rome. Additionally, to ensure an Italian monopoly for the wine going to the Celts in Germany and France, in 154 BCE Rome passed regulations prohibiting vineyard cultivation north of the Alps (Grout, 2015).

By 146 BCE Italy surpassed Greece as leading wine producer with more vines on the Italian peninsula than on the Peloponnese and its islands. Writing in 70 CE, Pliny the Elder noted at least 80 different varietals of wine available in Italy (Standage, 2005).

As the plebs swelled Rome, increasingly the politicians were using wine as bribes – delivered in amphorae – to encourage them to vote one way or another. This was usually *mulsum* wine, normally a *vin ordinaire* sweetened with honey just prior to drinking (Grout, 2015). This increased demand for wine, in turn, relaxed some of the restrictive vineyard growing laws. In turn, this allowed for vineyard development in southern France, starting around Narbonne and working its way westward, with subsequent plantings heading up the Rhône River valley towards Lyon.

By the first century CE, wine production, and writing about it, by Varro, Columella, Pliny and others, was becoming quite sophisticated. Discussions of vineyard practices must have helped to improve the quality and production around the Empire. More and more wine presses were utilized (Grout, 2015) to both maximize the yields and enhance the flavours. Fermentation, maturation, usually in dolia, aging of wine, and which wines could and should be aged, were discussed. The best wines were, apparently, aged in tightly sealed amphorae, the pitching of the interior giving the wine a resinous taste (Grout, 2015).

In a manner similar to many of today's wine-growing countries, and despite growing their own grapes, Rome continued to import wine. The Empire's money was being skimmed off and hoarded by the politicians and elite in Rome to purchase wines from the best vineyards and the most prized vintages for their own cellars. Wine arrived in the city in amphorae, offloaded at the sea-side port of Ostia into smaller boats to be moved up the Tiber River. It was then transferred again to large ceramic jars, or dolia, within the wine merchant's cellars, and buried in the ground to keep it cool. When sold and distributed to clients, smaller amphorae were again used (Standage, 2005).

Having the money to purchase the very best wines, the well-to-do Romans became wine snobs. Wine author Tom Standage notes:

> Wine became a symbol of social differentiation, a mark of the wealth and status of the drinker. The disparity between Roman society's richest and poorest members was reflected in the contents of their wine goblets. For wealthy Romans, the ability to recognize and name the finest wines was an important form of conspicuous consumption; it showed that they were rich enough to afford the finest wines and had spent time learning which was which.
>
> *(2005: 75)*

By a number of accounts, the best Italian wine was *Falernian*, grown in the volcanic soil hills of the Campania, near Naples (Pliny the Elder, 1855; Beard, 2008; Grout, 2015). The grapes grown at the top of the vineyards were termed *Caucine Falernian*, while the middle tier was *Faustian Falernian*, and lowest just *Falernian*. Marketing, it would seem, was alive and well even in Roman times.

The prized wines of the Falernians were the whites, which were aged for up to ten years, usually in larger types of amphorae, turning golden in the process. A 'best vintage' was described – the 121 BCE Opimian Falernian (Standage, 2005).

By 161 BCE, Roman wine snobbery – the drinking and spending on the premium wines – was considered to have become excessive. One law was enacted to restrict the use of gold cups, pitchers and kraters, which some haughty Romans apparently employed to flaunt their wealth. These most valued items were to be reserved for religious ceremonies only, not for private use (Standage, 2005).

Romans mixed their wine with several parts of water within the kraters; considering others – the Celts in particular – who did not, 'barbaric' (Grout, 2015). Despite this diluted wine, at the Roman's *convivium* – their equivalent to the Greek's *symposium*, which was a social gathering, usually of men, to drink and discuss the issues of the day – they apparently made an effort to get drunk.

Wine for the Roman troops

A culture of drinking wine spread and became ingrained with the Roman troops as well the elite and the plebs. Here again, the amphora was the primary container to supply the millions of litres required for the soldiers and their officers, stationed at forts scattered throughout the vast empire. The wine for the troops, however, was a daily ration of *posca* – a diluted, rather acidic wine with added herbs (Klenina, 2005).

Studies of the Roman army – the ruins of their camps, historical records, anecdotes and the like – provide a lens from which to view the amphorae in use. Like the rivers Rhône, Saône and Rhine to the north, and the Aude and Garonne to the west, the Danube was also an important river highway, utilized to supply the Roman troops who had conquered the lands to the northeast of Italy. Wherever they were located, the defensive camps along the boarders were termed *limes*. An important one on the eastern Danube was at Novae, located in what is now northern Bulgaria and situated about four kilometres east of the modern town Svishtov. This particular limes was about 250 kilometres upriver from the Black Sea. A detachment from that Novae garrison was also stationed on the Crimea peninsula, to the east on the Black Sea.

Archaeologists who have excavated the Novae limes, as well as studied information about the other outlying forts, estimate that the legionnaires drank about one litre of posca per day (Klenina, 2005). This would have required some two million litres a year just for those soldiers quartered up on those north and western sections of the Black Sea. To supply this quantity for the thousands of troops, enormous numbers of amphorae, containing posca, were shipped. About one third of the required stock was transported directly from Italian vineyards, while the remainder was sourced locally. Supply ships

FIGURE 2.4 A replicated cache of amphorae in the Bibracte Museum
Henry H. Work

brought the Italian wine through the Bosporus to the Black Sea and hence up the Danube. Otherwise, *mercatores*, the vendors who could lease and fill an entire ship, bought and shipped it, in amphorae, from vineyards around the Aegean and Black seas, such as the port of Herakleia of Pontos, an ancient city on Turkey's northern coast east of the Bosporus, and from Georgia's eastern shores (Klenina, 2005). The detachment on the Crimean Peninsula received the majority of their wines and posca locally (Stolba, 2015; Rybintsev, 1995).

Decline in use of amphorae

Around the Mediterranean, the use of amphorae diminished as the Roman Empire crumbled. Without the enormous demand for the traded goods – the wine, posca, olive oil, fish garum, etc. – for which the amphora was the primary package and shipping container, their need decreased.

As the political and military aspects of the Empire fell apart, so did the infrastructure of the hundreds of towns and cities which Rome controlled. Without the Roman bureaucrats and military garrisons, and as importantly, their payrolls funding the communities' services and craftsmen, the demand for the imported goods declined. Historian Peter Frankopan (2016) has observed that the majority of trade became local; the need for the millions of amphorae to ship the commodities up and down the rivers and across the Mediterranean simply dried up. At least in Europe, the increasing use of wooden barrels also diminished the demand for amphorae (Marlière, 2013).

By the ninth century CE, without the Roman Empire's demand for wine, coupled with the difficulty of growing grapes in northern Europe, many of those vineyards were abandoned or grubbed up to plant other crops. The drink of choice was generally beer in northern Europe, while wine remained predominant in the southern regions where the vineyards flourished; a trend which has persisted into current times (Standage, 2005).

On the eastern side of the Mediterranean, another factor impacted the trade of wine amphorae; the rise of the Persian Empire. There, without the vast seas and long, navigable rivers, the amphorae were not as useful. Coupled with the rise of the Muslim culture, which to some extent also diminished the wine culture, the need to use and ship amphorae declined. In 600 CE, Islam was on the rise, and its teachings prescribed abstention from alcoholic drinks. Islam's founder, Muhammad, issued the decree after becoming distressed over witnessing two of his disciples fighting while drunk. This ban was enforced more heavily in the Middle East and northern African coastline, rather than to the west in Spain or Portugal (Standage, 2005).

Only 60 years earlier, the Bubonic plague had hit Persia, moving steadily westward, subsequently impacting the peoples of Europe in about 530–40 CE. It also helped to decimate trade as fewer people were left to tend the fields and make the crafts (Frankopan, 2016). The battles between Persia and Rome, ensuing during 550 to 600 CE, added further to the destruction of the trade routes and to the use of the amphorae. Frankopan states that "There is also growing consensus that Muhammad was preaching to a society that was experiencing acute economic contraction as a result of the Perso-Roman Wars" (2016).

Where trade did improve was in the shipping of slaves. Slavery had almost always been an active part of the inter- and intra-country commerce. It is estimated that the Roman Empire needed some 200,000 to 400,000 new slaves per year (Frankopan, 2016). By the ninth century, the income from the sale of slaves was great enough to begin lifting the European economy. The reinvigorated economy created an increasing demand for wine, its movement now largely in barrels, and primarily being shipped to the northern European cities.

As one of the cities which early on threw off the stifling mantle of the Dark Ages, Venice earned its initial wealth from dealing in slaves (Frankopan, 2016). This new-found wealth created an elite who desired, and could afford, luxury items. Thus, the opportunity for greater development of the craftsman class was created. Later, in the eleventh and twelfth centuries, as the Crusaders were attempting to take Muslim Jerusalem, Venice secured exclusive trading rights to the east; providing backup forces and supplies for the European fighters via its vast armada of Mediterranean-going ships. These spoils from the shipping of troops and materials added to the cities already increasing wealth (Frankopan 2016).

Specialization in bottles, particularly wine bottles, was still in the future. However, the Venetian glass craftsmen did add greatly to the knowledge of glass blowing fabrication, design and decoration. We will see this knowledge utilized around Europe when we examine the growing use of wine bottles in Chapter 5.

Comparing apples to apples

Professor of Packaging Diana Twede notes: "As a rule, the efficiency of packaging depends on maximizing the net volume to weight ratio, especially for a heavy product such as liquid" (2002: 99). In Table 2.1, all three primary wine containers are compared, with the standard size wine barrel having the largest ratio, thus showing it as the most efficient in terms of containing the greatest volume per the packaging weight.

Conclusion

The ceramic amphorae emerged in the lands around the Mediterranean from a multitude of proto-types as the package to age and ship wine and other liquids due to their torpedo shape and ability to be tightly closed. The amphora was a primary container for some 5,000 years, but its use declined as barrels more efficiently took over that role in Europe, and the rise in Islam decreased the need to ship wine in the Middle East and northern Africa.

TABLE 2.1 Comparison of amphora, barrel and glass bottle containers by weight

	Container size: litres	Container weight: kilograms	Ratio: volume/weight
Amphora	24[1]	24	1
Wooden barrel	225[2]	45.4	4.96
Glass bottles (case)	9[3]	4.5	2

1 Dressel 1 (from http://vindolanda.csad.ox.ac.uk/reference/measures.shtml); for these smaller amphorae, the volume of the amphora in litres roughly equals their weight in kilograms
2 Standard size wine barrel
3 One case of 12 x 750 ml bottles with the bottles at 500 grams each

Note

1   More recently, in 2014 another similar grave was found with a smaller wine krater, yet one equally embellished with Greek motifs (Westfreid, 2015). In this tomb, 60 kilometres north of Vix, at Lavau, a suburb of Troyes, were found other Celtic nobility – a Prince and a woman, probably his wife. They too wore gold torcs, and had wine paraphernalia with them, and they died at roughly the same time as the Lady of Vix (Urbanus, 2015).

References

Anonymous (2013). Mon dieu! French Wine is from Italy. *New Scientist*, [online] 218(2920), p. 17.

Beard, M. (2008). *Pompeii: The Life of a Roman Town*. London: Profile Books.

Bevan, A. (2014). Mediterranean containerization. *Current Anthropology*, [online] 55 (4), pp. 387–418.

Caesar, G. J. (1869). *Gaius Julius Caesar: Commentaries on the Gallic War*. (McDevitte, W. A. and Bohn, W. S. trans.). New York: Harper & Brothers.

Casey, D. M. (2013). *Oppida*. Ipswich, MA: Salem Press Encyclopedia.

Chaume, B. (2013). Le complexe aristocratique de Vix/le mont Lassois. *L'archéologue: Archéologie Nouvelle*, Plantin et Moretus: CIPEC, pp. 52–59.

Cooper, E. (2000). *Ten Thousand Years of Pottery*. Philadelphia, PA: University of Pennsylvania Press.

Frankopan, P. (2016). *The Silk Roads: A New History of the World*. New York: Alfred A. Knopf.

Gallimore, S. (2010). Amphorae production in the Roman World: a view from the papyri. *Bulletin of the American Society of Papyrologists*, [online] 47, pp. 155–184.

Giannopoulou, M. (2010). *Pithoi; Technology and History of Storage Vessels through the Ages*. Oxford: BAR International Series 1240.

Klenina, E. (2005). Supply of the Legio I Italica at Novae (Moesia Inferior) and Tauric Chersonesos/Limes XIX. *Proceedings of the XIXth International Congress of Roman Frontier Studies*, Pécs, Hungary, 2003. (Edited by Zsolt Visy) Pécs, Hungary: University of Pecs.

Knüsel, C. J. (2002). More Circe than Cassandra: the Princess of Vix in ritualized social context. *European Journal of Archaeology*, 5(3), pp. 275–308.

Krausz, S. (2007). La topographie et les fortifications celtiques de l'oppidum biturige de Châteaumeillant-Mediolanum (Cher). *Revue Archéologique du Centre de la France*, [online] 45–46, p. 53.

Loughton, M. (2014). *The Arverni and Roman Wine: Roman Amphorae from Late Iron Age Sites in the Auvergne (Central France): Chronology, Fabrics and Stamps*. Oxford: Archaeopress.

Lukacs, P. (2012). *Inventing Wine: A New History of One of the World's Most Ancient Pleasures*. New York: W. W. Norton & Co.

Marlière, E. (2013). Les campagnes militaires et l'expansion de l'usage du tonneau dans l'Empire romain. *De la cave au vin: une fructueuse alliance*, Rencontres du Clos-

Vougeot, Dijon: Chaire UNESCO Culture et Traditions du Vin and Université du Bourgogne, pp. 47–61.

McDevitte, W. A. and Bohn, W. S. (translators) (1869). *Gaius Julius Caesar: Commentaries on the Gallic War*. New York: Harper & Brothers.

McGovern, P. E. (2009). *Uncorking the Past: The Quest for Wine, Beer, and Other Alcoholic Beverages*. Berkeley: University of California Press.

McGovern, P. E., MirzoianA., HallG. R., and Bar-Yosef, O. (2009). Ancient Egyptian herbal wines. *Proceedings of the National Academy of Sciences of the United States of America*, 106(18), pp. 7361–7366.

Pliny the Elder. (1855). *The Natural History of Pliny*. (Bostock, J. and Riley, H. T. trans.). London: H. G. Bohn.

Quercia, A., Johnston, A., Bevan, A., Conolly, J., and Tsaravopoulos, A. (2011). Roman pottery from an intensive survey of Antikythera, Greece. *The Annual of the British School in Athens*, 106(1), pp. 47–98.

Rybintsev, V. (1995). Viticulture and oenology in the Ukraine: a survey of their history, ecology and economic development. *Journal of Wine Research*, 6(1), p. 35.

Salač, V. (2010). De la vitesse des transports à l'âge du fer (Translated from Czech to French by G. Pierrevelcin) *Celtes et Germains au 1er s. a.C. en Bohême et en Europe centrale* (n°405/11/0603), la Grantová agentura de République tchèque (GAČR).

Standage, T. (2005). *A History of the World in Six Glasses*. New York: Walker and Co.

Stolba, V. and Andresen, J. (2015). Unveiling the hinterland: a new type of Hellenistic rural settlement in Crimea. *Antiquity*, [online] 89(10), pp. 345–360.

Twede, D. (2002). Commercial amphoras: the earliest consumer packages? *Journal of Macromarketing*, 22(1), pp. 98–108.

Twede, D. (2005). The Cask Age: the technology and history of wooden barrels. *Packaging Technology and Science*, 189(5), p. 253–264.

Tylecote, R. F. (1976). *The History of Metallurgy*. London: The Metals Society.

Urbanus, J. (2015). Eternal banquets of the Early Celts: an extraordinary 2,500-year old tomb offers vital evidence of trade, ritual, and power in fifth century BC France. *Archaeology*, 68(6), pp. 45–49.

Westfreid, M. (2015). La stupéfiante tombe princière celte de Lavau. *L'Express*, [online] 4 March 2015.

Website

Stillwell, R., MacDonald, W. L., McAlister, M. H. (eds). (1976). Mediolanum Biturigum (Châteaumeillant) Cher, France. *The Princeton Encyclopedia of Classical Sites*. www.perseus.tufts.edu

Blogs

Grout, J. (2015). Wine and Rome. *Encyclopaedia Romana: Rome, The Home of Empire and of all Perfection*. www.romanhistorybooks.typepad.com

Kauffman, R. (2010) Amphorae – a summary. *Anticopedia.* www.anticopedia.fr November.

Wernick, R. (2005) *The Lady of Vix; Life at the Top Drawer in 500 BC.* www.robertwernick.com

3

WOODEN BARRELS
Origins to 1500 CE

The earliest barrels

Simplicity of design, full functionality and longevity of use are some of the attributes by which our various machines and appliances are judged and rated. But there is an underappreciation of those items which have been around for hundreds or thousands of years. As Hicks (2011) notes, many people nowadays underestimate or misunderstand the innate skills, professionalism and expertise of ancient craftsmen. Possibly this is because they are reluctant to concede that such talents may be possible from people living one, two, or even three thousand years ago.

With barrels certainly in common use well before the fourteenth century, where did they come from? Unlike the ceramic amphorae, pots and jars, but like the animal hide sacks, finding the remains of ancient, organic wooden barrels is extremely difficult. The oldest barrel remains found so far, dated to the first century BCE, have been located along the major river ways and sea ports in what are now Germany, Belgium and France (Marlière, 2001). For example, those found in the German oppida of Manching, located near the Danube River city of Ingolstadt, in Bavaria, and in Mortantambe in Charente-Maritime were typically just some heads and portions of the connecting staves.

At about this same period, barrels were starting to be commented upon by the Roman writers. For example, Caesar, in discussing his mopping up

FIGURE 3.1 Roman-era barrel head and portions of staves found near Oberwinterthur ZH-Unteres Bühl, Switzerland
Kantonsarchäologie Zürich: Martin Bachmann

operations against some of the Centre-of-France Celtic tribes in 52 BCE, mentioned barrels. His description is purely pragmatic, noting that the barrels were being used defensively by the Celts, rather than in relation to their use for transporting wine or beer. He further explains that they were stuffed with flammable material and rolled down the hills at his legionnaires to be used as a distraction to some of the defenders hoping to slip away under the cover of the smoke (Caesar, 1869).

The fact that there were enough barrels to make a formidable attack, as well as a note in Caesar's diary, indicates that barrels must have been, by the time of his commentary, in everyday use. It is also worth noting that sites of the earliest found barrels and the site where Caesar had the barrels hurled down upon his men are a significant distance apart. The barrels could not have suddenly shown up. It would have taken years for them to be incorporated within the trade systems; initially for the tradespeople to realize and appreciate their advantages and begin to demand them, and then for the infrastructure required to gather the woods and develop the tools and skills to produce them in sufficient quantities to be put in place. An even longer period would have been required for them to become common enough to be traded and shipped to distant regions.

From this premise, we can make a reasonable assumption that barrels were developed at least a hundred years prior, and possibly as early as several hundred years before, perhaps in the fourth or third centuries BCE. Actually when, and where, they were originally designed and fabricated is still uncertain. Nor have archaeologists found a progression of prototypes – some sort of early styles of barrels leading up to the form which Caesar observed, which is basically the same style as we see today. Because we know so little about their earliest origins, as Andrew Bevan notes, wooden barrels are "an archaeologically invisible iceberg of barrel-borne goods" (2014).

Origins of the barrel

With the origins of wooden barrels still in the realm of pure speculation, one archaeologist has certainly narrowed the options. As part of her investigations of the past 20 years, Elise Marlière[1] has been looking into their beginnings. Instead of attempting to conduct a search for the first barrel ever made – most likely a futile exercise – she attacked the issue from another direction. The question she posed was: If you were a supply officer in the Roman army and needed to deliver thousands of litres of wine to your troops, what containers would you use: amphorae or barrels? As we observed in the last chapter, initially it was the amphorae. However, by the first century CE barrels begin showing in greater numbers in the Roman limes at the edges of the expanding Roman Empire (Marlière, 2001).

The artefacts and data further indicate that the majority of barrels were crafted in the cities lining Europe's major rivers rather than the Mediterranean's sea ports (Marlière, 2013). Lyon, on the Rhône, has been cited as a prime example. As a large commercial centre, the need for the barrels to ship or trans-ship wine, and possibly beer, existed. The raw materials for making the earliest barrels – trees of fir, spruce or larch – were readily available nearby. Additionally, there was a nexus of the craftsmen with the skills to fabricate the barrels: blacksmiths to manufacture the tools, the loggers to obtain the wooden staves, heading, and hoop material, the wheelwrights with the knowledge to bend wood, and carpenters to shape and assemble the pieces into a barrel. In the early stages of barrel manufacturing, it is not clear whether these several crafts were collaborating to make the barrels or whether just one man made them from start to finish. The stela, in particular those grave stones depicting coopers, the men who made the barrels, do not appear until several centuries into the current era.

While Gaul is the most likely place to have developed the barrel – barrels have been found in Roman Britain with marks indicating that they were made in Lyon – the Celtic craftsmen living in what are now Germany, Raetia (northern Italy), Spain and Britain could all have an equal chance as the developers of the wooden barrels (Marlière, 2013).

It is fairly evident that wooden barrels evolved from wooden tanks and pails. Wooden buckets and tubs – those wooden containers with straight sides – have been in use for many millennia. The vessels have been found in Egyptian tombs, and tanks have been depicted in murals, all dating to about 2500 BCE (Twede, 2005). Therefore, the concept of, and the techniques for, placing several wooden staves together around a circular bottom, and lashing the staves together with strips of wooden saplings, were well known. The question remains: when did the jump from using straight staves for an open bucket or tank develop into bending the staves, and adding a second end to enclose the container?

Another important point in searching for the barrel origins is that barrels most likely arose in order to *transport* liquids, rather than just store or age them. This is not an easy concept to imagine in today's world. Most current photos of barrels show them quietly resting in a wine cellar or whiskey (or whisky) aging house. Nevertheless, up until the 1950s, barrels were extremely common containers; being one of the most used containers to transport wine, and certainly other liquids, such as beer and whiskey, as well as numerous other commodities, such as food, gunpowder, cement, and tobacco (Work, 2014).

Wooden tanks and vats can be made any size required. However, because of their straight sides, whether vertical or tapered, they are difficult to move, and moving the larger ones without disassembly is impossible. As civilization expanded, the idea of moving large volumes of liquids naturally arose.

The amphora, as noted in the last chapter, was the container and package of choice, holding that role for several thousand years. Nonetheless, other containers with much greater capacities than the amphorae were in limited use. Animal skins, such as ox hides, could be stitched together to form large bladders. One was depicted, in a mural on a Pompeii bar wall, on a horse drawn cart. Presumably it was used to deliver wine to the city's inns. Dolia, the large ceramic pots, were also used to transport quantities of liquids on ships. However, both had disadvantages: the ox hide bladders were unwieldly due to a lack of structure and the contact with the animal skin could possibly impact the flavours of the wine, and the dolia, because of their weight and relative fragility, could only be utilized on ships or barges.

Several factors must have culminated to develop the barrels sometime in the several centuries prior to the current era: The vintners and wine merchants, and probably the Roman army, wanted a method to transport larger quantities of wine efficiently. The technology to make the iron and even more durable steel tools arose. These were necessary to cut the staves and plane smooth edges that would join tightly together. These tools were also required to cut the notches into the ends of the staves in which to fit the heads. The skills to bend wood with heat also came to fruition. The bent staves enabled the barrel to be easily rolled and manoeuvred, resting as it does just on a small section of the bilge, the bulge in the middle. All these created a package with a large capacity relative to its weight, especially as compared to amphorae or dolia.

What we do know – Marseille as an example

In Europe, an Etruscan fresco in the Tomb of Jugglers in the ancient city of Tarquinia, painted about 510 BCE, shows a wooden tank for treading grapes, but no barrels. Either barrels had not yet been invented, or had not by then reached into the northern Italian trading networks (Marlière, 2001).

Marlière speculates that barrels were around at least as early as about 125 BCE (2001). Around that time, Marseille (then known as Masalia) was a Greek colony, heavily involved in grape growing and wine making. In order to ship all their wine, thousands of amphorae were required. She notes a rise in amphorae production at the end of the second century BCE, but by 125 BCE a dramatic decline in amphorae production. One possibility for this decline, Marlière believes, could have been due to the increased use of barrels (2001).

Then, 75 years later, the evidence indicates that Marseille reverted back to shipping wine in amphorae. Within that interval, the Romans had sacked Marseille in 49 BCE. While many of its vineyards were ruined, a few of the top-rated ones survived. The cities' vintners turned to selling those premium wines, stored and shipped in amphorae.

Several scenarios for these shifts are possible, either individually or collectively. Perhaps, with less wine, the amphorae made more suitable containers. Or the barrels themselves, or the raw materials for making the barrels – the staves and heading – were not obtainable. I would like to propose another idea; that the quality of the coopering for the barrels – i.e. the jointing of the staves – was still in its infancy and poorly done. Those Marseille vintners wanted the best containers for their superior wine; leaking barrels would not have passed muster.

The joining surfaces of the staves, the edges where they were placed together to form a circle, for the earliest barrels – in fact barrels up until the eighteenth century when primitive machinery was first utilized in cooperages – were joined using hand tools. We know from artefacts that the late Celtic and early Roman coopers had a full array of hand planes and adzes. The question is how sharp these tools were, and possibly more importantly, how many staves they could join before the tool needed re-sharpening.

Various historical notes indicate barrel quality problems. For example, even into the fifteenth century, the Port of Bristol's (Britain) log books denoting the ship arrivals, along with their cargo, indicate that of the wine barrels delivered from France, often at least ten per cent were leaking, some so badly that they were actually empty (Pitt, 2006). Part of this could be attributed to shoddy workmanship, which has probably existed since man started making things. Nonetheless, two other issues must have added to the difficulties of making and keeping leak-free barrels: rolling barrels on rough surfaces and sharp tools.

Certainly, in an era when wine was being drunk all day in lieu of water, and life was still rather cut-throat and brutal, for the average cooper or craftsman the concept of quality control may have difficult enough to envision let alone achieve. If life was rough, so were the streets, wagons and boats upon which the barrels were rolled or transported. Before steel hoops, barrels were held together by wooden hoops. These hoops, made from various species of tree saplings, were tough but expanded when they were wet and contracted as they dried out. Despite placing numerous wooden hoops around a barrel, the staves which were the barrels' sides, could still move; especially so when rolling a heavy full barrel even on the smoothest of surfaces. If wine could seep out, oxygen could enter; causing not only loss of the liquid, but degradation as well.

However, from my experience of making and using barrels, and the more I learn about these oldest barrels, the more I tend to think the main reason for leaky barrels was the cooper's tools. Attempting to laboriously carve each stave – curving the outside, dishing the inside and then planing a continuous, super-smooth, angled edge on the two sides – was time consuming. Hand planing, especially when attempting to make the perfectly flat, nick-free edges needed to completely seal a barrel in the tougher woods such as oak, would have been difficult.

EXPLORATION 3.1
ROMAN TOOL MAKING

For the tools themselves, the coopers either made their own or relied upon their local blacksmith; there was no running down to the local hardware store. Nonetheless, as British archaeologist and metallurgist Ronald F. Tylecote notes,

> the Roman world knew all the types of hand tools that are in exis-tence today, with the possible exception of the wood screw. We see, for example, iron smoothing planes, just like those available in modern hardware stores, spoon bits [a bit with a long spoon shape with sharpened edges] (but not twist drills), and the most amazing complicated locks.
>
> *(1976)*

Yet, despite the array of available tools, the quality control in the smi-thing of the metals used for the tools would have been difficult. The raw materials would not have been as well differentiated or refined as today's ores. Nor could the forging itself be constantly successful with the limited methods to control the heat of the fires; the early smelters being basically hand-dug holes in the earth lined with clay (Tylecote, 1976). Finally, hand forging – essentially repeated beating of the potential blades with heavy hammers – would have further added to the variables of whether a blade could last the many hours of use.

Using methods similar to McGovern's analysis of the wine residue in amphorae, archaeologists are now examining ancient metal pieces with an array of extremely sophisticated technology. The results are mixed. Some recent tests examined Roman army metal arrowheads (Salvemini et al., 2014), the manufacturing of which would have been similar to making any hand tools. The tests, incorporating high-tech, neutron tomography, revealed that the finished products had numerous small defects; tiny holes, minute bits of slag imbedded within the metal, and separations where the metal was repeatedly hammered, folded over and hammered again to anneal it together (Salvemini et al., 2014). Most probably, the tools were experiencing similar defects to those in the arrowheads. This indicates that, however dedicated the cooper, it must have been difficult to continuously hand-make leak-free barrels day after day with the tools of that era.

This is not to say that tool quality did not improve. Marlière (2001) noticed a general, region wide shift to oak barrels in the third century CE. Perhaps by that time the Romans, Gauls and Germans had sig-nificantly improved their metallurgy. A Roman-era metal punch has been found in Heeten, north of the Rhine in the Netherlands, dated to between 315 and 340 CE (Godfrey and van Nie, 2004). It is believed to have been made by the Germanic tribes living in that area. Tests by electron probe microanalysis and scanning electron microscopy shows a high degree of carbonization during the smelting in the furnace, and tempering by the smith, both of which indicate to metallurgy professors Evelyne Godfrey and Mathijs van Nie a tool of "maximum strength and minimum brittleness" (Godfrey and van Nie, 2004).

Making wine in Marseille

Returning to Marseille, that shift from amphorae to barrels after 125 BCE has one small problem, but it is easily solved. If the Marseille vintners were using barrels to move their wine, where did their coopers source their wood for the staves and heading? Being in southern France, the area around Marseille tends to be drier than northern France or Germany. There are, and probably were trees from which to make barrels, but they were not plentiful. The forests which contain sufficient quantities of the suitable species for barrel making, such as Silver fir (*Abies alba*), European beech (*Fagus sylvatica*), European larch (*Larix decidua*) and English oak (*Quercus robur*), are further to the north.

However, wine from Marseille was being shipped up the Rhône in amphorae, as well as other trade items. We observed this with the finds of amphorae in Châteaumeillant and Bibracte, and the great krater and wine accoutrements in the tomb of the Lady of Vix. It is possible that wood for the staves, or even pre-made barrels, could have been shipped to Marseille, along with the tin, slaves and cattle, on the return trips in the trader's boats.

Marlière also notes that Caesar was known to have been concerned about, and was astute in his leadership towards, making sure his troops were well fed and supplied (Marlière, 2001). The army marched on the stomach, as the saying goes. Marlière speculates that with barrels becoming more common, Caesar might very well have directed his supply officers to incorporate them into his supply chains for shipping wine and posca to his legionnaires (Marlière, 2001). By the time of Caesar's death in 44 BCE, the barrels were apparently commonplace enough that they were being shipped up the Rhône and Danube to troops stationed in northern France and Germany, as well as going from Bordeaux to Britain.

Where to look for the ancient barrels

For archaeologists like Marlière, as they search the ancient ruins for evidence, one of the important specific sites in which to find the remains of the ancient barrels has been in the water wells. Large barrels, with their circular shape, were an ideal object to place into the holes to keep the sides from caving in. The majority of discoveries of barrels in wells have been where the Roman troops have been stationed. These forts and outposts needed relatively clean water, particularly in places where the soldiers were going to remain for some time. With barrels, like the amphorae before them, a somewhat dispensable item, using a few as well casings must have seemed like a good way to 'recycle' them (Marlière, 2001).

While the cool or cold water and the eventual silt tended to preserve the barrels, the dating of them is problematic. For one thing, they were being reused. This makes it difficult to fix a date as to when they were initially built and utilized. For example, when were they initially constructed? Were they utilized prior to being placed in the well for one year or fifty? Barrels, particularly those made of oak, can, under the right conditions, last 50–100 years. While historical dating may not be able to pin down the exact year a barrel was built, we would like to know closer than just what century the item was manufactured. Further, they lack the heads, which occasionally have a cooper's stamp upon them, again pining down where, and when, they might have been produced.

Additionally, the refuse fallen or thrown into the wells in the ensuing years creates a hog-podge of variously aged artefacts which add to the confusion when dating. However, where the barrels have been reasonably dated, the time-line does tend to follow the known expansion of the Roman troop movements (Marlière, 2001).

The barrels used in the wells have an additional problem in helping us piece together the development of the barrels. That is that we are getting only a snapshot of the barrel size which may have been in use; the barrels placed in the wells would have only been of the largest sizes. Nonetheless, they are one of the better sources of artefacts to assist in developing the timeline of the earliest barrel use.

If barrels were developed before the Romans invaded into the northern countries, one would think that the existing centres of commerce – i.e. along the river ways and sea ports – would be the logical sites for the factors contributing to developing a new container to ship liquids. This is supported, but only partially, by the fact that up to now no ancient barrels have

FIGURE 3.2 Barrels for wine and supplies sculpted into Trajan's column, 113 CE, Rome
Karen Work

been found in central Gaul (Marlière, 2001). Nonetheless, this lack of evidence does not constitute proof.

There is some thought that barrels were originally developed for beer (Marlière, 2001). I would feel comfortable with that theory if the beer barrels were intended to be shipped or transported, even if just down the street from the brewery to the tavern. The Celts had breweries for years before the Romans came calling, as a find in Kasendorf, near Kulmbach, Bavaria, dated back to 800 BCE shows(Oliver, 2012). There, a large amphora was found with the remains of black wheat ale flavoured with oak leaves. Additionally, there are Roman records of a brewery in Manching.

As it would have been difficult to move the large amphorae full of beer, perhaps people came to the brewery to fill up their own jugs or skin sacks. Somewhere along the line, the brewer or his patrons must have wished for ways to more easily transport greater quantities of the beer. The same would have been true with the wine being shipped to the Celtic nobility.

Thus, at some point during the ensuing ages, the barrel design was developed. We can imagine that it might have been a carpenter who made the wooden pails and tanks. Perhaps he and his Celtic mates were sitting around having a beer after work, ruminating on how to move great quantities of liquids. If the model for the barrel shape did not emanate from something local, perhaps it came from a design originating in the styles of the art and crafts filtering into the Celtic communities from the Mediterranean cultures. The round kraters and bulbous styles of ceramic pots may have sparked their imagination. Likewise, the style of an actual ceramic pot, of the type seen in the older Middle Eastern wineries may have been the source of the idea. A jar, such as the ones at Godin Tepe embossed with rope around them, also might have been the impetus (Cooper, 2000; McGovern, 2009; Morris, 2013).

The cooperage industry commences

While we still do not know where or when the original barrels were designed and built, we can see that by the first century BCE, barrels were starting to appear within the trading and supply systems.

Moving this potential nexus of the what and where the barrel was designed a step further, Marlière (2001) suggests that, by Imperial times, significant cooperage making facilities were located in the major shipping centres. Lyon is a logical first site. It was there that wine from Italy and Spain, and from the recently planted wine grapes in south-eastern France, was being shipped up the Rhône. It was transported in amphorae, or in the larger capacity ceramic dolia and possibly ox-hide sacks, and then probably transferred into barrels for distribution to the limes. Lyon is a plausible barrel manufacturing site because the city had access to the silver fir and larch – straight grained woods for the staves and heading, and the hazel wood from which the hoops were made. Further evidence has been found within the city; branding irons with the cooper's names or mark, wood punches to note the cooper or product, and funerary stele for the coopers, the men who crafted the barrels (Marlière, 2001). Additionally, the *Allobrogica* grape, grown by the Vienna, France vintners, was most probably shipped in barrels as no amphorae have been found carrying that grape.

Bordeaux also became an important centre for barrels. Near the city, a stela of a cooper and an epitaph for another cooper have been found (Marlière, 2001; Aubin et al., 1996). I have noted that the cities' traders and boatmen were transhipping Italian wine up the coast in the third and second centuries BCE. Amphorae workshops were started in the first century BCE, but were shortly phased out, possibly due to the increased use of barrels (Aubin et al., 1996). Bordeaux also grew and shipped the *Biturica* grape, perhaps the forerunner of Cabernet Sauvignon.

Barrels in the Middle Ages

It took several hundred years for Europe to recover from the decline of the Roman Empire. Wars – political and religious – and plagues all contributed to years of suppression. By 1000 CE, slowly things were beginning to change; cities were redeveloping and expanding hand-in-hand with increased trade.

Wine again became important. Both the church and private proprietors were re-planting vineyards, expanding their acreage into Bordeaux, Burgundy, and the Rhône valley. As the Muslim influence in Spain and Portugal waned, vineyards there were re-planted. England's *The Domesday Book* listed 42 vineyards in Britain during late eleventh century (Phillips, 2000).

In between the numerous wars, growth in the trading markets created wealthy middle and merchant classes. Besides the rulers and clergy, they were the ones who increasingly were purchasing wine, primarily in barrels. For those living in Paris, the wineries could ship the barrels on barges via the Seine, Marne, and Yonne rivers (Phillips, 2000). Bordeaux, and later La Rochelle, were shipping wine on boats which hugged the Atlantic seaboard as they sailed north to Britain and other European cities. Germany's vineyards along the Rhine and Mosel shipped their vintages down the Rhine in casks primarily to Flanders and to some extent Britain and the Scandinavian countries (Cunliffe, 1997).

Like all commercial enterprises, over the centuries Bordeaux saw the fortunes of its wine industry wax and wane. The chess games – including wars, taxes, marriages, divorces and murders – played by the alliances of Europeans royalty only served to exacerbate these cycles.

For example, in 1152 Eleanor of Aquitaine, who controlled the territory of Gascony which included Bordeaux, married Henry, the Duke of Normandy. He subsequently became Henry II of England. That alliance provided greater access to the British markets for the Bordeaux wine traders (Phillips, 2000) who were shipping barrels of wine to London and Bristol. However, it also opened up those same markets to wine coming from La Rochelle, 150 kilometres to the north. Bordeaux's négociants won this skirmish when Eleanor's son John lowered the taxes on the Bordeaux traders in return for them supplying materials for his war with the king of France.

One hundred years later, historical transaction data from England's King Henry III, indicates that in one year his household purchased some 1,445 casks of Bordeaux wine (Phillips, 2000). By such a purchase, the royalty gave de facto acknowledgement of the quality of the product, and certainly raised its status. This boost towards the English market helped expand Bordeaux's vineyards, including Graves and the Entre-Deux-Mers (Phillips, 2000). The now-famous Medoc had not yet risen to prominence.

Even in the Middle Ages, the wines from the regions of Gaillac and Cahors were important. Barges brought the wines down the rivers in barrels. As Phillips notes, "It is from about this time that the lighter-coloured wines of the region closer to the coast became known as *clairet* (claret), to distinguish them from the darker reds produced in the high country of Spain [and Cahors] that were shipped from Bordeaux" (2000).

By 1335 roughly 60% of Bordeaux wine was being shipped to England, with the balance being sent to Spain, Flanders, Germany and other areas of France (Phillips, 2000). This business was immensely important to the economy of both France and it trading partners, so much so that between 1446 and 1448 wine made up nearly one-third of England's entire import trade (Vintners Hall, 2018). Typically, the Bordeaux négociants would send some 100 to 200 shiploads to England just after the fall harvest, and then another armada would sail with aged wine after the New Year. These increased sales encouraged vineyard expansion, along with an increase in the need for barrels to age and ship the wine.

To provide some comparison of production, in the 1300s Bordeaux was filling and shipping some 20,000 to 30,000 barrels annually, from a high in one year of 102,000 (Rose, 2011). (The unit of measure of the barrel was at that time 900 litres.) While an exact comparison is not available, in general the Bordeaux region is now shipping between 200,000 and 250,000-barrel equivalents per year, or roughly 20,000,000 to 25,000,000 cases of wine annually (FranceAgriMer, 2018; Millar, 2017)

By 1310, shipments had dropped to 51,000 barrels due to a poor crop, again in 1324 there was a decrease due to the war between England and France, a demise seen also to recur in the 1330s with the Hundred Years War. By the 1350s, the norm was between 10,000 to 15,000 barrels per year (Phillips, 2000). These decreases further illustrate the cycles, attributed to both vintage variations as well as the period's economic circumstances; cycles which we still see today, albeit to a lesser extent.

Making all these barrels was not a simple task, complicated by a high demand for the containers to ship and store many more commodities than just wine and beer. The needs from the vintners and other trades created a lucrative business for the cooperages. And, as did all the European governments of the time, the French government wanted a share of the profits. The French coopers, and separately the stave makers were listed as some of 121 craft and trade organizations in the *Le Livre des Métiers* (The Book of Trades) published by the French government in 1268. Inclusion was recognition, but also put the cooperage businesses on notice that the tax men would be at their doors (Work, 2014).

Further problems

Despite the growth in the wine trade, life continued to be difficult for the vintners. Like the plagues in the Dark Ages, the Black Death in 1340s curtailed production, and with it the trade in wine (Phillips, 2000). Wars

FIGURE 3.3 The earliest cooper's hand tools would have looked similar to these, in use up until the late 1900s
Kauri Museum, New Zealand

continued to impact not only the markets but the vineyards themselves as troops trampled through vineyards and most likely appropriated, or just stole, wine from any cellars they came across.

If those were not enough, poor vintages and/or bad barrels frequently created further turmoil in the vintner's life and disarray to his efforts. Earlier we discussed the rough treatment the barrels encountered. Despite the use of sometimes as many as 18 sapling hoops encircling a barrel, these did not have the strength to hold the barrels extremely tight, and the steel hoops we see today did not become common until the nineteenth century. If the wine went off, the inn keeps and wine merchants devised all sorts of ways to avoid throwing it out – adulterating bad wine with good, and adding pitch, wax, gum, powdered bay, or turnsole (a purple dye). To counteract some of these onerous practices, taverns were not allowed to sell both red and white wine (Phillips, 2000).

As bad wine was also a common problem for households, or at least the wealthier ones that could afford barrels of wine aging in their cellar, pamphlets and instructions were written to attempt to fix undrinkable wine. A booklet written in the late 1300s, entitled *Le Ménagier de Paris* was penned by a knight employed by the Duke of Berry (the region in middle France around the city of Bourges). It included advice for keeping wine in barrels sound by having the household staff check the household's casks every week and take urgent steps when any had gone bad. (One can suppose that the servants did not mind *that* weekly task.) If in winter, an off-barrel should be placed outside in the frost; the cold would at least slow down the bacterial action. For all the good it would do, people were advised to stuff black grapes through the bung hole for wine gone sour, or to add bags of elder wood and powdered cardamom if it smelt bad (basically an aromatic cover). To clarify it, they could add hot whites and shells of eggs to the barrel. I am not sure how redness would develop in white wine, but to remove it, holly leaves could be added to a barrel. Finally, the pamphlet noted, bitterness could be neutralized by adding hot boiled corn or a basketful of clean sand (Phillips, 2000). I have not tried these methods, so I cannot recommend them.

Barrels in the age of sail

Shipbuilding and barrels went hand in hand; the woods used in their fabrication, the technology and tools which crafted the final products, and the barrels containing the supplies for the long-range voyages of discovery.

Additionally, the trade, and occasional plunder, would have been extremely difficult if barrels were not available to store the ship's provisions and items of exchange, in both of which wine was an essential commodity. This will be discussed in the next chapter.

Conclusion

The oldest remnants of wooden barrels have been found along the river shipping routes of northern and western Europe, dated to the first century BCE. However, by the turn of the millennium, apparently barrels had become a common packaging container. In the ensuing years, because Europe had the forests to supply the timber for the barrels, and because the barrels were more efficient than the amphorae for shipping larger quantities, they began to surpass the amphorae as a shipping container.

Note

1 As of this writing, Elise Marlière is the Co-Director of the Antiquarium – Arqueológia y Patrimonio, in Ibiza, Illes Balears, Spain, and a researcher with the Université de Paris X, Archéologie.

References

Aubin, G., Lavaud, S. and Roudié, P. (1996). *Bordeaux vignoble millénaire*. Bordeaux: L'Horizon Chimerique.
Bevan, A. (2014). Mediterranean containerization. *Current Anthropology*, [online] 55 (4), pp. 387–418.
Caesar, G. J. (1869). *Gaius Julius Caesar: Commentaries on the Gallic War*. (McDevitte, W. A. and Bohn, W. S. trans.). New York: Harper & Brothers.
Cooper, E. (2000). *Ten Thousand Years of Pottery*. Philadelphia, PA: University of Pennsylvania Press.
Cunliffe, B. (1997). *The Ancient Celts*. Oxford: Oxford University Press.
Godfrey, E. and van Nie, M. (2004). A Germanic ultrahigh carbon steel punch of the Late Roman-Iron Age. *Journal of Archaeological Science*, [online] 31(8), pp. 1117–1125.
Hicks, C. (2011). *Girl in a Green Gown: The History and Mystery of the Arnolfini Portrait*. London: Chatto & Windus.
Marlière, E. (2001). Le tonneau en Gaule romaine. *Gallia* 58, pp.181–201.
Marlière, E. (2013). Les campagnes militaires et l'expansion de l'usage du tonneau dans l'Empire romain. *De la cave au vin: une fructueuse alliance*, Rencontres du Clos-Vougeot, Dijon: Chaire UNESCO Culture et Traditions du Vin and Université du Bourgogne, pp. 47–61.

McGovern, P. E. (2009). *Uncorking the Past: The Quest for Wine, Beer, and Other Alcoholic Beverages.* Berkeley: University of California Press.

Millar, R. (2017). Top 10 Bordeaux export markets in 2016. *The Drinks Business,* [online] 5 April 2017.

Morris, S. P. (2013). From clay to milk in Mediterranean Prehistory: tracking a special vessel. *Backdirt: Annual Review of the Cotsen Institute of Archaeology at UCLA,* [online] pp. 70–79.

Oliver, G. ed. (2012). *The Oxford Companion to Beer.* Oxford: Oxford University Press.

Phillips, R. (2000). *A Short History of Wine.* London: Allen Lane.

Pitt, C. R. (2006). *The Wine Trade in Bristol in the Fifteenth and Sixteenth Centuries.* MA. University of Bristol.

Rose, S. (2011). *The Wine Trade in Medieval Europe 1000–1500.* London: Continuum.

Salvemini, F., Grazzi, F., Angelini, I., Vontobel, P., Vigoni, A., Artioli, G., and Zoppi, M. (2014). Morphological reconstruction of Roman arrowheads from Iulia Concordia: Italy. *Applied Physics A; Materials Science & Processing,* 117(3), pp. 1227–1240.

Twede, D. (2005). The Cask Age: the technology and history of wooden barrels. *Packaging Technology and Science,* 189(5), pp. 253–264.

Tylecote, R. F. (1976). *The History of Metallurgy.* London: The Metals Society.

Work, H. H. (2014). *Wood, Whiskey and Wine: A History of Wine.* London: Reaktion.

Websites

FranceAgriMer. (2018). Etablissement National des Produits de L'Agriculture et de la Mer. www.franceagrimer.fr

Vintners Hall. (2018). www.vintnershall.co.uk

4

WOODEN BARRELS

From 1500 CE to current times

Increasing demand for barrels, both for wine and other commodities

In the late 1400s and early 1500s, Portuguese sailors were establishing sea routes to India, Christopher Columbus crossed the Atlantic, and the Magellan-Elcano expedition circumnavigated the globe. On these voyages of discovery, as well as the numerous subsequent ones following in their wake for trade and exploitation, the wooden barrels played a lowly but integral role, containing the wine and other supplies and the items of trade.

This opening of the seas – via new maps and larger ships able to handle rougher seas – spurred fishermen to venture further out into the oceans. By the fifteenth century, the Dutch were 'mining gold' in the North Sea; the vast schools of herring and cod. Their ships delivered the catches to the nearby Scottish ports where the fish were dried or placed in brines, all packed into wooden barrels to be shipped to British and European markets. The British pushed farther afield, finding the cod along the New England and Canadian coastlines. They too used barrels to transport the salted cod to eager markets (Work, 2014).

Whalers, as well, quickly followed in the wake of the early sailing explorers. By the sixteenth century, the whaling ships were stuffed with barrels containing the fresh water and supplies on their outgoing voyages, returning with whale oil filling those same casks. We have noted this type of recycling previously; the amphorae were being reused as tiles and as pipes, and the earliest wine barrels were being reused to line water wells. In this golden age of sail, many of these barrels were recycled for the same or different products or uses.

On a similar note, some unscrupulous wine merchants placed wine in used barrels, which having once contained olive oil, molasses, meats, fishes or other foods or liquids, would degrade the flavours of the wine.

By the nineteenth century, an exponential rise in the use of barrels arose from an unlikely source: the need to transport the crude oil being found in the American state of Pennsylvania. This jump in demand – from needing some 2,000 barrels in 1859 to requiring some three million barrels just three years later – was unprecedented in the annals of product container production. It prompted companies, such as Standard Oil, to purchase vast tracks of forests to ensure a supply of the oak needed for the barrels, and to build large cooperages where hundreds of men could turn out thousands of barrels per day.

Ironically, it was shortly discovered that wooden barrels were not the ideal container for the crude oil. Even with the heavy crude they leaked; or at least the hastily made barrels attempting to satisfy the increasing demand seeped excessively. The crude oil companies quickly turned away from the use of the barrels to large wooden tanks placed upon railroad cars, then to steel tanks, then rejecting the tanks and railways altogether to lay pipelines. Nonetheless, it is from this short-lived use of wooden barrels for the crude oil that our term 'barrel of oil', with its capacity measurement of 42 US gallons or about 159 litres, originated.

As the European and North American populations expanded, so did the demand for wine. However, in northern Europe, and especially Britain and Germany, it was superseded by the demand for beer, partly due to tradition, as well as a lower cost of the liquid for the working man. In North America, whiskey flourished, also due to minimal cost as the bourbon companies were getting surplus corn at low rates. With the demand for all these products, so rose the demand for barrels to age and ship those commodities.

EXPLORATIONS 4.1
WINE BARRELS IN THE AGE OF SAIL

In the fall of 2014, Karen and I were staying the month in Bordeaux's Chartrons district. One day, with hundreds of Bordeaux citizens, we gathered along the banks of the Garonne River to witness the arrival of *L'Hermione*, a replica of the original 1779 French sailing ship.

The ship came into view as it passed La Cité du Vin. It then slowed, awaiting the centre-section of the elegant, newly built, vertical-lift bridge, the Pont Jacques Chaban-Delmase, to slowly rise. Up it went, some 50 metres, allowing the tall masts of the ship to easily pass under and continue its journey on up the river. The 44-metre long, 32-gun frigate subsequently moored at the Quai Richelieu, just upstream from the Chartrons district.

(The original ship is famous for transporting French General Lafayette (1757–1834) in 1780 to the emerging United States to assist in the American Revolutionary War against the British.)

The following day the *L'Hermione* was open to visitors. With many others, I lined up for a chance to tour the ship. In particular, I wanted to see how barrels were an integral part of the ship's equipment. As this replica ship was on a training voyage, in preparation of a re-enactment of the eighteenth-century journey to America, it was carrying only a limited amount of supplies. Nonetheless, several displays within the ship showed that, for the original journey, an extensive supply of stores – food, water, wine and gun power – would have been packaged in barrels for the several months round-trip voyage. While most were stowed in the lower decks to help ballast the ship, to fit in the required number of barrels, others would have been stuffed in every nook and corner throughout the ship.

The original *L'Hermione* did not visit Bordeaux. Over the years, however, thousands of other ocean-going sailing ships did, taking with them much of Bordeaux's wine on their outgoing voyages. By the sixteenth century, sailing ships had circumnavigated the globe and were more frequently sailing to the East Indies and the Americas. During this period in the days before plastic containers or refrigeration, barrels proved to be the ideal containers for wine and the ship's other stores, as well as the many items of trade, and/or the spoils from their conquests.

Constructing barrels and ships

Recently, while in Melbourne, Australia, I passed by its large port. Several giant, stork-like cranes were loading and off-loading the metal shipping

Barge Nebraska discharging 4245 Barrels of Wine into American Hawaiian S.S. Co's Arizonan; San Francisco Oct 10 1913

FIGURE 4.1 Loading barrels with California wine in San Francisco
Courtesy of the Unzelman Collection, Santa Rosa, CA

containers from the ships, while forklifts on the wharf were busy organizing those boxes; placing them on truck trailers for local delivery or rail cars for delivery further afield. From my vantage point, I could clearly see the stern of one of the massive container ships, the focus of much of this activity. On it, I counted a wall of containers – six high by 16 across – stretching to the outer edges of that ship. By estimating the distance of those 16 containers across the back of that ship, I could determine that just the *width* of that container ship (about 39 metres) was roughly the same *length* as the *L'Hermione* and of most of the other sixteenth century, ocean-going sailing vessels!

Nonetheless, by the sixteenth century, serious ship building had been going on for thousands of years. I use the word 'serious' because, despite being made largely of wood, the building of those ocean-going sailing ships was both highly intricate and complicated, no less so than the mechanics of today's container ships and their support equipment of cranes, forklifts, trucks and trains. Those early shipwrights were extremely skilled men, incorporating the experiences of hundreds of ancient boatbuilders with the latest technology of their day.

Construction of those ships typically started with a dense framework of heavy timbers – usually made of oak as are wine barrels. These structural members were adapted to the curves of the ship's design by bending the wood, as is done with barrel staves, by splicing pieces together, or by actually sourcing the joints in trees to match where the ship's divergent form needed to come together, such as the stern keel post. The exterior of the massive framework was overlain with strakes of waterproof woods, while on the interior the shipwright used lighter woods. Additionally, the intricacy of the rope or hemp rigging used to stabilize the masts and hoist the numerous sails would make all but the most experienced seamen's heads spin. These complex frame and support systems were designed – by trial and error over the centuries – to counteract the tremendous forces of the seas and take maximum advantage of the only means of propulsion, the wind.

Wine barrels, on the other hand have no internal framework; this would take up space and make cleaning the interior a nightmare. Their external framework, basically the hoops, is non-obtrusive in order for the barrel to be rolled. They are the epitome of simplicity crossbred with efficiency.

Oak for wine barrels

In the previous chapter, I noted that the earliest barrels had been made of softer woods, such as silver fir and larch. That changed relatively quickly as the advantages of oak were discovered, and the iron and steel tools to cut and plane the wood came into general use. By the third century CE, French forest engineer and author Jean-Paul Lacroix estimates that oak was the primary timber being used for barrels (Lacroix, 2006). Further, he states that "the strength and durability of oak, as compared to softwoods, was a critical asset" (2006). We can now add that the flavours the oak provides to the wines are complimentary as well.

If the evidence of our ancestors placing terabinth in wine to be a preservative, as found by McGovern's examination of the residue of the amphorae, is any example of their willingness to experiment, then, too, it is probable that every type of wood has been tried for the wine barrels. The earliest barrels used softer woods most likely because sharp, hard steel tools were not yet available on a general basis to cut and plane the oak or other hardwoods. Other woods have been tried for wine barrels because they were the only trees available, such as; birch, chestnut, Cyprus, Douglas fir, elm, jarrah, karri, locust, maple, palm, red gum and spruce (Schahinger and Rankine, 1999). Moreover, some were tested because it was thought that they might provide a difference to the vintner's wine; an advantage to their marketing.

EXPLORATIONS 4.2
USE OF DIFFERENT OAK SPECIES

As an example of this latter rational, on an early trip to Bordeaux, Karen and I were provided with a rare chance for a personal tasting with the cellar masters at both Château Lafite and Château Mouton-Rothschild. Both wineries are in Medoc's Pauillac, and not more than a kilometre from each other, with vineyards which are almost contiguous.

At each winery, the tours started in their fermentation rooms. Being the middle of winter, the open-top wooden tanks were empty but clean; the fermented wine having been pumped to the enclosed wooden tanks in subsequent rooms for settling before being barrelled down. We then moved into their chai. Those cellars contained hundreds of brand-new chateau-style barrels, all resting quietly with a year-old vintage. In both wineries we were able to taste directly from the barrels. Although the wines were young, we could still detect subtle differences.

During our tours, discussions with the cellar masters got around to the forest sources for the oak each used for his wineries' barrels. One noted that he requested Limousin oak, obtained from the forest tracks around the city of Limoges, in the centre of France. The other demanded wood from the Nevers forests, a bit further north, but southeast of Paris. The growing conditions for the Nevers oaks are slightly cooler – due to slightly higher elevation – slowing the tree's growth resulting in tighter tree rings (more rings per unit of distance, i.e. millimetre or inch).

The oak in both forests falls under the general, common name of European white oak (*Quercus robur*). More and more, however, as wine-makers and scientists gain exacting information about the details and physical locations of the species, the oak from the Limousin, the more southerly forest, is being referred to as *Quercus robur*, while that from the centre of France (Nevers and Vosges forests) is *Quercus sessiflora* (Goode, 2014). With their ranges overlapping, silviculturists are now recognizing that both their individual species ratios within any forest, and their flavour profiles, vary. Additionally, the terroirs in which those oaks grow provide delicate and understated distinctions which are passed to the wine. It is these differences, along with those in the grape growing and winemaking, which provide the nuances to make the wines from both these famous vineyards different, yet equally sought after.

Oak forests

As Lacroix noted, early on, European oak had become the wood of choice for barrels. The desire to build wine barrels with oak, however, was competing with the demand for oak to construct the thousands of ships and all sorts of medieval equipment – wooden tools, furniture and barrels for other commodities – as well as the beams for increasingly large buildings such as cathedrals. Europe's oak forests could not keep up with the expanding demand. As early as 1543, England passed laws to curtail the overcutting of their oak and minimize building of large casks (Kilby, 1990). France followed shortly thereafter, when in the seventeenth century, under Louis XIV's Secretary of State of the Navy, Jean-Baptiste Colbert, the government enacted strict laws about cutting oak, and set aside significant forest areas to be used solely for building its naval ships (Logan, 2005). Later, periodic wars and/or embargos forced the European wine barrel coopers to source European oak from the Polish port of Memel, on the Baltic Sea, and occasionally American white oak (*Quercus alba*) from the United States.

When the Europeans arrived in the United States, they found vast tracks of hardwood forests, with numerous species of oak. Among the early settlers were some who had experience as coopers. As they started to work with these American oaks, one species, American white oak (*Quercus alba*), stood out for its attributes to make sound barrels. It had many similarities to the European oaks with which they were familiar, but it also had one important difference. Because of its internal cell structure, American oak could be sawn instead of split. This advantage allowed cooperages working with American oak to speed up the process of making the staves, thus enabling some large cooperages to produce thousands of barrels per day.

Barrels and European wine making

In terms of wine, by the sixteenth century Europe had largely settled into many of its wine-making traditions, with barrels playing a major role. The wine was aged in casks and barrels, and shipped primarily in barrels. Glass was used for tableware – pitchers and glasses – and was still several hundred years from being commonly used for wine bottles.

Wars and harsh weather continued to disrupt production, but the demand for products from across the country and around the world usually quickly overcame the periods of hardships.

As the trade increased, slowly the one or two-man cooperage shops began to increase in size. Many skilled coopers and unskilled labourers sought work in the developing cooperages which were building the thousands of barrels required for the salted fish and whale oil industries. Additionally, huge casks and tanks were being built for wineries. For example, built deep within the bowels of the Heidelberg castle, a cask was installed capable of containing 220,000 litres of wine. In Strasbourg, an equally large one was built (Robinson, 1997). These casks are so large, and designed to take advantage of the total space within the confines of their respective cellars, that they had to be assembled on site.

The European craftsmen guilds – including the cooperage guilds in England, France and Germany – became stronger. This served two purposes. The first was to set a minimum standard for their products by controlling their member craftsmen and tradesmen. By extension this created virtual monopolies for those trades within their respective communities. Secondly, the guilds acted to present one uniting voice; especially so in attempting to protect their members from exorbitant taxes and or onerous government rules.

The guilds could not, however, protect the wine barrel craftsmen from all the natural or political storms. For example, grape phylloxera (*Phylloxera vitifoliae*) is a root louse which, over a few years, can devastate vineyards. Accidently brought in from America, it hit the European plants starting in the mid-nineteenth century. Like America's Prohibition Amendment later on, phylloxera ravaged both the vintners and in turn their coopers, as in many cases there was no need for barrels because there was no wine to place in those casks. The vintners must have been dissolute at seeing their vines shrivel up and die, and the coopers equally so, unable to pay their workers or purchase staves and heading for future years.

Wine, only one of many products put into the barrels

Barrels, integral in the trading and freight transportation systems of the times, came in a myriad of sizes. Various charts list upward of 50 different variations, each with their own individual name and usually built to contain a specific commodity. However, amongst all of these, there are basically two types of barrels; *tight* and *slack*. The *tight* barrels were for wine, whiskey and beer, as well as any liquids or products which required a completely sealed container. Products and commodities such as grains, tobacco, potatoes, salt, salted fish and meat, gun power and cement all would have

FIGURE 4.2 A drinking party in a wine cellar; etching by Nicolas van Aelst, circa 1600

required tight barrels; to contain the products, and as importantly, to keep the environment – bugs, dust, and rain – out. (In those early days, warehouses or even sheds were an extravagance. The barrels were almost always exposed to the elements; freezing in the winter, boiling in the heat of the summer, soaking up water in the rain or the staves drying and shrinking if left out in the sun.) *Slack* barrels were for such items as apples, pears, nails, and crockery (cushioned in straw).

EXPLORATIONS 4.3
EXAMINING THE USE OF BARRELS IN CALIFORNIA AS AN ABBREVIATED VERSION OF HOW THE EUROPEAN WINE CULTURE EVOLVED

Ideally, we would like to say that barrels were specifically developed to transport wine, with aging thrown in as a side benefit since transportation modes in the first millennium CE were rather slow. This would be a great idea except that we have no proof, at least not yet. Gradually, archaeologists and scientists like Marlière and McGovern, and their colleagues, do seem to be closing in. Stay tuned.

Nonetheless, with the historical data available, we can make educated guesses. Some idea of what must have taken place, albeit in a vastly condensed time frame, can be gleaned by examining the rise of today's relatively young wine culture in places like California. The development in Australia, South Africa and Chile would be similar. The wine industries' history within these regions provides a window onto what factors might have influenced Europe as the barrels were developed and introduced in those later centuries BCE, and have evolved ever since.

California has a wild grape variety, *Vitis california*, which produces a rather sour grape. The native Indian tribes may have eaten it, although it was probably not high on their desirable fruit and berry list. There is no evidence that they made a 'wine' from the grapes. The first wines, as we know them, would have been brought in with the explorers, and later with the Spanish missionaries arriving in the 1770s. The padres brought several varieties of the Criolla wine grape (*Vitis vinifera, species*) from Spain, and planted it around their missions. These priests eventually built a series of 21 churches and facilities, stretching from San Diego to Sonoma, a small town 100 kilometres north of San Francisco.

The Cirolla grapes acclimated well to this range. The missionaries' containers to make, age and store their wines would have been any barrels or ceramic vessels, large or small which accompanied them on the ships. Additionally, most likely they also made use of animal hide sacks. Until the missions became established, the padre's winemaking efforts would have been difficult at best.

As the missions grew, the friars, perhaps wanting to earn some money from making and selling wine to the growing Spanish ranchos, would have turned to larger vats, casks and tanks. Any oval or round casks (those with curved sides) would have had to have been imported from Europe, but the tanks (those with straight sides), could have been made from California redwood (*Sequoia sempervirens*) which grew along the coast, northward from the area around Carmel. This wood provided a straight grain, easy-to-work timber, which was resistant to most liquids including wine, making it ideal for tanks to contain wine or water.

In the eighteenth and nineteenth centuries, the lure of opportunities – farming rich lands, freedom from the stifling traditions in the East Coast and Europe, and gold – drew emigrants from around the world to California in search of its 'treasures'. A number of the Europeans luckily brought their winemaking skills, because panning for gold, as with many entrepreneurial endeavours, was not a sure thing. These people could and would fall back on their homeland trades, including starting California's now famous wine industry.

For example, in the early nineteenth century, one young French man, Jean-Louis, with the appropriate surname of Vigne, planted a vineyard in the Los Angeles area. It was at that time just a sleepy little community surrounding the nascent mission. Once his grapes had matured and wine had been made, he needed a method to transport his vintage to the main markets on America's eastern seaboard (Kilby, 1990).

He had grown up in Cadillac, a village on the Garonne River, not far upstream from Bordeaux. There, besides learning grape growing skills, he had also apprenticed as a cooper. With his knowledge of barrel building he sought oak from the hills north of LA and built a small cooperage to construct the barrels needed to ship his wine.

The railways had yet to connect America's east and west coasts. This necessitated shipping his wine in the barrels on a sailing ship. In those days, the Panama Canal had also yet to be built. The ships in which he sent his wine had to make the several-month voyage – south along the western coasts of Mexico and South America, rounding Cape Horn at the tip of Argentina, and sailing north along the eastern sides of those regions in the Atlantic Ocean – in order to reach the Baltimore and New York markets (Kilby, 1990). He probably shipped his wines as soon as they finished fermenting; they certainly would have aged during the long voyage.

Other immigrants, especially the large numbers heading to the gold fields in the 1840s, found the rich volcanic soils in northern California suitable for planting vineyards. There, they built stone wineries and installed redwood tanks, had oak casks shipped from Europe, or reused wine or whiskey barrels which delivered those products to the miners.

By the 1870s the rail lines had connected the country. Barrels of wine could be shipped east to St. Louis and Chicago, there to connect with rail or river transportation in order to distribute the wine further afield.

Initially, the wine was shipped in barrels which had brought wine and whiskey to the miners. Some of these immigrants, had, like Monsieur Vigne, barrel making skills, and set up cooperages, including the California Barrel Company in 1883, and the Carl Cooperage Company, both in San Francisco, and one in the Napa Valley's town of St. Helena. However, California was not blessed with great oak forests suitable for barrel making. Thus, on their western runs, the trains brought staves and heading from the vast eastern hardwood forests to these budding cooperages.

While California held a moniker of 'the promised land', that was mostly marketing. In a shortened-time frame, the vintners and coopers saw their share of economic and cultural turmoil akin to that experienced in the long history of Europe. They were a long way from the eastern markets. Transporting their products was problematic; firstly, getting their barrels delivered in a timely manner, and secondly, having the wine still palatable if barrels were transported in the heat of the summer in non-refrigerated box cars. Closer to home the turmoil created by the fights to oust the Spanish and make California a state also disrupted the fragile economy. By the early twentieth century, American's temperance groups finally had enough power to pressure Congress to pass the Eighteenth Amendment prohibiting the manufacture and sale of alcohol in 1920; the Amendment was repealed in 1933. Wineries were restricted to making only 'sacramental' wines. While some wine certainly slipped out the backdoor to not-so-religious customers, it certainly put a crimp on total wine sales, and in turn, the need for additional cooperage. Finally, war, especially America's Civil War and World Wars I and II, created economic hardships, not to mention the loss of military age personnel to engage in the viticulture, wine making, and cooperage building.

Nevertheless, the Californian wineries survived. By the 1970s, they were starting to make a name for themselves within the greater world of wine. The Judgement of Paris, a tasting at which several Napa Valley wineries scored extremely well with French judges, placed California on the oenophile's map.

Current uses of wine barrels

As we get into a discussion of today's wine barrels, a quick look again at Bordeaux's changing wine cooperage scene might provide some perspective.

EXPLORATIONS 4.4
WINE TRADE DISTRICT

In the 1980s, still scattered amongst the wine négociants' cellar within the Chartrons, Bordeaux's wine-trading district, were a few barrel cooperages. They were sited in this wine trading precinct to make the barrels for each new vintage as well as to repair and maintain the older ones.

During my first visit to Bordeaux, I made a courtesy call at one of those cooperages. This particular barrel maker, besides fabricating the barrels for their French winery clients, had recently started to export to California; the beginnings of the huge demand created by the growth of the United States, and particularly the Californian wineries noted above. At that time, the Napa Valley company where I was employed was representing their line of barrels. I wanted to meet the owners and see how they were crafting the barrels.

What Karen and I found as we drove into Bordeaux in the 1980s was a grimy city. It was more than just the grunge of a cold January day. Hundreds of years of accumulated mould and dirt were covering its beautiful limestone buildings, and all too many Citroens, Peugeots and Renaults were adding to the pollution and clogging the narrow streets.

At that time, the Chartrons was still the wine trading area of the city, as it had been for the past several hundred years. We encountered a dark warren of small alleys, along which ancient brown wooden doors, just large enough to pass barrels through, led down stairs or ramps into the wine cellars. The cellars were generally owned by négociants, who purchased the wine from the various Bordeaux regional wineries. In their cool, dimly lit cellars this wine would age in casks before it was shipped to clients in France, Europe and the rest of the world.

Le quartier des Chartrons is adjacent to the Garonne River. The area takes its name from a fourteenth-century monastery built by the Carthusian monks on a site of what was then just outside Bordeaux's town walls. As the monastery gained in importance, and the swamps around it were drained, a settlement grew up. Being near to the river, the area attracted the river trade, of which the buying and selling of wine became an extremely important and lucrative enterprise. Slowly, wine traders and brokers, including some from England and the Netherlands, developed companies within the area. Cellars were built, and more and more wine passed through the Chartrons

By the Middle Ages, the wooden barrels had long since replaced the amphorae as the container of choice for the wine. The wineries and vineyards would ship their wine by river boat and barge. These conveyances would tie up near to the négociants' caves which were to receive the barrels. Most of the river boats were basically just material-hauling barges, called *argentat*, for the town where they were first built. In addition to the barrels of wine, they also brought oak staves and heading for the cooperages, as well as grape stakes for vineyards, down the Dordogne River from the forests in the Corrèze. The Dordogne meets the Garonne River at the Gironde Estuary. At this juncture, the area is tidal and the boats could facilitate a left turn to sail up the Garonne to Bordeaux on an incoming tide.

Situated upon the left bank, the Chartrons fronts a straight stretch of the Garonne River. Just upstream is the large Bordeaux public space, the Place de Quinconces. Then the river makes a sweeping curve to frame the classical eighteenth-century limestone buildings, such as the Place de la Bourse or, with its narrowly pointed spires, the whimsical fifteenth-century Porte Cailhau building, of the central city.

The river is still tidal to this point. In the early days of the Chartrons trading centre, when the tide was out, the barrels were rolled up and down the mud flats to reach the barges and boats. Perhaps boards were laid down upon the mud to aid in pushing the barrels up the river's inclined shoulders. Later, the river's edge was cobbled, and then rock quays and concrete docks were subsequently built to receive and dispatch the barrels full of wine. By the sixteenth century, sugar was another important trading item, and unfortunately, so were slaves

My visit to the cooperage was well before the days of GPS maps on our phones, much less the cell phones themselves. Now, having re-visited the Chartrons several times, and even having lived in its environs for a month, I have learned the confusing maze of alleys and small streets. I cannot begin to imagine how my wife and I actually located the cooperage on that initial visit.

Nonetheless, once we had entered the building, we encountered piles of sawdust cluttering the floor and found the walls blackened with years of the accumulated smoke from the barrel-bending fires. The techniques of barrel fabrication we saw on that visit had changed little in hundreds of years. The only improvements we observed were a few more machines – albeit rather ancient ones – with which to ease some of the cooper's labour. Had we been able to walk into a Roman cooperage we would not have seen much difference.

Barrel wood

Discerning wine drinkers, as far back as the Greeks and Romans, have been debating the merits of one vineyard over another as they smell and sip their wine. Serious scientific examination, however, of the timber employed for the barrels as well as the toasting regimes used to bend the staves, has only received traction in the past 50 years. These more rigorous investigations were enabled by the advent of hi-tech scientific equipment capable of probing and measuring the compounds within, and the morphology of, the various wood species, as well as accurately monitoring toasting temperatures.

Equally, the demand to understand how the oak impacted the wine came from the winemakers. The increasing number of university-trained winemakers were not content to rest on 'tradition'. They wanted scientific answers as to what were the causes of the flavours and how they could influence and nuance them. The growth of universities with oenology and viticultural departments has helped to satisfy these needs.

Additionally, recent wood and toasting research developments were prompted and encouraged by the increased wine competition worldwide. This started in the 1970s as new world wineries started to make a name for themselves. With marketing pushing wine consumption, wine drinking became more and more popular outside Europe. Winemakers felt the pressure to make better and better wine; they wanted answers, which only rigorous science could provide.

Historically, when purchasing their barrels, wine makers would select a cooperage, usually a local one, and accept what it offered in terms of wood origin and toast level. Typically, the regional cooperages were limited, primarily in terms of the transportation costs, in how far afield they could source their timber. Those winemakers had accepted the traditional methods for the length of time for air drying their lumber and the processes by which they would manufacture the barrels.

However, as the wine industry has become more diverse and competitive – as we observed with Châteaux Lafite and Mouton-Rothschild – the need to find the best barrels to enhance each individual wine increased dramatically. In the 1970s, many American winemakers started producing both Burgundian and Bordeaux style wines in their wineries, say a Chardonnay and Cabernet Sauvignon, or a Pinot Noir and Merlot. They would connect with a French cooperage and request *both* styles of barrels, even though traditionally these coopers normally made only *one* style or another. As the American winemakers learned about the various French forests, they also began requesting the different woods. These demands crossed the established boundaries, and prompted the cooperages to dramatically diversify their offerings of both forest sources and barrel styles.

Today, it is estimated that roughly 800,000 new wine barrels, made from both European and American wood sources, are annually sold worldwide (Dekker, 2017). The main wine barrel cooperages are located in France and America, while other important ones are located near the wine regions in Spain, Italy, Portugal, Australia, South Africa, Chile and China.

Flavours from oak wine barrels

Winemakers have known for centuries that oak has many aromas and extracts which contribute and compliment the wine flavours. But researchers have now only recently identified the numerous chemicals that are the sources for these compounds. They come from the oak species itself, as well as the terroir in which they are grown. Further enquiry has illuminated how the oak's compounds are also changed and modified by the air-drying and toasting regimes the coopers use to process the wood and build the barrels. Wine's hundreds of flavours combine with those of the oak during fermentation and/or the barrel aging, building upon one another producing the complexities which are so appealing.

Oak and its terroir

The several species of European and American oaks fall under the general common name of *white oak*. When they were classified years ago, however, the scientists were not considering that these species might have significant flavour differences. I will confine a discussion of these differences to general terms.

The researchers, coopers and winemakers now know that European oak typically provides more tannin compounds. These contribute to mouthfeel in wine (Scollary, 2014). Additionally, barrels made with European oak tend to yield their flavours slower, not overwhelming the wine. This may be partially due to the fact that European oak is split rather than sawn, minimizing the broken cells in the wood (Crawford, 2014).

American oak, on the other hand, is higher in coconut and fresh wood aromas (Badet-Murat et al., 2016; Goode, 2014). To a lesser degree, the vanilla aroma is apparent in American oak, as is a 'whiskey' aroma, due to the association of American oak with bourbon barrels. Air drying both species of woods softens the tannins, and toasting can precipitate flavours ranging from clove to smokiness (Robinson, 2015).

European oak in general, and French oak in particular, is held in the highest regard for aging wines. American oak just does not have the same panache. In defence of American oak, however, from my years as a cooper, I believe that part of this is due to the lack of care which American oak originally received when it was beginning to be used for wine barrels. Barrels of American oak were primarily being made for the bourbon industry which has an entirely different set of requirements.

With the different variations in compounds, American oak needs a longer period of air drying to wash out the tannins and other bitter compounds. Splitting the oak and employing unique toasting regimes may also enhance the flavours. As researchers continue to study the effects of American oak, I believe we will see an increasing acceptance.

Cooperage manufacturing influences

Air drying the staves and heading

Oak, when used for making barrels or similarly for fine furniture, needs to be dried prior to use in order to minimize shrinkage once the barrel, or the piece of furniture, is assembled. For wine barrels, rather than utilizing kilns, the wood is normally dried in the open air. This is to allow the wind and air flow to evenly evaporate the moisture from within and between the cellular structure, and, as importantly, to permit the rains and snows to wash out some of the tannins. Normally two to three years are necessary to decrease the moisture levels in the woods to acceptable levels and minimize the tannins.

Leaving wood out to air dry for longer periods to decrease the tannins, which contribute harsh or bitter tastes, is one of the techniques cooperages are utilizing to 'soften' the tastes imparted by the oak. Nonetheless, to speed the process up, and provide some reliability, a few cooperages have taken to sprinkling the staves with water, and/or actually soaking the staves for several weeks in huge water baths.

Toasting

After several years of air-drying, the staves arrive at the cooperage as rough, rectangular blanks. They are then machine planned and their edges bevelled. The still straight slats are placed within a circle of several heavy-duty steel hoops. These hoops are reused over and over to maintain a consistent barrel size. Within these hoops, the splayed array of staves is then placed over the bending fire with a cable encircling the spread end. The fire heats the remaining interior moisture turning it to steam to provide the flexibility for the staves to be bent without breaking while the cable is slowly tightened. The cable pulls the wide end of the staves together, thus developing the curvature and the *barrel* shape.

Once the staves are pulled together, the barrel is removed from the fire and additional hoops are placed on it to hold the staves in position. It now has its barrel-looking form, minus the ends, and is then placed back on a fire for the toasting process. The original main purpose of this secondary firing was to *set* the staves in their curved positions. However, it has now been realized that various flavours can be drawn from the wood depending upon the heat of the fire and the time the barrel remains on the blaze. During this period, the interior of the barrel becomes *toasted*; increasing in interior colour and wood caramelization with the heat penetration.

Time on the toasting fires and/or adding fuel to the fire raises the barrel's interior temperature. Winemakers can request a light toast, in which the interior wood usually does not reach 150°C, producing flavours which are sappy, scented, spicy, leather, clove and coconut. A medium toast is generally considered in the temperature range of 150–190°C, developing butterscotch, sawdust (oaky) and the vanilla flavours. Leaving the barrels on for longer periods pushes the temperatures to greater than 190°C, which develops a heavy toast with toffee, coffee, almond and smoky flavours as the heat changes the wood sugars (Scollary, 2014).

Winemakers have become extremely creative in nuancing the flavours from their wines with requests for the various oaks, their origins, air-

TABLE 4.1 Wine flavours from oak type and toasting[*]

	Light toast	*Medium toast*	*Heavy toast*
American oak	vanilla, dill, coconut	vanilla, honey, caramel, toast, roasted nut aromas, strong coconut, roast coffee and cocoa	strong roast coffee, espresso, caramelized sugar, tiramisu, wood smoke and vanilla
French oak	vanilla bean, caramel, holiday spice flavours like nutmeg, clove, allspice and dried ginger	cedar, cigar box, milk chocolate and baking spice	crème brûlée, cedar, charcoal, and Asian spices like cinnamon, ginger and clove
Hungarian oak	vanilla, herbal flavours, sweet spice flavours like clove and cinnamon	stronger butterscotch, banana, sarsaparilla and sweet spice	strong spice, vanilla, butterscotch, toffee and molasses

[*] Thanks to Carter, Donald A., 'Pass the Toast – The Maillard Reaction in Wine Barrel Toasting', http://winesnark.com/pass-the-toast-the-maillard-reaction-in-wine-barrel-toasting/

FIGURE 4.3 Wine barrels on seven-inch, Western Square metal pallets
Courtesy of Western Square

drying regimes and toasting times and temperatures. For example, one Napa Valley winemaker, noted for his Cabernet Sauvignon, placed an order for 150 American oak barrels from the cooperage at which I was the General Manager. Even with this significant number of barrels, ours were just part of a mix of both American and European barrels at this winery. In the case of our barrels, he requested a heavy toast; not a typical toast level for aging Cabernet. When questioned, he explained that he wanted the heavy toast to provide spices – that of coffee and vanilla – to *accent* his wine.

Barrel size and length of aging

Barrels provide significantly more oak flavour than do large oak wine tanks or casks, primarily due to the increased surface area ratio to the volume of wine. While most European and American wineries incorporate 225 litre sized barrels, for winemakers in Australia 300 litres is the norm, while some winemakers do utilize larger, 500 litre barrels, especially for aging more delicate wines such as Sauvignon Blanc and occasionally Chardonnay, when a minimal influence of the oak is desired.

Wine making influences

Micro-oxygenation

In the mid-1990s, while on one of our trips to Bordeaux, we met up with a Napa Valley winemaker friend. He had just returned from a fact-finding trip into the Madiran wine region in south western France. This area is part of Gascony – spread over the departments of the Gers, Hautes-Pyrénées and Pyrénées-Atlantiques. Over glasses of wine, he related what he had found.

Madiran's principal red grape is the Tannat variety. As its name implies, Tannat produces a thick, strong tasting, tannic wine, which generally needs three or more years of barrel maturation to soften. This long aging requirement placed the Madiran vintners at a disadvantage; they were having difficulty commanding the higher prices needed to offset the costs the extended aging necessitated.

In searching for how to soften their wines and/or age them faster, they found that by introducing minute amounts of oxygen into the wine while it was in tanks, they could simulate, in a reduced time-frame, the aging which occurs in the barrels. They called this process micro-oxygenation, or micro-ox for short.

But by not placing the wines in barrels, they were not getting the oak flavour. They solved this dilemma by using a combination of aging the wine for a period in tanks using the micro-ox system, and then placing it in barrels for final aging and picking up the oak flavours. In some cases, vintners actually installed individual oxygen diffusers in the barrels.

As our winemaker friend took this information and techniques back to the United States, he and other winemakers there started experimenting with the process. Subsequently, micro-ox has radically transformed how low-end, supermarket wines are made. The winemakers utilized it to rapidly make inexpensive wines in tanks; incorporating the micro-ox to mimic the aging process which normally occurs in the barrels, and adding chips or pieces of toasted oak (oak alternatives) to provide the oak barrel flavours. Additionally, many winemakers are using micro-ox to finesse very heavy wines or to correct problem wines.

Consistency in flavours

Of the millions of today's wine drinkers, few have a good understanding of the factors involved in the growing of the grapes. In particular, there is a decreasing awareness of the concept of *vintages*, partially due to improvements in grape growing and winemaking, minimizing the need to 'age' bottles of wine in one's home. As a result, many imbibers expect every bottle of Chardonnay, or whatever wine they purchase from a particular winery, to taste the same as the previous one.

Certainly, viticulturists have done much to minimize the impact of the year-to-year weather variations. Trellising, leaf-pulling, drip irrigation, and frost protection systems are just some of the innovations vineyards are now utilizing to produce relatively consistent harvests, or at least minimize the dramatic swings experienced just a few decades ago. Many innovations in winemaking have helped to enhance the best flavours and even correct many flaws.

Along these same lines, the cooperages are also taking steps to manufacture barrels which produce consistent flavours. Above, I noted the use of sprinklers or water baths to help remove tannins as the wood dries. The removal process can then be controlled more precisely than when relying upon the weather.

In the cooperage, another major change has been to control the amount of heat each barrel receives while it is on the bending and toasting fires. As a result, the fires are becoming increasingly automated; employing devices to deliver specified amounts of fuel, and measuring the amount of heat the interior of the barrel receives. This data is stored for future use. The entire effort is to ensure that if a winemaker orders 100 medium toast barrels, each and every one will be almost exactly the same. When he or she places a similar order the following year, those barrels too will be almost identical in terms of the flavours passed into the wines.

How much consistency is desirable? This provides great fodder for discussion in winemaker tasting groups and blogs. Should wine growers and winemakers be more traditional, natural, in their approach, or is this new technology producing better wines? The consistency in the tastes coming from the barrels is only one small part of the equation. Not all cooperages have embraced the newer techniques, so winemakers can still purchase barrels with more or less variation.

Fermentation

One of the side effects of grape fermentation is the heat generated. For red wine this is not usually a problem. However, for white wines, a cooler fermentation results in crisper wines. Thus, Chardonnay is frequently fermented in wooden barrels. Their small size and large surface area allow the heat to dissipate. Additionally, the flavours derived from the oak barrels are slowly and gently integrated into the fermenting wine.

Normally, only white wine is barrel fermented. Those wines have been separated from the grape skins and pulp, so are easier to handle with only the barrel's small bunghole available to introduce and remove the wine. However, there has been some interest in fermenting more delicate red wines, such as Pinot Noir, in barrels. This is typically a labour of love, rather than for large scale commercial winemaking (Robinson, 2015).

Chardonnay (French Chablis) is ideally suited to barrel fermentation and aging as the oak flavours meld nicely with the flinty, steely and apple characteristics of the typical Chardonnay flavour profile. The oak adds a buttery tone and rich mouthfeel.

Small barrels also facilitate lees stirring. Lees are the yeast cells and other particulates which are left over from the fermentation. They slowly fall out of the wine as it ages. By stirring the barrel daily with a long wand, these lees increase the richness of the wine. My wife, Karen, did daily lees stirring when making the Sauvignon Blanc from our Napa Valley vineyard, although she was fermenting the wine in stainless steel barrels. This procedure added body to her wines.

Barrel aging

In today's modern wineries, with the exception of wooden barrels used for fermentation, barrels are primarily used just for aging wines. These are mostly reds: varieties such as Cabernet Sauvignon, Pinot Noir, Merlot, Syrah, Zinfandel, Malbec, Grenache, Nebbiolo, and Bordeaux blends. Typically, the aging period is between 12 to 24 months in the barrel. Some reds, particularly the heavier reds of Spain, are aged in barrels for longer periods, whereas whites, such as Chardonnay and Sauvignon Blanc that are barrel aged usually are aged for shorter periods. Any barrel aged wine, with the time and labour involved, typically commands a higher price.

The headiest of wines can be aged in 100% new barrels, but most wineries use some combination of new and used barrels; the new supplying the oak flavours, and all providing the *aging*, i.e. the interaction with minute amounts of oxygen for which the barrels are uniquely suited. Of course, there are many permutations of all these options; coming under the general term of the 'winemaker's toolbox'.

Oxygen is critical to improving the wine. It helps to connect the short molecules, which contribute to what we taste as sharpness or bitterness, into long strings, creating the mouthfeel of a softer, mature wine. Additionally, oxygen helps to fix the wine colour, and generally stabilize the wine, developing the balance and characteristics which we associate with pleasant aromas and flavours (Del Alamo-Sanza and Nevares, 2015)

There is still some controversy about how oxygen actually exactly interacts with the wine. Initially, researchers believed that the majority of oxygen was picked up as the barrels were opened for topping and/or the wine transferred from one container to another. Further experimentation has revealed that some oxygen is introduced through the wood of the barrel – an interaction between the wine penetrating the interior of the wood meeting the oxygen which has entered the wood from outside the barrel. Surprisingly, barrels with air-tight seals show greater oxygen pickup than those without. This seems to be due to the negative interior

FIGURE 4.4 Wine barrels in chai
Glenn Cormier

pressure 'sucking' the oxygen in. The negative pressure is created as the water in wine evaporates from the barrel (Del Alamo-Sanza and Nevares, 2015).

The more current thinking is that oxygen pick-up is a combination of these factors – some through the bung and some through the wood. Additionally, researchers have found that the type of oak – American or European – allows more or less oxygen into the wine (Del Alamo-Sanza and Nevares, 2015). Due to the different cell structure of American white oak and its European counterparts, oxygen ingress in American oak is slightly greater than that in the European barrels. American oak has within its cell structure *tyloses*. These help to block the movement of liquids from one cell to another. As wine writer and researcher Wessel du Toit explains, "The tyloses, although preventing wine leakage, are not impermeable to gasses and more oxygen thus comes into contact with wine in American oak barrels, compared to French oak barrels" (du Toit, 2016). Further, it has been found that barrels with fine grain oak, especially those used for the Chateau style barrels (those with the sapling hoops and which typically have thinner 22 mm staves) tend to age wine faster, i.e. have oxygen interact with the wine, than barrels with thicker, 27 mm staves of the transport style barrels (Salmaggi, 2017).

Spanish wine chemists Maria Del Alamo-Sanza and Ignacio Nevares placed oxygen probes into the barrels through the bung. They found that "21% of total oxygen entered through the bunghole, 63% of oxygen entered between the staves, and 16% of oxygen entered through the wood itself" (2015).

The traditional method for winemakers to follow the progress of oxygenating the wine was to periodically sample, by tasting and by measuring the oxygen. Now, however, there are some tools to provide real-time measurement of oxygen while the wine is in barrels (du Toit, 2016). Along these lines, the French-based Taransaud cooperage is introducing a device which is attached to the barrels and can provide continuous monitoring of the dissolved oxygen in the barrel.

Conclusion

By the Middle Ages, wooden barrels became extremely important, particularly in Europe, to transport wine and numerous other commodities. More recently, the new winemaking tools – stainless steel tanks, micro-ox, oak alternatives – have decreased the use of wooden barrels; however, the barrels continue to play a vital role in premium wine production. Wine is no longer transported in barrels, and for that we will explore glass bottles in the next chapter, and other containers in subsequent ones.

References

Badet-Murat, M.L., Vicard, J. C., Watrelot, A. A. and Kennedy, J. A. (2016). Innovative tools for stave selection and toasting: uncovering the impact of oak on wine style and composition. *Wines & Vines*, [online] 97(2), p. 44.

Crawford, K., Benton, A. and Dreger, A., (2014). The effect of grain orientation on extraction of oak flavor compounds. *Wines & Vines*, [online] 95(1) p. S20.

Dekker, A. (2017). *Moderate Growth in 2016 for French Cooperages.* [online] Fédération des Tonneliers de France. 30 June 2017.

Del Alamo-Sanza, M. and Nevares, I. (2015). Oxygen transfer rate in oak barrels: annual evaluation for dynamic oxygen intake and entry. *Wine & Vines*, [online] 96(12), p. 58.

Goode, J. (2014). *The Science of Wine: From Vine to Glass.* Berkeley: University of California Press.

Kilby, K. (1990). *The Cooper and His Trade.* Fresno: Linden Publishing.

Lacroix, J.-P. (2006). *Bois de Tonnellerie: De la forêt à la vigne et au vin.* Chartres: Editions du Gerfaut

Logan, W. B. (2005). *Oak: The Frame of Civilization.* New York: W. W. Norton & Co.

Robinson, J. ed. (1997). *The Oxford Companion to Wine.* Oxford: Oxford University Press.

Robinson, J. ed. (2015). *The Oxford Companion to Wine.* Oxford: Oxford University Press.

Salmaggi, P. (2017). Personal communication. 14 May 2017.

Schahinger, G. and Rankine, B. (1999). *Cooperage for Winemakers: A Manual on the Construction, Maintenance and Use of Oak Barrels.* Adelaide: Ryan Publications.

Scollary, G. R. (2014). Grapevine: oak and wine flavour. *Chemistry in Australia.* May 2014, p. 39.

Work, H. H. (2014). *Wood, Whiskey and Wine: A History of Barrels.* London: Reaktion.

Blog

du Toit, W. (2016). *Oxygen Permeating through Oak Barrels – New Results.* Wineland Media. www.wineland.co.za

5

GLASS BOTTLES AND OTHER GLASS VESSELS

A 1,700-year-old bottle of wine

The next time you are in your local wine shop or supermarket, take a look at the shapes of the wine bottles on the shelves. For example, focus just on the bottles for the Cabernet Sauvignon, normally placed in a Bordeaux-style bottle; those which are tall, and straight-sided with sharply curved shoulders. Even within just this one bottle-shape, the nuances between the designs and hues of the glass are almost as endless as the wine labels themselves. Despite the tradition of placing Bordeaux-type wines in a Bordeaux style bottle, it seems that each winery utilizes a slightly different colour and shape for their bottles. Add in the various coloration of the plastic or tin foils, and the diversity increases exponentially.

Examining any of the other traditional bottle styles of the wine varieties will show vast differences as well. Considering the thousands of wineries, each trying to present a stylistically different image, well, the variations are endless. Unfortunately, while all this packaging is eye-catching, it does not make our task, as consumers, of choosing a wine for tonight's dinner any easier.

Back to the bottles; descriptions of all the styles have been done well in other books. Rather, let us examine the general time-line and types of bottles, and explore some of the more unique aspects of using glass bottles for wine.

The oldest bottle known to have contained wine – because it contained a residue – was a 1.5 litre bottle discovered in a Roman tomb. The grave was located near the German Rhine River town of Speyer, about 20 kilometres southwest of Heidelberg, hence this particular magnum has been suitably named the *Speyer bottle*. The bottle has been dated to between 325 and 350 CE, just past the prime of the Roman Empire, and about 400 years after its craftsmen first started blowing glass vessels

The tomb was found in 1867, and the bottle inside was among the items for the hereafter of a man and woman, thought to be a Roman Legionnaire and his wife. It was one of 16 bottles; all but this one empty. Journalist Bonnie North described having wine in your tomb as a "BYOB [bring your own bottle] afterlife" (North, 2016).

Analysis of the contents indicates that olive oil was also in the bottle (Dal Piaz, 2010). Oil was frequently added; sitting atop the wine it protected the wine from interaction with oxygen. For some reason this bottle had more than the necessary amount to cover the wine. The top of the bottle was sealed with wax.

Experts examining the bottle suspect that a small amount of wine was initially in the bottle; perhaps the remainder after toasting the dead. To keep it drinkable for the deceased, the bottle was topped with the olive oil. This mixture had, over the past 1,700 years, slowly turned into a resinous clump (German Wines, 2017).

The shape of the Speyer bottle combines the style of the future Bordeaux bottle – straight sides and tall neck – with the ancient, amphora-like aspect – small handles where the neck meets the bottle's body (Jackson, 2014). Besides the fact that the bottle still contained wine, it is also surprising that it was used for wine. Most of the other Roman-era bottles that have been uncovered have had thin walls, suggesting that they were too fragile to contain wine (Jackson, 2014), or certainly for being used to ship wine. This one may have been an exception. Nor is the origin of the bottle known. Was is made in Italy or Germany? If it was used to transport wine from Italy to northern Europe, perhaps it was designed to be a bit tougher.

The beginnings of glass

The history of glass making appears to have evolved out of the ceramics industry. As the craftsmen and potters of the Mesopotamia region, some 5,000 years ago, developed coatings and glazes for their pots, mosaic tiles and beads, it is believed that they also discovered the secrets of making

FIGURE 5.1 Roman-era wine bottle (circa 325 CE) found in tomb of Roman soldier near Speyer, Germany
Historical Museum of the Palatinate, Speyer, Germany, by Peter Haag-Kirchner

translucent materials (Klein and Lloyd, 1984; Rasmussen, 2012). Upon gaining the knowledge of what materials melted into glassy-like solids, it would not have then been too far a stretch to make small glass vials and vases in moulds. Moulds were already in use to manufacture amphorae and similar ceramic pots and jars. It is entirely possible that there could have been a cross-over in the techniques.

The second-century CE Roman writer, Pliny the Elder, relates his version of the origin of glass. Somewhere along the coast of what is now Syria, nitrate traders were building a cooking fire on the beach. Lacking other rocks to support their pot, they were using pieces of nitrate, or natron as it is known today. (Nitrate/natron removes oxygen from materials, and is believed by historians to have been traded for the purpose of curing meats (Binkerd and Kolari, 1975)). Additionally, and why it is important to the story, nitrate is a natural soda and, along with silica (sand) and lime makes up the three basic ingredients of glass. Presumably, according to Pliny, when the nitrate was heated it combined with the sand and flowed (Tait, 1991).

Pliny's tale makes a good story despite the lack of a date and the questionable accuracy. It is probably as close to the truth as we will ever get to the first origins of glass making. Glass was known to the pharaohs of Egypt and the early kings of the Middle East, but the best that could be made in those eras were small vials and jars to contain beauty creams and medicinal lotions (Klein and Lloyd, 1984).

Sometime later, probably in the second or first millennium BC, a *rod and core* method of making small vials, jars, bottles and drinking glasses evolved (Klein and Lloyd, 1984). The glassmaker would initially form clay and straw around a metal rod. This lump was then dipped into the molten glass to enclose it. When the glass cooled, the rod and bulk material making up the shape were removed, leaving a space for whatever liquid the vial was intended (Van den Bossche, 2001). These rough looking vessels, usually without bases, were the humble beginnings of the elegant bottles and glassware which have been developed in the ensuing years.

As with the historic 'experiments' to add ingredients to wine to improve or preserve it, glassmakers also learned to add metal salts to create colours (Rasmussen, 2012). Various copper ores would render a red or green in the finished product; cobalt created the blues; combinations of copper and iron became blue green; while lead and antimony resulted in a yellow hue. However, it is believed that much of the colouring was hit or miss, as the consistency of stained glass did not show up until the tenth century (Rasmussen, 2012)

Glass and wine came together with the Greeks. By virtue of the Empire's unprecedented love of wine, they raised the standards of wine glassware (Kahn, 2014). Wine and food were part of their cultural experience; a social practice which dictated elegant tableware that could match the higher level of civilization to which they aspired. Glass drinking cups, pitchers and possibly some kraters were used for serving and drinking the wine (Klein and Lloyd, 1984).

The Roman expansion into the Middle East set the stage for commercial glass production by virtue of their unprecedented transportation and communication systems. Combining these with the cultural eruption, "the late Hellenistic period [was where] such values were shaped by social practice, specifically the consumption of wine that contributed greatly to the development of glassware" (Kahn, 2014). Kahn goes on to elaborate:

> Wine-related artifacts virtually fill our modern museums, including Eastern and Greek ceramic and metal wares for storage, transport, cooling, mixing, serving, drinking, and also, without doubt, impressing others…. Roman ceramic fine wares continued this practice with the ongoing production of Hellenistic ceramic types of cups, bowls, and beakers to serve similar functions.
>
> *(2014)*

By the first century BCE, these two traits of 'civilization' – commerce and culture – were melded together to encourage the discovery and improvements in glass blowing, rather than just using moulds. The evidence points to the first glass blowers in the Middle East, probably not far from where Pliny placed his traders.

Roman bottle development

As the early Middle Eastern glass craftsmen expanded their styles and techniques – developing new shapes and colours – their creations were traded and appreciated across the Empire. Seeing these new and innovative products, the Romans in Italy wanted their own glassmakers doing the same things. The techniques and technology of glass blowing quickly spread around the Mediterranean (Van den Bossche, 2001; Kahn, 2014). The glass blowing and production processes could be utilized as free-form or via moulds. These advanced techniques allowed the craftsmen to create larger and more varied versions of the glasses, vials, bottles and jars; expanding the uses of the numerous glass containers.

The advantages of serving wine in a glass, as opposed to ceramic or wooden vessels, even if the glass was not completely transparent, became obvious. One could actually see the various hues of colour of the wine. Nor did the glass impact the flavour (Kahn, 2014) as would drinking vessels, those such as wooden or stoneware cups, or animal hide sacks. This enhanced appreciation of the wine encouraged the elite to request larger bottles; at first, most likely to serve the wine instead of pouring out of a pitcher or krater.

Bottles for wine could theoretically have been made by these blowing processes. However, there were several limitations which restricted the production, and thus kept the cost relatively high. The elevated temperatures required to melt the raw materials consumed significant amounts of fuel, primarily fire wood, restricting the actual production sites (Kahn, 2014). Additionally, until a long, hollow metal or ceramic rod could be developed – to both keep the workers at a safe and workable distance from the heat of the fires, and to allow the craftsmen to inflate the molten glass by blowing – the bottles were understandably small, made by using either the rod and core or mould methods (Kahn, 2014).

Moreover, for the bottles at that period, blowing produced only thin-walled vessels (Rasmussen, 2012). This may have been fine for elegant glassware, or bottles to be used to serve wine at a table, but not tough enough for the rougher handling a bottle would experience if used to ship and store wine.

The enhanced trade around the Mediterranean, and demand by the elite who could afford the early prototypes of glasses and bottles did, however, encourage further glass production. The use of longer rods, and developments in using the *sagging* process – by which a hot glob of glass was placed over a mould and allowed to sink into the form – became commonplace. By improving the production efficiency, these techniques lowered the price and increased the availability of the glass products (Kahn, 2014).

The blowing process, even with the use of the long iron rod, had not reached the point of making wine bottles commercially available. Apparently, the ones that were made, at least the ones that have been found, were generally too thin to withstand much handling (Van den Bossche, 2001). Although, McKearin and Wilson note, that, "It seems safe to say that from about 1 AD [CE], whenever and wherever glass bottles were made, some of them functioned as vessels from which wine, spirits, and other beverages were served" (1978). However, the development of the blowing process did allow for much more diversity in the bottle variations (Kahn, 2014).

Over the several hundred years of the Roman Empire, its glass makers not only expanded the numbers of people who could own and utilize glass objects – bottles, vases, and window panes – but developed an elaborate trading system for obtaining the raw materials (Velde, 2009; Fraser, 2004). Not that this system continued into the 500 to 1000 current era – it had to be pretty much started anew – but at least the basic technology was somehow kept alive. While some of the knowledge was lost, later glass craftsmen could draw on tradition and lore, as well as see the glass objects which had been made during the Roman period.

At the height of the Empire, Materials Chemistry Professor Seth Rasmussen notes that "A middle class Roman family probably owned glass storage containers, drank from glass vessels, and brought souvenir glass cups with the names of their favorite gladiators molded into them. Even the final resting place of many Romans was a glass funerary urn" (2012). The Roman glass industry must have been, while not huge as compared to the numbers of workers making amphorae, still a sizable group of craftsmen spread throughout the Roman Empire.

The early glass factories

As the Roman Legions conquered the tribes and civilizations living around the Mediterranean coastline and in Europe, more often than not they embraced the craftsmen of those various cultures. For glass making, at least, that trade flourished with well-to-do Romans wanting to emulate the Greek style of lavish hospitality and dinners with fine dinnerware and glass wine services.

During the Roman era, there were glass making centres as far afield as Boulogne, Trier, Cologne, Manchester and Leicester. These were all near heavily forested areas capable of supplying the essential fuel for the glass furnaces. In particular, the hardwoods such as oak and beech could provide the higher temperatures needed for melting the raw materials. However, the centres were far from, or totally without, access to certain raw materials, particularly the soda which, to a great extent, was still being sourced from Egyptian dry lake beds. When making glass without the soda it became *waldglas* – forest glass; a dark green with impurities (Rasmussen, 2012).

Throughout northern Europe, pieces of glass have been found that do not exhibit the *waldglas* trait. This has prompted archaeologists to seek further answers as to how the glass ingredients could have been transported to the far-flung areas. Until sources could eventually be found in Italy, France and Germany, archaeologists believe that the Romans had an elaborate trading system to supply glass factories in the northern and western Mediterranean (Velde, 2009). Middle Eastern kilns, those at specific sites near the sources of the materials, made the basic raw glass. As a more efficient trading process, these blobs were then shipped and traded around the Mediterranean to the finishers who re-melted the blobs to manufacture the window panes, table ware and bottles in moulds or by blowing (Velde, 2009).

Besides the obvious advantage for the glass blowers of not needing to procure the several raw materials, by sourcing from specific raw glass suppliers they could began to learn the properties of that glass; the colours, transparency, and hardness which came from a particular area. It is theorized that they could have possibly requested raw glass from different supplies in order to vary the final products (Velde, 2009). Re-melting may have minimized their fuel needs as well.

To the degree that such a trading scheme existed, and with the Romans' penchant for organization, as well as their active Mediterranean and river transportation systems, it would have been very similar to today's manufacturing, with factories sourcing their materials from known suppliers, often on a just-in-time basis (Velde, 2009).

The Dark Ages – for glass and everything else

As the Roman Empire slid into disorder so did the demand for, and ultimately, the manufacturing and use of glass bottles. Few bottles have been found dated to the Dark Ages, roughly the fifth to the tenth century.

We previously observed that, during the decline of the Roman Empire, the economy of Britain (Fraser, 2004), certainly the furthest removed in the Empire's western section, as well as the economies of France, Spain, Germany and Italy, suffered. When the services of the Roman troops were no longer required, and the Roman administrators dismissed, the demand for the goods and services which the merchants in the towns had been providing were no longer needed. In this downturn, the area's craftsmen, as historian Rebecca Fraser states, and "[t]he famous pottery factories, which gave so much employment because the Romans used pots the way we use plastic bags, as containers and transporters for every kind of commodity, vanished – and so did the art of making glass" (2004).

It took several hundred years for the dust to settle and for Europe to get back on its feet. Britain lost much of its glass making knowhow. The glassblowers in Italy and France retained the technology, and it was those craftsmen who were the first to begin anew the now fledgling industry. This was helped by the demand for glass panes in the churches and cathedrals of Europe; first clear glass and then panes in colours (Fraser, 2004). For example, in Britain in the 670s, warrior and nobleman Benedict Biscop wanted to build a church for a monastery in Northumbria, northern England. He imported stonemasons from France, but circumvented importing glass by hiring a Gaul glassmaker. This man built a glass factory and crafted the first windows for an Anglo-Saxon church.

The Renaissance of glass bottle making

In the eleventh century, Venice staged the comeback by developing a powerful fleet of ships and encouraging trade. Among the many items of trade, the Venetians started accumulating was glass. Originally it was glass for mosaics, but with the technology gained from its trading contacts in the east, and after its military sacked Constantinople in 1204, they stole their glassblowers as well (Rasmussen, 2012).

However, the glass makers could not build their factories in Venice proper. Upon realizing the danger from out-of-control glass kiln fires, the Venice city administrators wisely isolated their glass making facilities on the island of Murano, just north of the city (Tait, 1991).

By the fourteenth century, having taken over the role as the pre-eminent glass blowing craftsmen from the Islamic glass centres of Damascus, Aleppo and Egypt (Tait, 1991), the Venetian enclave of Murano had been producing high-end glasses and vases for several hundred years. Through their trade contacts, its craftsmen had found sources in Egypt and Syria for sodium carbonate which could produce the clearest glass available in Europe (Henbest, 2015). Murano's specialized and respected craftsmen were able to make crystal glass vases and glassware surpassing anything else being made at the time. Decorative tin-glazed *maiolica* glassware was also being produced (Tait, 1991).

Additionally, the Murano craftsmen were also blowing glass bottles. By 1268 they were producing water-bottles, flasks for perfumes and scents

(Tait, 1991), as well, perhaps, as some bottles for wine to be used in lieu of table decanters.

Over time, glass factories flourished in other European countries; France and Spain in particular, developed by their craftsmen's skills, by illegally stealing secrets or the craftsmen with the technical knowledge from neighbouring countries (Tait, 1991).

To place glass making in some context, Holland was also a centre for glass making, but with a focus on pieces primarily for scientific pursuits. In addition to making glassware for serving and drinking wine, Rasmussen (2012) observes that the Dutch glass craftsmen helped to develop another extremely important attribute in wine production. He states: "Perhaps one of the greatest of such cases was the utilization of the improved glass distillation equipment for the isolation of alcohol from wine. The successfully isolated distillate then found a variety of uses – as a solvent, preservative, and the basis of brandy, at first taken medicinally, later recreationally" (2012).

European glass bottles

It was not until the fifteenth and sixteenth centuries that the interest in bottles was revived, with decanter-like bottles being used on tables in estates, castles and abbeys. To a lesser degree, other bottles were occasionally used in homes and taverns.

Glass was being made for decanters; however, the populace drinking wine used ceramic jugs, salt-glazed stoneware (made by throwing salt on the pots while in the kiln), wood, pewter, tin, or even sacks made from animal skin or intestines (Johnson, 2004). With use, however, the bacterial build up negatively impacted the wine in these non-vitreous vessels,

1660   1700   1720   1730   1780   1810   1840

FIGURE 5.2 Progression of wine bottle shape designs
Lisa Caron

exacerbating the problems of a poor vintage, substandard winemaking, and/ or degradation of the wine during transportation.

For those who could afford to drink wine, especially in northern Europe and Britain, the early bottles were inconsistent in size. This was due to the still primitive hand-blowing techniques. In fact, inaccurate quantities were such a problem that laws were passed in England making it illegal to fill the tavern's glasses or bottles directly from the barrels. People brought their own containers to be filled (Johnson, 2004; Robinson, 1999), and the wine was sold by measure. Often the patrons had their own personal labels or stamps to identify their containers, as well as their capacity, noted on the vessel (Robinson, 1999).

Several factors led to a resurgence in glass making and glass bottles. The dawning of the Renaissance brought a general interest in things scientific, including glass blowing. The increasing population throughout Europe created a larger nobility and aristocracy, classes of people who wanted and could afford the finer accoutrements. After the religious orders had kept the growing of grapes and enjoyment of wine alive, to a certain extent, northern Europe finally become a wine drinking society. Additionally, the building of churches, which flourished starting in the mid-eleventh century, gave the glass foundries sufficient work to exist; making all the stained-glass window panes (Scott, 2011).

By the seventeenth century aristocrats in England and elsewhere in Europe were drinking more and better wine (Ludington, 2013). And they started using bottles to bring wine from the barrels in their cellar to their tables (Johnson, 2004).

Fuelling the glass furnaces

To meet the growing demand for the bottles, the problem for the glass blowers, like that for the metal smiths, were the enormous amounts of fuel, primarily wood, needed to create the fires hot enough to melt the ingredients. Europe had extensive forests. Nevertheless, increasing demands were being placed upon them for timber to build the ever-larger sailing ships, wooden barrels and household utensils, huge beams for cathedrals and other buildings, as well as carts and bridges. The wood cutters had to go further and further afield. As the distances increased, transportation, and the associated costs, did as well.

As noted in Chapter 4 on barrels, in 1543, England started passing laws to curtail the overcutting of their oak (Kilby, 1990), and by 1617 banned the use of wood as fuel for glass making as well (Johnson, 2004; McKearin and Wilson, 1978). France followed shortly thereafter, enacting strict laws about cutting oak in 1669 (Logan, 2005).

Unable to utilize wood for fuel, the glass makers turned to coal. However, in Britain it was not that simple. The King, James I, had banned the use of wood, and at the same time sold the rights to make glass to just one individual, Naval Commander and Member of Parliament, Sir Robert Mansell (1573–1656). Mansell had established himself at the best coal mines, those in Newcastle-upon-Tyne (Johnson, 2004). Having found that coal produced hotter fires making stronger glass, and the clearest, numerous small glass operations sprung up, paying Mansell for the coal *and* the right to make glass.

Despite the monopolistic policies of the glass industry at that time, the situation did prompt one individual to improve upon the fuelling system. Sir Kenelm Digby (1603–1665) perfected the methods to utilize coal in order to melt the raw materials required for glass (Johnson, 2004).

Glass technology was low on the list of accomplishments and adventures for this seventeenth-century Renaissance man (Mellick, 2011). In fact, only because he dabbled well in almost everything, was he able to make a significant contribution to ongoing evolution of the glass bottles.

Digby's father, Sir Everard Digby, was involved, and eventually killed, in the Guy Fawkes debacle. Young Digby was placed under the guardianship of William Laud, who later become the Archbishop of Canterbury, and then his uncle, Sir John Digby, and accompanied Sir John when he took up the post of Ambassador to Spain in Madrid.

These learned men offered young Kenelm incredible insights into the latest thinking and politics of the times. Subsequent training at Oxford honed his already brilliant mind. A large endowment from his father's estate allowed Kenelm to pursue his intellectual interests (Mellick, 2011). He is noted for a number of achievements, especially so in the fields of medicine and mathematics. He anticipated calculus and developed a numbers theorem which has been only recently proven (Mellick, 2011). His endeavours in the glass industry, while making an important milestone in the evolution of glass bottles, including acquiring a glass company in the 1630s, have become almost an overlooked footnote in Digby's own history and exploits.

How he got into this business is not clear. However, from his interest in numerous endeavours, it is not hard to imagine Digby as a man who was well read, travelled, and who corresponded with many of the important men of his day. The decimation of the forests would have been in the news, as would the switch from wood to coal to fire the glass furnaces. The spark to pull these changes into his consciousness was perhaps that he or his butlers had broken more than a few of the generally thin, fragile bottles, losing what they thought was good wine. His inquiring and creative mind could have found both an intellectual satisfaction and the potential for economic gains if he could devise a stronger bottle.

Understanding that coal would provide more heat than wood to melt the raw materials for glass, Digby set about to find how best to do so, and then heat the fires even hotter. For this, he developed a fan to stoke the fuel. The hotter temperatures made the glass stronger, and the coal ash created blacker – browns and dark-green – colours. These darker bottles were seen as a sign of strength and also had, unbeknownst to Digby, the unintended consequence of shielding the wine from light (Johnson, 2004). The bottles were still being hand blown. However, Digby additionally changed the traditional bottle shape from a bulbous, onion-like shape to one more flattened in order to better nest together. He also added a longer neck to enable pouring, and a ridge at the bottle's opening around which to tie on the cork. Most importantly, the bottles made in his factory were cheaper.

After, several set-backs, including being placed in jail, in 1662 Digby was eventually awarded the patent for this more efficient bottle making process (Johnson, 2004). It took another eight years and 37 years respectively for the Netherlands and France to incorporate his processes.

In the 1600s, to enhance their bottles for their customers, producers would occasionally place a button of glass attached to the bottle. These *seals* indicated the name, initials or address of customer (or organization like an abbey) and sometimes the date. Sir Kenelm Digby placed some upon the bottles for his customers (McKearin and Wilson, 1978). The bottles are now termed by collectors *sealed bottles*, and not to be confused with bottles for which the openings are sealed with corks or wax or other stoppers.

Digby's bottles were a mallet shape but many others in the marketplace were still in the style of an onion (Robinson, 2004). These bottles appeared by the sixteenth century, often with a wicker cover for protection, and were probably packed with a lot of straw. By the seventeenth century, as the use of bottles spread, there was a realization that some wines could 'age', i.e. get better over time if they were well-sealed in a bottle. This prompted the glass makers to alter the shape to the longer, narrower, straighter bottles – the shapes we recognize today in the Bordeaux and Burgundy bottles (Dominé, 2000) – in order that they could be laid upon their sides, thus keeping the corks moist and tight.

Once Digby's bottles got into the trading system, the London wine merchants, who had imported their wines in barrels, started bottling the wine for their customers. Later, this process shifts again; the merchants, disliking the additional time, labour and costs required to top up the wine barrels sitting in their cellars, start shipping bottles to Bordeaux and other wine sources for bottling at the wineries or the ports (Debas and Orsini, 2006; Pitte, 2008). Eventually, glass plants were built in or close to the wine regions.

Bottle size

As the shape of the glass bottle changed in the sixteenth and seventeenth century the size remained roughly at 750 millilitres. This capacity had evolved from what is believed to have been the largest size the glass blowers could create with one lung full of air (Flewellen, 2012).

While the concept of moulds was certainly well known, up until the 1820s bottles where largely blown by hand. This meant variations in size and capacity. Finally, in 1821, Ricketts Glassworks in Bristol patented a glass moulding machine (Robinson, 1999). For the first time, standard size bottles could be consistently manufactured.

FIGURE 5.3 A range of bottle sizes
Courtesy of the Society of Historical Archaeology/Bill Lindsey

Glass bottles in Bordeaux

In the late 1600s and early 1700s, the Bordeaux wine industry was expanding exponentially. The vintners and négociants wanted to ship more and more of their best clarets in glass bottles, rather than tin pots (Le Mao, 2009) or barrels to domestic and overseas customers. These bottles were generally shipped from factories in northern France or Britain. Seeing an expanding need right in Bordeaux, the coal-fired Mitchell Glass factory was set up in the Chartrons area to specifically make wine bottles. These bottles were the Bordelaise-style – those with a tall, thin shape and long neck.

To meet their growing demand for bottles, France, and Bordeaux in particular, encouraged the immigration of people who had glass making skills. France's glass factories were outdated, with some still attempting to utilize the diminishing supply of wood to fuel their furnaces (Le Mao, 2009). The majority of France's glass factories were in the north. This added to the cost of transporting the empty bottles to the Bordeaux wineries and the négociants even before they were filled.

One of the immigrants was Irishman Peter Mitchell (1687–1740), who arrived in 1721. Better known to his French *amis* as Pierre, he initially started work as a cooper (McNally, 2016). Within a few years, and realizing the demand for glass bottles, he persuaded some Irish glass blowers to immigrate as well and set up a factory, complete with a huge kiln in which to melt the raw materials for the glass.

Along with importing the workers, he also imported English coal, as it was cheaper and better than that he could obtain from northeast France. Also, from the Irish and English coastlines, he imported *salicor*, the ash of burned kelp which was rich in potash and soda (Dungworth, 2009). When salicor was added to the raw materials for the glass, it lowered the melting point thus reducing the need for the coal fuel. Despite the costs of importing these products for fabricating the glass, he still could make his Bordelaise bottles stronger and less expensively than his French counterparts. The rugged bottles helped to develop the shipping of more wine in bottles, individually nestled in wooden cases, as opposed to bulk in barrels.

Mitchell built his factory in the southwest corner of the Chartrons. It featured a unique cone-shaped furnace, a replication of a style he had seen in Dublin, which towered above the surrounding neighbourhood, becoming part of the eighteenth-century landscape.

For the sake of its consumers, France wanted to standardize the capacity of the bottles. This was certainly not a new concept; Rome had done the same with amphorae, and, later the individual European governments demanded the same of the cooperages for the wooden barrels. Along with the French government giving permission to Mitchell to establish a company came the requirement to fabricate his bottles to a consistent size and weight (Le Mao, 2009). It even sent out inspectors to check on the production. Certainly, there were difficulties, since the glass bottles were still being hand-blown rather than made in moulds. However, the adherence of Mitchell's products to the government's requirement must have been close enough as his company was still going strong, and dominated within the industry even up into the middle of the nineteenth century (Le Mao, 2009)

Being a cooper, and then wine bottle maker, showed Mitchell's penchant for diversification. As his glass bottle company expanded, he diversified by also becoming a vintner. He purchased what was to become Chateau de Tertre, near Arsac in the Medoc, in 1736. He later bought into a shipping company to have control over the exportation of his wine and the importation of the raw materials required to make the bottles

His Bordeaux bottle shape still survives, as witnessed on all the wine shop and supermarket shelves. In the Chartrons, however, only the *Place Mitchell* and the *Rue de la Verrerie*, both in the area where Mitchell's glass factory once stood, are the current reminders of its historic wine culture (McNally, 2016).

Development of wine bottles in America

Not unexpectedly, the wine bottle development in early America paralleled that going on in Europe. There was a logical reason for this: some of the émigrés were glass blowers; seeking a way to make a living, they were eager to start the fledgling glass companies (McKearin and Wilson, 1978). With their skills, they were able to build the kilns, source the raw materials, and blow the bottles.

The first bottles identified as being for wine started appearing in the 1630s, with the initial American-made 'claret' bottle in the United States produced in 1798 by Christopher Trippel & Co., in Philadelphia. By that time, other small glass works had commenced operations in Cambridge and Salem, in Massachusetts, and in New York city (McKearin and Wilson, 1978). As befitting their training, the craftsmen were blowing English style bottles, with a capacity of about 2.5 quarts (2.4 litres), with a squat body and a short, tapered neck. By the late-1750s, wine bottles were fairly common, such that advertisements were being placed in publications for various types and quantities. As an example, a 1789 ad in *New York Packet* (an Albany newspaper) declared for sale '*Brown Wickered Demie John's* fit for shipping'. The wicker was apparently being produced by local Native American Indians. Early on, the demijohns were used for products other than wine, but later specific wine bottles were being produced. Another ad, this one in 1848 from the company of Benners, Smith and Campbell of Dyottville, New Jersey attests to 'Manufacturers of Carboys, Demijohns of all sizes, Wine, Porter, Soda and Mineral Water, Lemon syrup and Ink Bottles, Jars and Druggists' Bottles and Vials of every description' (McKearin and Wilson, 1978).

By the 1800s, and in a manner similar to the barrel cooperages of that period, machinery was being developed to improve the efficiency of manufacturing, the consistency of the products, and to reduce the labour costs. One man who made a big impact on glass production in the United States, and eventually in Europe, was Michael Owens (1859–1923).

Owens, like Pierre Mitchell in Bordeaux, was of Irish descent, and had worked his way up through the labour ranks to achieve success in the glass packaging industry. While Mitchell hired Irish glass blowers to help him set up a factory, Owens, in 1889, was hired by Edward Libbey (1854–1925) to become his Toledo glass plant superintendent (Twede, 2012). (Many in America will at least recognize these two names as being synonymous within the glass industry. Their last names are now heading some very different companies. One at least, the Owens-Illinois Glass Company, is still much involved in producing bottles for the wine industry.)

With Libbey's backing, Owens was able to conceive the ideas for many machines to mechanize the glass bottle industry. They were successful not only in developing the machines, but with their subsequent patents, in selling machines to other companies both in the United States and Europe (Miller and Sullivan, 1984). Interestingly though, Owens being basically illiterate, could only devise the concepts; he had to have the plant engineers draw the plans and formalize how such machines could actually function (Twede, 2012). After much trial and error, his initial success was in automating the narrow-neck bottle blowing process. Subsequently, he added more machines to continuously form bottles and he built kilns to supply several machines simultaneously (Twede, 2012). Some of the machines were huge, weighing over 100 tons, with the mould for each bottle style costing several thousand dollars.

Through a series of mergers and acquisitions Owens and Libbey eventually acquired the factories to make bottles for beer, whiskey, milk, soda including Coca-Cola, medicines, and glass bottles for fruits and vegetables (Twede, 2012). By the early 1900s Libbey and Owen were selectively selling their patented machines to specific companies. The Northwestern Ohio Glass Company purchased one to manufacture wine and brandy bottles (Twede, 2012).

The demand for wine bottles was minimal against those needed for the beer, soda, whiskey and food industries (Twede, 2012; Miller and Sullivan, 1984). Only the largest companies, with orders for huge numbers of bottles, could afford new moulds in order to change styles or sizes. In the 1800s, the American wine industry was fledgling, with much wine still moved around in barrels. By 1850, total US production of wine was a mere 250,000 gallons (9,462 hectolitres). Nonetheless, an advertisement in 1862 by the Whitney Glass Company of Camden, New Jersey, was offering an assortment of wine bottles: ones in dark glass and those 'very heavy', jugs with handles, demijohns, Rhine flasks with handles, champagne bottles and carboys (McKearin and Wilson, 1978). By 1860, wine production had jumped dramatically to just shy of 1.5 million gallons (56,775 hectolitres), with California becoming a major contributor (Sumner et al., 2001). The American wine industry realized continual increase in production, albeit slowly, until the 1970s, when it took off and rose to about 528 million gallons (about 2 billion litres) in 2000 (Sumner et al., 2001). Naturally, the demand for glass bottles increased as well, as the wineries phased out the selling of their products in barrels. However, there was a limited choice in the styles available (McKearin and Wilson, 1978). It was not until the early 1900s, when the glass bottle automation started to bring down the price of the moulds, that US wineries started to branch out and offer different styles. As California became a major grower, by 1958 the Gallo Winery had grown large enough to commence making its own bottles for its numerous wine brands (Gallo Glass, 2018).

The shapes and colour of wine bottles

Bordeaux versus Burgundy

As noted, the wine bottles morphed from onion-shaped to a cylinder in order be laid down for aging and then to facilitate shipping. The earliest wine bottles from France's Bordeaux and Burgundy regions were the same shape; a shape easy to blow, round with a bulbous belly, sloping shoulders and slender neck, and a punt, the dimple at the bottom which assists the bottle to remain upright, as well as collect some of the sediment when the bottle is upright (Pitte, 2008).

Additionally, as Université de Paris-Sorbonne professor Jean-Robert Pitte suggests, there was a more important reason for the differentiation between the bottle styles of the two important wine regions (2008). Despite settling the wine in tanks and barrels before bottling, the heavier Bordeaux wines threw sediment whilst in the bottles. He theorizes that the glass makers modified the Bordeaux bottle to have a more angular shoulder in order to help catch this sediment as the wine was being decanted. The Burgundian vintners kept the same gentle sloping shoulders, as they considered the sediments of the Chardonnays and Pinot Noirs 'softer'; i.e. not needing extensive decanting (Pitte, 2008).

Other bottle shapes

In a manner similar to the evolution of the amphorae and wine barrels, wine bottle manufacturing evolved in the various countries for the numerous wines and wine regions; start and stop, hit and miss, and generally without overall design. There must have been a give and take on what the

FIGURE 5.4 Various bottle sizes and shapes
Glenn Cormier

glass manufacturers could produce, what the vintners wanted, with a dash of what shipping methods were employed, as well as the customer's desires.

Some regions decided to stick with the onion shape, or a variation of the onion shaped bottle; consider today's Mateus Rosé or the Chianti bottles. The reasons run the gamut from sticking with tradition, the disinterest or lack of funds to change glass moulds, consumer recognition, and the realization of a successful marketing niche. The German style hock bottle – the tall, thin bottle, evolved for much the same rational. Small bottles, such as the *demi* (375 ml), were developed for higher alcohol wines, such as the sweet dessert wines.

Large bottles did not come into the market until moulds and mechanical methods to blow bottles were invented in the 1800s. From the standard 750 ml size, Austrian wine jumped to a one litre bottle, while France added a magnum, one of 1.5 litres, double the traditional and standard of 750 ml.

Then we get to the large bottles, named for Biblical kings, rulers or royalty: the 3 or 4.5 litre *Jeroboam*, or *Rehoboam* depending on the French region where it is used: the 6 L. *Imperial* or *Methuselah*; the 9 L. *Salmanazar*; the 12 L. *Balthazar*; and the 15 L. *Nebuchadnezzar*, the largest I have ever seen. There are other sizes, including a 30-litre bottle, the *Midas*. Additionally, grander ones have been created for some champagnes, including a 26.25 L. *Sovereign* in 1988 for the champagne house of Taittinger to inaugurate the launch of the world's then largest cruise ship.

Lifting and pouring full bottles of these larger sizes is like pouring from an amphora; hard on the back. Plus, they are definitely only for special occasions, as they cannot be filled on normal bottling lines, and require unique corks and capsules.

Bottle colour

At the dawn of the current millennium, after owning a vineyard and selling the grapes for a number of years, my wife starting making wine, a Sauvignon blanc, from the grapes of our vineyard. When the question came as to what style and colour of bottle to place it in, she chose a dead leaf green, Bordeaux shaped bottle.

The colour provided two advantages. The first was to minimize the exposure to UV rays which can hasten the deterioration of the wine, as opposed to using a clear white, flint bottle. Secondly, rather than the traditional darker greens – antique or champagne, or amber which is typical of

Alsatian styles – the semi-translucent dead leaf hue allowed the consumer to see that it was a white wine.

She varied the Bordeaux shape slightly, choosing one with a bottom diameter slightly smaller than the shoulders, providing a more elegant appearance. For large wineries, running thousands or millions of bottles on several lines, this less stable, top-heavy shape of bottle is not practical. However, for her small bottling runs, on a portable line, it posed few problems.

Today, the choice of bottles for any winemaker or wine marketer is enormous. One glass manufacturer's catalogue I perused noted 23 possible Bordeaux shapes, 21 in the Burgundy range, additional ones in hock shapes and other styles, all in almost as many colour variations. At the top of the neck, one could also choose from 11 variants of the rim and/or threads, depending upon the closure one chooses – cork, screwcap, crown, champagne, etc. Bottle companies are also offering lighter weight bottles and have stepped up processes to recycle the glass bottles, both to provide a more environmentally conscious foot print.

Conclusion

After using amphorae and wooden barrels for thousands of years to package our wines, we are now in the age of the glass wine bottles. Their increased use came about as glass manufacturers employed the hotter coal to melt the raw materials, then developed machines to increase production. Glass has many attributes over the more porous ceramics and wood, enabling it to effectively store wine for long periods. Additionally, glass is recyclable.

References

Binkerd, E. F. and Kolari, O. E. (1975). The history and use of nitrate and nitrite in the curing of meat. *Food and Cosmetics Toxicology*, 13(6), pp. 655–661.

Debas, D. and Orsini, A. (2006). De la bouteille bordelaise. *Verre*, [online] 11(1), pp. 46–55.

Dominé, A. ed. (2000). *Wine*. Cologne: Könemann.

Dungworth, D. (2009). Innovations in the 17th-century glass industry: the introduction of kelp (seaweed) ash in Britain. In: *Les innovations verrières et leur devenir*. [online] Nancy: Actes du Deuxieme Colloque International de l'Association Verre & Histoire. 26 March 2009.

Flewellen, J. (2012). Wine bottle shapes. *The Oxford Wine Blog*, [online] 30 July 2012.

Fraser, R. (2004). *A People's History of Britain*. London: Pimlico.

Henbest, N. (2015). The universe, decanted. *New Scientist*, [online] 228(3052/3053), pp.73–75.

Jackson, R. S. (2014). *Wine Science: Principles and Applications* (4th ed.). Waltham, MA: Food Science and Technology Series; Academic Press.

Johnson, H. (2004). *The Story of Wine; New Illustrated Edition*. London: Mitchell Beazley, Octopus Publishing.

Kahn, L. C. (2014). Herodian innovation: the glass industry. *Near Eastern Archaeology*, 77(2), pp. 129–139.

Kilby, K. (1990). *The Cooper and His Trade*. Fresno: Linden Publishing.

Klein, D. and Lloyd, W., eds. (1984). *The History of Glass*. London: Orbis.

Le Mao, C. (2009). Un établissement pionnier dans la capitale du vin: la verrerie Mitchell au XVIIIe siècle. *Verre Historie*, [online] 26 March 2009, p. 401.

Logan, W. B. (2005). *Oak: The Frame of Civilization*. New York: W. W. Norton & Co.

Ludington, C. (2013). Walpole, Whigs & wine. *History Today*, [online] 63(7), p. 42.

McKearin, H. and Wilson, K. M. (1978). *American Bottles & Flasks and Their Ancestry*. New York: Crown Publishers, Inc.

McNally, F. (2016). Bottling it in Bordeaux – An Irishman's Diary about one of the lesser-known Irish gifts to France. *The Irish Times*, [online] 7 July 2016.

Mellick, S. A. (2011). Sir Kenelm Digby (1603–1665): diplomat, entrepreneur, privateer, duellist, scientist and philosopher. *ANZ Journal of Surgery*, [online] 81(12), pp. 911–914.

Miller, G. L. and Sullivan, C. (1984). Machine-made glass containers and the end of production for mouth-blown bottles. *Historical Archaeology*, [online] 18, pp. 83–96.

North, B. (2016). 2,500 years ago, this brew was buried with the dead: a brewery has revived it. *National Public Radio*, [online] 24 October 2016.

Pitte, J.-R. (2008). *Bordeaux/Burgundy: A Vintage Rivalry*. Berkeley: University of California Press.

Rasmussen, S. C. (2012). *How Glass Changed the World: The History and Chemistry of Glass from Antiquity to the 13th Century*. New York: Springer.

Robinson, J., ed. (1999). *The Oxford Companion to Wine*, (2nd ed.). Oxford: Oxford University Press.

Scott, R. A. (2011). *The Gothic Enterprise: A Guide to Understanding the Medieval Cathedral*. Berkeley: University of California Press.

Sumner, D. A., Bombrun, H., Alston, J. M. and Heien, D. (2001). An economic survey of the wine and winegrape industry in the United States and Canada. Agricultural Issues Center, University of California, Davis [online].

Tait, H., ed. (1991). *Five Thousand Years of Glass*. London: British Museum Press.

Twede, D. (2012). The birth of modern packaging: cartons, cans and bottles. *Journal of Historical Research in Marketing*, 4(2), pp. 245–272.

Van den Bossche, W. (2001). *Antique Glass Bottles: Their History and Evolution (1500–1850) A Comprehensive, Illustrated Guide with a World-wide Bibliography of Glass Bottles*. Woodbridge, Suffolk: Antique Collectors' Club.

Velde, B. (2009). Roman blown glass compositions: following supply patterns in the manufacturing chain. In: International Colloquium of the Association Verre & Histoire, 26–28 March 2009, [online] Nancy, France.

Websites

Gallo Glass. (2018). Gallo Glass Company. www.galloglass.com
German Wines. (2017). Deutsches Weininstitut. www.germanwines.de

Blogs

Dal Piaz, G. (2010). Old wine: An ancient timeline for great old wine. Snooth. www.snooth.com. 8 November 2010.
Robinson, J. (2004). Will our grandchildren need a corkscrew? Janice Robinson. www.jancisrobinson.com. 11 June 2004.

6

LARGE FERMENTING AND STORAGE VESSELS FOR WINE

Dolia

The excavations by archaeologists of the most ancient winemaking sites in the Middle East have uncovered many amphorae-shaped ceramic jars and pots, including some larger ones set partially or entirely in the ground. The earliest of these have been in the 5 to 20 litre capacity range, just large enough for making wine for a family. Over time, the size increased, indicating commercial winemaking activities were advancing. Some dolia are as large as 5,000 to 15,000 litres, although the 200 to 2,000 litres range seems more the norm.

Today, with more than a few wineries in a number of countries still employing dolia, or having re-introduced them into their production, each country has its own term for the large ceramic vessels: France (dolium), Spain (tinajeria), Portugal (talhas), Italy (dolium), Greece (pithos), Georgia (tvevri or qvevri). I will use dolium (plural dolia) unless referring to those of a specific country.

Unsurprisingly, there are potters in the various countries still carrying on the ancient skills of building these large vessels. Most, however, are adding modern accoutrements, such as refinements in the ceramic material and stainless steel doors and valves, as well as firing them in electric kilns.

It is romantic to consider the ancient winemakers using these extremely basic vessels, but what were the practicalities? How, for instance, were or are they kept sanitary? How well do they deal with oxygen interactions for the wine? And what do they contribute to a wine's structure as it ferments and ages?

Despite being the workhorse container of the ancient winery, making wine in today's dolia is rather a niche industry. Thus, the impetus for scientific research into the best practices of utilizing dolia in winemaking – why they work or do not – is limited. Certainly, there are many traditions which the winemakers incorporate to make quality wine in dolia, but understanding why these traditional methods are successful has yet to be clearly delineated.

EXPLORATIONS 6.1
FEW DOLIA IN BORDEAUX

The findings of Roman era dolia, typically the very largest of the ceramic vessels, and which were normally imbedded in the ground, are relatively common in eastern France: the Celtic Oppidum d'Ensérune, near Narbonne, and the Roman-era Toulons villa are just two examples. As well, they were common in Spain, Italy and the wine growing regions further to the east.

Around Bordeaux, however, the findings of dolia are scarce. One reason could be that by the time the people of Bordeaux started planting vineyards and making wine, they had no need of large dolia because wooden vats and barrels were available. Nonetheless, the region certainly has its share of ancient amphorae and wine drinking equipment – pitchers, cups, glasses, and kraters – as the finds in the region's Roman-era villas attest. These vessels were common artefacts in the Gallo-Roman villa of Plassac, about 20 kilometres by river north of Bordeaux, and that of Vesunna, near Périgueux. Dolia, however, were not to be found. Archaeologists have discovered that Bordeaux did have several amphorae production facilities operating for several centuries around the turn of the first millennium BCE and the initial millennium CE. However, apparently production was limited to the standard size amphorae and not the larger dolia.

With the dolia so important in the early wineries, and still in use in more than just a few wineries today, it is worth examining the processes by which they are made and utilized.

FIGURE 6.1 Wine storage dolia, with their tops sticking above ground
These were uncovered at Villa Rustica, Boscoreale, Italy, a city near Pompeii, after being covered with ash from the 79 CE Mt Vesuvius eruption
Wikimedia Commons

Making the dolia

With a cone-shaped base, few if any dolia were thrown on a potter's wheel. They were, instead, made by laboriously stacking and smoothing clay, coil upon coil, to build up the sides of the dolium (Barisashvili, 2011). The potter has a coil of clay the size of an Anaconda snake slung over his shoulders. Slowly walking backwards around the developing pot, he moulds and forms this coil into the sidewall. A large dolia could take a day or more to build as some drying is required before piling on more clay. Over the years, individual potters and ceramic manufacturers have developed variations, including making the body and rim separately, and making the dolia in moulds.

Firing a completed dolium would have been difficult, especially so with the largest styles. Generally, a 'portable' kiln of bricks would be built *around* such a dolium. As the building and firing was laborious, the dolia were expected to last many years. The largest dolia being made today are typically no bigger than the largest kilns, and are moved in and out using forklifts.

As the size of the dolia increased, the clay would occasionally develop cracks, due either to uneven drying of the large, thick surfaces or from handling during the manufacturing (Peña, 2007). Rather than scrap the whole piece, ingenious methods were devised to minimize the crack and keep it from expanding. One method was to cut a double dove-tail mortise on either side of the crack prior to firing. After the firing, these channels would then be filled with lead or other ceramics, basically 'bridging' the gap to hold it together (Peña, 2007).

Moving

Where possible, dolia were made as close to where they were to be used as practical. Otherwise, in the days before the availability of forklifts, cranes and massive trucks, wooden carts, many men, ropes, slings, pulleys all must have been employed to transport the largest vessels.

Protecting the outside of the dolia

In many early wineries, even into Roman times, the dolia were set into the ground. The main purpose appears to be in assisting to keep the temperature of the wine stable and cool. An additional benefit was providing easier access to the tops – no need for scaffolding or ladders to climb up in order to accomplish the various winemaking and maintenance tasks of filling, lees stirring, emptying, cleaning, and recoating the interior when necessary. For those dolia set into the earth, a thick wash of lime was applied to the exterior of the dolia prior to setting it in the ground. This helped to reduce the naturally occurring mould in the soil (Barisashvili, 2011).

In the Villa Regina de Boscoreale, uncovered near Pompeii, a number of dolia were found set in the ground in the middle of the villa's enclosure (Beard, 2008). Some present-day wineries in France, Spain, Portugal, Italy, Georgia, Greece, Canada and America are still employing dolia with their winemaking processes (Caillaud, 2014).

Lining the inside

Because the ceramic materials utilized for the dolia or qvevri typically are porous, most are coated on the inside. Historically, the two main coatings used were beeswax, utilized by Georgian vintners (Barisashvili, 2011), or pitch, employed by the Romans (Peña, 2007). In the past hundred years, paints and now more inert epoxies and non-porous ceramics are being utilized.

These newer oxygen-excluding technologies certainly aid in keeping the vessels sanitary, acting like the inert surfaces of a stainless steel tank rather than a wooden cask or barrel. However, by impacting the oxygen exchange are they changing the traditional methods by which the dolia functioned for wine maturation? This is another question for the researchers.

Cleaning

Typically, once the wine is emptied, for most dolia this would require someone (small) to climb into the tank to remove the final residue, and then wash the interior with a lye or ash (Barisashvili, 2011), a mild alkali solution which not only cleans but sanitizes. Even with the coatings, there are minute cracks, allowing bacteria to grow in the nooks and crannies. And despite the most rigorous cleaning, nothing short of a gas can access these micro-organisms. Therefore, today, sulphur is introduced into the dolia – either by burning a wick or from a gas cylinder. The sulphur gas kills the bacteria hiding within these cracks, keeping the vessel sanitary (Barisashvili, 2011). This is a method similar to that used in wooden tanks and barrels.

Covers for the opening

For traditional dolia, while the wine was fermenting, a wicker cover would be utilized to allow the gases to escape, enabling easy access for punching down the cap, while keeping insects and vermin out. When finished fermenting and into the aging phase, tight-fitting wooden or stone covers were employed. They might be laid upon a gasket of beeswax or clay on the rim of the dolia to provide a more positive seal. Most certainly, they were then completely covered with a thick paste of clay to form an air-tight closure (Barisashvili, 2011).

Unfortunately, this type of seal is not convenient for checking on the wine. Nowadays, more sanitary and easily accessed covers of stainless steel are incorporated (Caillaud, 2014).

Accessing the wine

Either the winemaker poured the wine in or it flowed via gravity from a trough above. Removing it was not as easy. If the dolia is set into the ground, in the days before pumps, the only method was to bucket it out. However, there is some evidence that even the Romans had simple pumps (Marlière, 2013; Marlier & Sibella 2002) which they used to pump wine to or from dolia on board ships. Perhaps the fanciest of Roman vintners would have incorporated such a pump. These were basically a revolving set of ceramic jars, or copper or lead cans, to remove the wine from the vat. However, most must have resorted to the bucket method. Modern dolia are set up on legs and have valves to which hoses and pumps can be connected, to aid the process.

Locations of dolia

Most of the dolia were located at winery sites, either set under grape stomping troughs or presses, or in an area of many dolia where the wine was fermented and/or aged. Surprisingly, they have been discovered in other venues. The Italian town of Herculanum was another village covered in the 79 CE eruption of Italy's Mt. Vesuvius. There, archaeologists have uncovered a tavern (*thermopolium*). Within the terracotta tiled bar were several 400 to 500 litre capacity dolia (Caillaud, 2014). Perhaps these were

FIGURE 6.2 Dolia inset within a Herculanum bar
Wikicommons – Jebulon

for dipping into to serve the patrons directly. In today's modern bars liquids are dispensed from pressurized kegs hidden behind the counter; however, how these dolia were fully utilized has not been discovered. Other dolia were placed in the centres of the early ships in order to transport significantly more wine with less weight than a boat load of amphorae (Marlière, 2013).

EXPLORATIONS 6.2
TASTING OF WINE MADE IN AMPHORAE/DOLIA

The Spanish Mediterranean beach town of L'Escala, formerly the Roman port of Empúries, is located about 125 kilometres north of Barcelona. In ancient times, this was an important fishing and trading harbour, initially used by the Greeks, and later by the Romans. After years of archaeological digs, the ruins of the two former towns are now open to visitors. One can walk amongst what were expansive Greek villas and the town's agora (marketplace), while up the hill in the Roman town, the outline and a few columns of its forum and an amphitheatre are still visible. In both ruins, archaeologists uncovered the remains of various factories, including the fish preservation works, which utilized salt. L'Escala, is still an important sardine and anchovy fishing community (and still packing them in salt), as well as a popular tourist spot for both the Catalans and the French.

In researching our visit to the Empúries ruins, Karen and I noticed that the site's museum was offering a tasting of wine made in amphorae. Upon reading this, the image of holding our glasses out to receive wine right from an upturned amphora sparked our interest. We made a reservation. Arriving on time, we joined the small group making its way to a room above the museum.

The ambiance for the tasting was perfect; an old stone building overlooking the Greek ruins, with a warm breeze blowing in from the blue Mediterranean Sea through the open windows. Joan Benejam Vidal, a young, knowledgeable Spanish sommelier presented the wines and described in detail how they were made. But, speaking in the Catalan language, which is just different enough from Spanish, we missed much. While we understood that the six wines – three whites and three reds – were made in amphorae, we were unable to determine the actual size of those vessels. To our disappointment, the wines were poured from bottles.

The several varietals – Macabel (Ugni Blanc) a white, Grenache (surprisingly in both white and red types) and a Syrah – were all well-made and individually interesting. The Macabel was especially crisp. Karen detected a bit of minerality, perhaps from the ceramics, running through them.

As we progressed through the wines, I was thinking that if these wines were aged in small amphorae, typically of the 20 to 30 litres size, they were fantastic. Could wineries still actually be storing considerable amounts of wine in such small amphorae?

At the end of the tasting, I learned that the sommelier could speak a little French, so was able to ask him the size of the amphorae the wineries were using. He described the amphora as the large dolium style, in the range of 1,000 to 5,000 litres, not the smaller amphora type. (I am still unsure as to why the tasting was advertised as 'wine from amphorae'.) Dolia, as noted previously, have been used for thousands of years, and in fact, on one of our first visits to Spain, Karen and I tasted wine dipped directly out of a dolium in a winery in the Valdepeñas wine region south of Madrid, as noted below. With all of today's winemaking technology, I could see how the wines we tasted at Empúries could be made using these large dolia.

A few days after the tasting I asked a California winemaker friend about aging wine in small amphorae. His opinion was that aging or storing wine in amphorae is to go backward; if those vessels do not ruin good wine, they certainly add nothing to it. Nonetheless, during the Roman era, the amphorae were used to ship millions of litres of wine around the Mediterranean, and the larger dolia, placed in ships, carried many more thousands of litres. It would be fascinating to see how this wine really tasted, although perhaps one might not want to drink a whole glass.

Back in L'Escala, since fishing and the processing of the catch was such a critical aspect of the city's history, it has developed a noteworthy museum to showcase the fishermen and their culture: the Museo de la Anchoa y de la Salt. What I found interesting was that up until recently, small wooden barrels were one of the containers into which the salted anchovy and sardines were packed. Now the salted fish are packed in glass, plastic or tin, while the barrels are relegated to memorabilia in the museum.

Impacting the wine

Qvevri, the Georgian term for dolia, even to this day still play a prominent role in that country's winemaking. In commenting upon how they change the wine, Giorgi Barisashvili, a Georgian viticulture and winemaking consultant, believes that "Wine produced using the qvevri is characterized by its unique type, stability, high potential for aging, natural brilliance, distinguished flavor and aroma, high tannin content, and other positive properties" (2011).

How does the use of dolia/qvevri compare with wine aged in wooden tanks? In the winter of 2011–12, an oenology student, now professor at the University of Milan, Luigi Armanino, trialled both a dolium and wooden tank with Barbera grapes from Asti, Italy (Armanino, 2014).

After the Barbera was harvested and fermented, 200 litres were placed in a non-lined, ceramic dolia with a stainless-steel cover. For comparison, a second lot was placed in a 1,500 litre once-used wooden tank. Since this dolium had unlined walls, they would have acted like those of the tank, allowing some exposure to the wine as the oxygen penetrated through the walls.

During the 14 months the wine spent in these two containers, the dissolved oxygen was constantly measured. In wine, as I have noted, dissolved oxygen plays a complex and an important role in aging, and insuring the colour stability in red wines. In this experiment, the wine in the dolium averaged 0.3 mg/l of oxygen while that in the wooden tank was slightly lower at 0.2 mg/l. Both, however, were within the normal range. With the difference in sizes of the containers, the wine in the dolium had much more exposure to the sides of the container. This may have been a large contributing factor to the slightly higher oxygen level. The wine in the dolium showed a sharp drop in the total acidity at the end of the aging period, as well as a slight decrease in the colour intensity.

Professor Armanino in an interview with wine writer Llaria De Lillo later drew the following conclusions:

> Comparing the same wine with these two different aging procedures it is immediately clear that the flavour/fragrance profile changes a lot. First of all, in the amphora [dolia] wine, the scent of wood that we are so used to perceiving in wines aged in barrels or large casks isn't there. In its place we find nuances of minerals, often a little ethereal but in any case, complex, together with an intense flavour in the mouth and a velvety softness, probably due to oxygenation and, perhaps, a slight

transfer of potassium from the terracotta which lowered the natural acidity of the Barbera wine.

(De Lillo, 2015)

More recently, in an unscientific comparison, Portland, Oregon winemaker Barnably Tuttle, of Teutonic Wines fermented a mix of Gamay and Pinot Noir in both an amphora and a wooden barrel, each roughly the 225 litre size. He stated to wine writer Rachael Signer that "the textual, flavor and aromatic difference is immense". The wine aged in the unlined amphora was "chewier, richer more complex with greater length" than the barrel-fermented and -aged wine (2017).

Notes of other wineries using dolium-style tanks

One of the attributes of ceramic dolia that few would dispute is that the thick walls tend to minimize external temperature swings. To a lesser extent, the same thing happens in cement tanks and wooden wine tanks. The actual physical shape of the dolium impacting the wine is a different story. Although the shape of the dolia vary from region to region and in era to era, some winemakers believe that the egg form contributes to wine clarity. During fermentation, Barisashvili believes that the shape concentrates the grape seeds at the bottom minimizing their additional acid in the wine, while the skins float to the top for positive contact (2011).

Okanagan Crush Pad Winery, in British Columbia, Canada incorporates a number of large dolium-sized concrete 'eggs' to ferment their wines. Winemaker Matt Dumayne noted that the oval shape results in more 'textural wines'. He believes that it "creates a kind of vortex, and it prevents the lees from sticking to the bottom of the tank, and the suspended solids get much more contact with the wine" (Signer, 2017). This seems to be in line with what Mr Barisashvili noted.

In France, owner/winemaker Guillaume La Garde of Bordeaux's Chateau Roland La Garde makes biodynamic wines. He has trialled some dolia to ferment his Merlot, Cabernet Sauvignon and Malbec, feeling they open faster than those fermented in barrels (Signer, 2017).

Researchers at the University of Milano's Department of Food and Nutritional Studies summed up some of the advantages and difficulties in working with dolia, especially those placed in the ground, as compared to stainless steel, wooden or concrete tanks. On the plus side, the dolia keep the wine temperature cool and minimize daily or seasonal fluctuations. The disadvantages include high maintenance costs due largely to the difficulty in cleaning the tanks; low tank capacity, as compared to other tank materials; controlling oxygen ingress; and controlling the fermentation/maceration conditions, including controlling the wine temperature (Tirelli et al., 2014).

Like so many other variables for winemaking, making wine in ceramic vessels is another 'tool' to nuance certain flavours, provide a specific taste profile for customers, and otherwise offer something different in the marketplace.

EXPLORATIONS 6.3
TASTING FROM DOLIA IN VALDEPEÑAS

Exploring the Valdepeñas region of Spain in the mid-1980s, Karen and I called in at Bodegas Miguel Calatayud, a large and, at that time, co-op type winery, where we requested a tour. This was in the days before most European wineries provided tours or tastings, so our arrival was quite unexpected. Nonetheless, the winery staff were extremely cordial and accommodating, directing one of their cellar personal to show us around.

Our tour guide was a gregarious man, probably in his fifties. Despite not speaking English, he was more than happy to show off the facility. The reality, as we discovered, was that he was much more pleased to have a mid-day tasting (probably more like drinking) of the wines than to be pulling hoses or cleaning tanks.

The visit was late February, still cold enough for sweaters and jackets. The wines had finished fermenting, and most were settling in the wineries' many fibreglass and large concrete tanks, as well as their ceramic dolia. All these containers were tall enough to require ladders to access their top openings. And we did. (This was also in the days before safety concerns about visitors walking around on the tops of the tanks.)

We climbed up to the top of a row of dolia. Standing upon the cat-walk, the rims of each of a number of dolia peaked up above its surface. Their openings – about 50 centimetres in diameter – were covered with beret-shaped, brown wicker hats. Apparently, with the cool temperature, and the small volume of wine at the top exposed to the air versus the huge volume of the tank, oxidation was of little concern. Perhaps, especially so, as these wines were intended to be everyday drinking wines for the mass market.

Karen could speak some Spanish, and I knew some of the wine terms. We could understand our host when he asked if we knew how they made their rosé. We replied, no. He then removed the covers off two of the dolia. We saw that one contained red wine, while the other a white. He then unpretentiously dipped a glass into the red, and another into the white and poured them together. "Aquí está", or voilà, instant rosé. The smiles on our faces produced a smile on his, obviously realizing that it was so easy to amuse gullible Yankees. We all then proceeded to enjoy the cold 'rosé'.

While we had seen dolia in photos of ancient wineries, at that time we were unaware of wineries still using them. This winery had quite a few placed in their various store rooms, and even had an enormous one propped up at their winery entrance. While wineries like this have been using and continue to use dolia, there has been a renewal of interest from a few winemakers around the Mediterranean and also in the new world countries employing them for aging and/or the storage of wine. Part of the interest is tied to making organic wines, as well as a 'getting back to the basics'.

Since I was in the cooperage business, I wondered whether the winery used barrels for aging. Yes, they did, and they had about 100 set off in a separate room. This would have been a tiny portion of their production; their better reds. We tasted from a few of the barrels, although our guide would have been more than happy to provide a tasting from every single one.

(As a side note, the barrels were made of American oak by a Spanish cooperage. This was extremely common, as purchasing American oak, even with the additional transportation costs, was less expensive than obtaining French oak for the manufacturing of the casks. Whether it was a cultural thing – hanging on from the hundreds of years of wars and trade competition with the French – or the lower price, or some combination of the two, I cannot say. The Spanish, and Portuguese for their port wines, however have a long history of utilizing American oak to make their barrels. It is changing somewhat today, as the Spanish winemakers are requesting French and European oaks from their Spanish cooperages.)

Back to the tour: by its end, our cheeks were flushed and our host's even redder. We thanked him generously and drove away carefully.

Concrete tanks

Once concrete came into general use, some wineries started shifting from dolia to concrete tanks. This was most likely a practical progression: a square or rectangular tank is more efficient, capacity-wise, than a round one. Many were open-topped, and used for fermentation. Others were completely sealed.

Concrete, like the ceramics of the dolium, requires coating the inside. This was not so much to minimize the oxygen interaction as to resist the acids in wine which can erode the cement within the concrete. In the 1950s, as epoxies came into use, and improving on the resistance and inertness of the paints, they were utilized to coat the interior walls.

Concrete tanks were used in bulk wine facilities in both Europe and the United States into the late twentieth century. The majority have subsequently been replaced with stainless-steel tanks. This is not because the round stainless steel tanks are space-saving, but because they are cleanable, require less general maintenance, and are easily adaptable to the many wine maintenance chores, such as cooling or heating the liquid. Further, should there be head-space at the top – i.e., not enough wine to completely fill the tank – a round tank exposes the wine to less area at the top surface than does a square tank.

Wooden tanks

Wooden tanks and casks have been a mainstay of western wineries, usually in conjunction with barrels and occasionally as the wineries sole cooperage. As winemaking expanded, first in Europe and then the rest of the world, the use of wooden containers, larger than barrels, made sense for a number of reasons. Their greater capacity minimized the labour required to fill, empty and otherwise maintain the cooperage. For lighter wines, such as the northern European varietals, the larger tanks did not overpower the flavours with oak. Finally, they were a more efficient use of winery space than the smaller barrels.

Over the past several thousand years, wooden tanks have been made in a variety of shapes. The forerunners were the circular troughs in which Egyptian workers are shown in murals treading grapes at harvest; a wooden bottom with vertical staves as sides, probably held together with fibre lashing. The wood of the tanks depicted in the Egyptian murals was most likely palm. Although it could also have been cedar, imported from the Levant with the wine. As these tanks are only depicted in murals, it is difficult to determine.

FIGURE 6.3 Wine casks in a modern winery
Glenn Cormier

As the wooden cooperage used in Europe evolved, vertical, straight-sided tanks in the shape of truncated cones may have been the connecting link between the open-topped troughs to the curved-stave barrels. An innovation in the design of these tanks was making the top, or head, slightly smaller than the bottom. The hoops, whether fibre, saplings, or eventually iron or steel, would then be assisted by gravity; any slackness or drying of the tank would allow the hoops to drop, becoming tighter and tighter.

Envisioning a cone shaped tank, one can surmise that a carpenter or wheelwright, the type of craftsmen who would eventually become the full-fledged coopers, might have created the idea of placing two of the tanks end to end and somehow bending the staves to connect them. It is very possible that the barrel was created from this image.

Another advantage of the cone shaped tank was in the use of riveted steel hoops. Celtic and Roman craftsmen were able to construct tools and fittings of steel. Although, like today's exotic materials such as carbon fibre or titanium, they utilized that material only in the most necessary instances, or for those who could afford it. The rims of chariot wheels were one situation where steel was essential. Those steel rims were riveted to the wooden wheel frame. For vintners, brewers or others who were utilizing wooden tanks, having the blacksmith make riveted hoops would not have been a stretch. Each of the steel hoops required for a cone-shaped tank would be made slightly smaller than the one below it. Securing the ends of the hoops together with rivets is a far less complicated method to fabricate than to forge or cut threads, and to make nuts upon which to secure the hoops.

**EXPLORATIONS 6.4
CLEANING A WINE CASK**

Dusty and dirty, terribly confined, often still with a strong aroma of the sulphur gas used as a sanitizer for the tank, cleaning the inside of wooden tanks and casks was not a job for your average worker.

The nastiest job I encountered in 30 years working as a cooper was cleaning out the interior of used wooden wine tanks. The worst were the oval casks, with their extremely small access hole. Before the days of settling wines in the stainless steel tanks or the use of mechanical washers, after fermentation some wineries settled their wines in the wooden tanks and casks prior to aging in small wooden barrels or bottling. Over the years, the tartrates in the wine would build up on the lower sides of the tanks, in some cases becoming several millimetres thick. Periodically, it was necessary to remove this build-up so the wine could actually interact with the tank's wooden surface. There was only one way to do this; have a person crawl into the tank, drag in some tools and a light, and grind and chip away at these tartrates. I did it more than a few times, regretting every instance.

Once the barrel shape evolved, they were made in a great many sizes to fit various needs and spaces. The largest barrels have become what we call casks, which are basically immovable. Often these are oval in shape, usually greater in height than width. They appear to have evolved in the Germanic countries, and are still prominent in Germany's wine caves today. It was in to these casks which I squeezed to clean them out. Talk about claustrophobic!

Since Roman times, tanks have been made in all sizes and shapes. Some as large as 500,000 litres, eight metres in diameter with staves six metres tall, requiring some sort of internal bracing to support the large head. Slowly, most of these are being replaced by tanks of stainless-steel or fibreglass. Although, like barrels, some wineries making premium wines still utilize the oak wood tanks for aging lighter or white wines, or in combination with barrels. In yet another permutation in the cask and tank sizes and styles, perhaps a reflection of a bridge between the ceramic dolia and the wooden tanks, the Taransaud cooperage has introduced wooden tanks in an egg shape.

EXPLORATIONS 6.5
WINE TANKS MADE OF REDWOOD

In California, many wine tanks for the early wineries were made of red-wood – from either the coastal redwood (*Sequoia sempervirens*) species or from that of the giant redwood (*Sequoiadendron giganteum*) of the Sierra Nevada mountains. Cut from huge, first-growth trees, it made clear, straight-grain lumber. Unlike oak, it is softer and without the similar strength, nor can it be bent. But by cutting the staves and heading thicker, adequate tanks could be produced. However, like oak, redwood contains tannins, making redwood extremely resistant to decay. In a large tank, however, the impact of those extra tannins on the wine is minimized.

By the time I became a cooper, and got into the wine business, redwood wine tanks were being phased out. In the Napa Valley, the old wineries, where the redwood tanks were prominent, were being taken over by new owners, intent upon upgrading the facilities. One of my cooperage tasks was to dismantle some of these redwood tanks to make way for the stain-less steel tanks and barrels. In one winery, the tanks had not been well maintained. There was a rank odour of mould from wine residue left under the tanks. It persisted for the several days while we removed the tanks.

A month or two thereafter, while on an airplane flight, I was served a red wine in a 375-millilitre plastic bottle. When I cracked the screw-cap and poured the wine out, it had the same smell as I had observed in the wine tanks. Checking the label on the bottle, I noticed that a Central Valley winery was the bottler. Thinking back to that tank dismantling job, I remembered that it was delayed until that same winery could remove the wine from those old tanks. They must have bottled it for the airlines, complete with the rank odour. Apparently, no amount of chemical fiddling by the winery's oenologists could remove it.

Stainless steel tanks

The new owners of the winery where I and my colleagues took down the tanks were well funded, enabling them to replace the old redwood tanks with new ones of stainless steel, and purchase new barrels as well. That was not the case for all winery start-ups. Many budding winemakers struggle to purchase their equipment. More than a few have resorted to purchasing tanks used by the milk or beer industries. They too, were stainless steel, however made to meet a different set of requirements; their shapes tended to be more horizontal than vertical. As a result, the wine was exposed to a large surface area, and more oxygen than necessary, as these tanks are filled or emptied.

Stainless steel, an alloy of iron and carbon, with chromium added to make it resistant to rust, corrosion and staining, has been around since 1915. It was initially used primarily for cutlery (Ranson, 2013). By the 1920s, its ability to be cleaned and sanitized encouraged the beer industry to start employing it for tanks, followed by the dairy industry for its milk hauling tanks set upon trucks, and the general food industry for tanks and other food-handling equipment (Ranson, 2013). The wine industry, a bit more traditional, really did not embrace stainless steel until the 1970s in its tanks as well as its grape handling and bottling equipment.

However, when it did, it did so with flash and pizzazz. The modern stainless steel tanks relieved much of the manual labour required for the dolia, concrete and wooden tanks. These tanks are usually set upon legs or upon ledges to allow troughs to be placed below their funnel-shaped doors which facilitate emptying the sediments after fermentation or settling. Not only do the tanks incorporate the ability to heat and cool the wine in the tank, they now allow the winemaker to monitor the temperatures, as well as set those temperatures remotely. Filling the wine and emptying it through numerous valves and fittings has become routine, as have become the mechanics for doing pump overs or stirring, as well as cleaning the tank once the wine has been pumped out. Some tanks have removable lids, above which is a track to support an apparatus to punch down the cap during fermentation.

FIGURE 6.4 Typical stainless steel tanks in a winery
Glenn Cormier

One of the lovely things about visiting today's modern wineries is the ambiance; the clean, glistening surfaces and the beautiful barrels. The stainless steel tanks most wineries have installed add to this environment with their sparkling surfaces, or attractive dimpled designs.

Stainless steel tanks and equipment are now the workhorses of almost all wineries. A few very premium facilities do not utilize them in the actual winemaking processes, but it would be hard to find any winery today that does not use a small stainless steel tank to at least hold wine before bottling, and all new bottling lines are made with stainless steel.

Conclusion

Throughout history, as wineries grew to making wine on a commercial scale, they have required larger and larger vessels. The dolia originally played that role. In areas of abundant forests, wooden tanks were the equivalent of those ceramic containers. In the past several hundred years, winemakers added tanks of concrete, and in the past 50 years, they embraced stainless steel. Nowadays, tanks of stainless steel are predominant, with wooden tanks coming in a far second. Nonetheless, to one degree or another all the various containers can still be found.

References

Armanino, L. (2014). Preliminary investigation on the evolution of Barbera D'Asti in terracotta. In: *1er Colloque International, La terra cotta e il vino*. Imprunta, Italy: Artenova, [online] pp. 89–108.

Barisashvili, G. (2011). *Making Wine in Qvevri: a Unique Georgian Tradition*. Tbilisi, Georgia: Biological Farming Association "Elkana".

Beard, M. (2008). *Pompeii: The Life of a Roman Town*. London: Profile Books.

Caillaud, C. (2014). Les céramiques et le vin: élaboration, stockage, commerce, de l'Antiquité à l'époque moderne, de l'amphore aux tinajas. In: *1er Colloque International, La terra cotta e il vino*. Imprunta, Italy: Artenova, [online]. pp. 4–89.

De Lillo, L. (2015). Wine in amphora vs wine in barrels: What are the differences? *Il Giornale del Cibo*. (Interview with Luigi Armanino, translated into English), [online] 2 November 2015.

Marlière, E. (2013). Les campagnes militaires et l'expansion de l'usage du tonneau dans l'Empire romain. In: *De la cave au vin: une fructueuse alliance*, Rencontres du Clos-Vougeot, Dijon: Chaire UNESCO Culture et Traditions du Vin and Université du Bourgogne, pp. 47–61.

Marlier, S. and Sibella, P. (2002). La Giraglia, a dolia wreck of the 1st century BC from Corsica, France: study of its hull remains. *The International Journal of Nautical Archaeology* 31(2), pp. 161–171.

Peña, J. T. (2007). *Roman Pottery in the Archaeological Record*. Oxford: Oxford University Press.

Ranson, E. (2013). Steel giving. *Materials World*, [online] 21(8), pp 47–49.

Signer, R. (2017). Beyond the barrel: unique ways to ferment wine. *The Wine Enthusiast* [online] 20 March 2017.

Tirelli, A., Gabrielli, M., and Piergiovanni, L. (2014). Caratterizzazione del Cerasulolo di Vitoria in terracotta. In: *1er Colloque International, La terra cotta e il vino*. Imprunta, Italy: Artenova, [online] pp. 109–147.

7

ALTERNATIVE PACKAGING

Bag-in-box, plastic bottles and aluminium cans

Alternative packaging

Any new containers for wine create controversy. Consider the ideas in these two quotes:

> With prices ranging from as little as $2 to more than $1000 per bottle, it is understandable that there is a significant variation in consumer's quality expectations.
>
> *(Reeves, 2010)*

> "The wine bottle is late-18th century technology," says Colin Alevras, sommelier at [New York restaurant] DBGB. "It's time to move on."
>
> *(Colman, 2009)*

These comments identify important issues for today's wine consumers; on one side, those of its visually appealing packaging and the perception of quality, and on the other how environmentally friendly the containers really are and whether they adversely impact the wine. The wine marketing gurus at the wineries are also concerned with these same attributes. For the winemakers, however, it is more a matter of protecting the wine, particularly from increased amounts of dissolved oxygen (Reeves, 2010), or the detrimental effects of sunlight. All these issues are being discussed as wineries struggle to decide in which containers of the various new materials to market their wines.

Glass of course is excellent at keeping the oxygen from the wine within, but its Achilles heel is the closure, be it natural cork, or now more and more synthetic stoppers or screw caps. The wine containers made of the newer materials – plastic bottles, or plastic-lined bag-in-box or aluminium cans – to one degree or another, also have a similar problem with their closures, nor are they as secure as glass over the long term at preventing the entry of oxygen. Additionally, there are questions about the long-term degradation of plastic.

As the bag-in-box was the first alternative packaging to make serious inroads into the glass bottles, its origins and make-up will be discussed first.

FIGURE 7.1 Typical bag-in-box
Glenn Cormier, Lisa Caron

What is bag-in-box?

In the past, bag-in-box has sometimes been referred to as *goon* sacks (short for flagon in the Australian vernacular), *jug wine*, or *bum wine* (Steeman, 2015). However, with significant improvements in the interior sack materials, better spigots, sophisticated marketing and actually filling the bags with better wine, bag-in-box is now coming into its own (Prestipino, 2015).

In France, a bag-in-box of rosé in the fridge is especially popular in the summer (Colman, 2009), they are a popular container in which to purchase wine in Italy (Cravero, 2016), and for the past 30 years wine in the boxes provided almost 50% of wine consumed in Australia (Prestipino, 2015). As of 2007, international acceptance put the use of bag-in-box at 9% in France and UK, 42% in Norway, 33% in Sweden, and 6% in the US (Reeves, 2010). An unofficial survey of a Safeway store near Seattle, Washington, revealed 15 different brands on the shelves, offered in a number of varieties, while another in Western Australia noted about eight different brands with a good selection of varieties. Overall, bag-in-box wines account for about 10% of the world wine market (Carvero, 2016).

There are a number of advantages to the box wines. First, like the barrels over the amphorae, they save in shipping weight as compared to wine in glass bottles. A case of wine in glass bottles, nine litres of wine, typically weighs about 15 kilograms (33 pounds) with the standard 500 gram bottles, and 13.8 kilograms (30.4 pounds) with the newer, lighter 400 gram bottles. Using standard bottles accounts for roughly half the weight of the total package full of wine. Shipping the equivalent in bag-in-box (three x 3 litre) containers dramatically reduces the carbon footprint (Colman, 2009), weighing only about 10 kilograms (22 pounds) total.

Additionally, once a bag-in-box is opened, the wine will stay fresh for at least several weeks. This is due to the fact that as the wine is released from the spigot almost no oxygen is allowed back in to the wine (Routledge, 2016). Wine in a glass bottle can also stay fresh, but the oxygen must be evacuated with a pump-type device, or displaced with nitrogen or other inert gas.

The bag-in-box has its downsides. Unlike bottles, one cannot see the amount of wine left in the container. Depending upon the materials incorporated in the bag's layers, it usually has a shelf-life of six months to a maximum of one year. Additionally, there is the lingering stigma of containing wines of lesser quality.

TABLE 7.1 Comparing container weights – bag-in-box, glass bottles and plastic bottles (each containing nine litres of wine)

	Weight of wine	*Weight of containers*	*Total shipping weight*
Case of 12 x 750 ml glass bottles (500 grams each)	9 kilograms	6 kilograms (cardboard nominal)	15 kilograms
Case of 12 x 750 ml glass bottles (light-weight – 400 grams)	9 kilograms	4.8 kilograms (cardboard nominal)	13.8 kilograms
Three x 3 litre, bag-in-box	9 kilograms	0.04 kilograms each	9.12 kilograms
Case of 12 x 750 plastic bottles	9 kilograms	0.3 kilograms (cardboard nominal)	9.3 kilograms

EXPLORATIONS 7.1
TASTING BAG-IN-THE-BOX WINE

A few years ago, while visiting friends who live east of Bordeaux, Karen and I were ushered on to their patio for aperitifs. They brought out a tray with four glasses containing a chilled Sauvignon Blanc, a traditional wine from the Graves region southeast of Bordeaux. A superficial smell and taste of the wine indicated body, some complexity, a hint of flint, but not overly grassy; a most pleasant wine, perfect for the warm afternoon. When we finished those glasses of wine, and knowing that we were to have barbecued lamb, we switched to red; this time a Merlot, another wine typical of the Bordeaux region. Again, our host brought out the wine, in glasses, on a tray. Tasting the wine, we found it very acceptable; not with any great depth, but with some plum flavours and without flaws.

I began to think something was a little odd. Why didn't our host bring out the bottle for either of these wines?

Standing around the barbecue as he was grilling the chops, he revealed the purpose of this exercise. Both wines were poured from bag-in-box which he had purchased at his local *supermarché* in 3-litre containers. Knowing our interest in wine, he wanted to confirm his own tastes, and appreciation of these wines. He sought an unbiased opinion, i.e. not showing us the packaging source for the wine. We found both wines perfectly acceptable for the relaxed afternoon visit, and the picnic-style meal.

What difference would it have made if we had seen the wine being tapped from the bag-in-box? I believe none. Over our years of wine tasting, we have been offered terrible wines from elegant bottles, and very enjoyable wine from jugs, bag-in-box, tanks, dolia and barrels. If it is good, we enjoy it. If not, it goes down the drain or is politely refused. The container certainly adds ambiance, but rarely masks significant flaws.

The quality of the bag-in-box packaging ranges from simple to high-end (Colman, 2009). Overall, the bag material itself is much improved from the initial efforts, as has the box designs and lithography, bordering on some of the imagination of wine bottle labels. For example, Astrapak, a South African company sells its sacks in the United States, one which even resembles a wooden barrel (AstraPouch, 2018).

Who invented bag in the box? And where?

Who first placed wine in an animal skin bladder is uncertain, but it is certainly the distant forerunner of the bag-in-box. Snow skiers in the 1960s and 1970s were often seen holding a *bota bag* of wine up in the air with a stream of red wine running into their mouth, or occasionally down their chest. These were a modern-day take-off on the goat skin bags used by early shepherds or other travellers, the more recent ones being lined with rubber.

Although many people and companies saw the benefits of placing wine in pouches within cardboard containers, it was Australian Tom (Thomas William Carylon) Angove (1917–2010) who is credited with inventing the bag-in-box for wine, or as he marketed it, the *wine cask* (Lower, 2010).

EXPLORATIONS 7.2
THE DEVELOPMENT OF BAG-IN-BOX FOR WINE

Angove was a third-generation Australian vintner. His grandfather, Dr William Thomas Angove (1854–1915) had emigrated from England to

Tea Tree Gully, set in the rolling hills of Adelaide, South Australian. A photo of this first Mr Angove on the Angove Wines website depicts a man with a wonderful twinkle in his eyes. Perhaps there was something about his seeming love of life, along with the feeling that he had been set down in a paradise as compared to his chilly Cornwall home, which prompted him to plant ten acres of vines (Angove Winery, 2018).

By 1886, he had formally established Angove Family Winemakers. His son, Thomas 'Skipper' Carylon Angove (1880–1952), Tom's father, carried on with the business by developing vineyards in Renmark, along the Murray River in the Riverlands region. As those vineyards came into production, Skipper expanded the exportation of their wines and distilled spirits (Angove Winery, 2018). Tom joined the business in the late 1930s after graduating with a degree in Oenology. He continued the development, helping to cement Angove into a substantial business, with one of the largest vineyards in the southern hemisphere (Clark, 2004). At almost 517 hectares, it is an enormous wine estate.

By the early 1960s, quality, varietal wines were coming into their own in Australia. Technological developments in vineyard management and cellar practices had improved the quality; the need to mask mediocre wines by making them into Sherries, ports and brandies was decreasing, as was the demand for those higher alcoholic liquids.

Large glass wine bottles were available, but they were heavy, and susceptible to breakage; a liability in the era when many Australian's enjoyed the wine while out on picnics or at a barbecue, especially so with everyone running around barefoot. Additionally, as with any bottle, if some wine was left in the bottle, it would become vinegar within a few days.

The idea of the bag, one which collapsed to keep air out of the liquid as it was withdrawn, was not new. People had incorporated similar systems for other materials, including Dr William R. Scholle who used it for battery acid[1] and Liqui-Box (Funding Universe, 2017), both in the United States. The bag, however, required some structure, either itself or around it. Thus, combining a recyclable cardboard support with the bag made good sense.

It took Mr Angove several years perfecting the packaging. By 1965 he was able to obtain a patent[2] for 'improved container and pack for liquids'. Shortly thereafter, he started production and marketing of his wines in what he termed a half gallon 'wine cask'.

The initial design was fairly rudimentary. Users of Angove's 'wine cask' were required to tear off a corner of the internal plastic bag in order to pour out the wine. They then sealed it with a wooden clothes peg. Nonetheless, seeing some success in this innovation, in 1967, Australian winery giant Penfolds introduced its own version. In association with inventor Charles Malpas, they improved the system by connecting a plastic tap to the metallised wine bladder. This latter adaptation is what we now generally see available in the 1.5, 2, 3, 4 and 5 litre sized bag-in-box packaging.

Apparently, all the bugs were not worked out of those early bags and cardboard packaging, as Angove Wines stopped offering its wines in the 'wine casks' in the 1970s. However, subsequent improvements prompted them to restart this packaging in 1984. At this time, they introduced a 5-litre box. It was entitled the 'Paddlewheel 5' in honour of the wood-fired, paddle wheel steam boats which had carried freight up and down the Murray River in the late 1800s into the early 1900s. It was those ships which took the early Angove wines from the winery in Renmark, downstream to the town of Murray Bridge, there to be carted overland to markets in Adelaide, or forwarded on to other Australian or overseas customers from Adelaide's port.

By the early 2000s, wine cask wine made up one half of all wine consumed in Australia (Clark, 2004). One of Australia's largest wine retailers, Dan Murphy, currently offers at least ten brands of wine in the boxes, available in most of the common white and red varietals.

Coincidentally, the man, Dan Murphy who started the retail shops, was also instrumental in improving the wine cask. He, with inventor Charles Malpas, developed a spigot which could be attached to the bag, enabling the wine to be released while preventing air from entering (Steeman, 2015).

Further enhancements have included square bags to fit more efficiently within the box, taps which do not have to be removed from the box, better printing to allow more creative labelling, and chemical improvements in the bag layers (Steeman, 2015).

Bag-in-box basics

Within the cardboard box, the crux of today's bag usually consists of five layers of various metallic and/or plastic films (Fradique et al., 2011; Reeves,

2010). Individually, they provide the barriers to oxygen and/or strengthening membranes for the bag itself (Reeves, 2010).

The results of a 2011 study by the University of Bordeaux found that multi-layer PET (Polyethylene Terephthalate) plastic materials combined with layers of a Gas Barrier Resin (an example being an ethylene-vinyl alcohol copolymer and MXD6 nylon mix) provided significantly improved protection from oxygen ingress, as opposed to a single layer PET container, over the generally short shelf life of bag-in-box wines (Yeamans-Irwin, 2011).

Some packaging suppliers make a bag which utilizes a metalized layer to provide a greater restriction of oxygen. This material is, however, more susceptible to the minute fracturing during shipment and handling, thus creating the possibility of oxygen ingress (Reeves, 2010).

The shelf life of wine in a bag-in-box is dependent upon a number of factors: rate of O^2 ingress, storage temperature, humidity, wine composition, bag size, film fracturing, and the rate of use (Reeves, 2010). In general, however, the recommendation is three to six months (Cravero, 2016).

Besides oxygen entering through the bag layers, two other possible sources of ingress are the plastic tap or valve and the seams. The potential for leaking air into the wine comes through the seam to which the tap connects to the bag and to the tap itself. Depending upon the storage conditions and the type of wine, researchers have found that volatile compounds in some wines are reduced, apparently caused by both absorption of the plastic material and the tap seal. Further, tasters in one study found the aroma of plastic after only 30 days of storage in bag-in-box (Cravero, 2016). Another study found that free SO_2, which acts as a preservative, was halved after three months of storage and reduced by 75% after six months (Cravero, 2016). Taste tests comparing wine in bag-in-box to that in bottles are mixed at best.

Plastic bottles

As water and soft drink companies shifted to using plastic bottles, the wine industry resisted, generally preferring glass bottles. Eventually, however, plastic bottles were found to have some practical uses in which to package wine. The two main criteria were that the wine would not remain long in the bottles – it would be purchased and drunk within months not years – and that the use of glass, with its heavier weight and potential for breakage, was problematic. To a lesser degree, individual serving was added to the mix. More recently, large supermarket chains, particularly those in the UK, have started marketing wine in plastic as a method to reduce their carbon footprint (Specter, 2008). We will examine the issues of the environmental impact for wine packaging and containers in Chapter 11.

The arguments against the use of glass bottles in certain locations made plastic bottles ideal for venues such as economy class on airlines; reducing the weight of the glass and eliminating a breakage problem. (In First and Business Class, wine is usually poured out of a 750-ml bottle which the flight attendant controls.) Also, plastic bottles are ideal for selling wine in theatre, sport and beach settings, with their individualized serving size and non-breakability.

With plastic bottles, oxygen ingress is a concern, hence the six-month to one-year shelf life as with the bag-in-box (Reeves, 2010). Like the bag-in-box, the plastic bottles have several layers of PET (Polyethylene Terephthalate) combined with a nylon layer for strength (Reeves, 2010). Additionally, 'oxygen scavengers', compounds that absorb oxygen, are incorporated in the packaging to catch whatever oxygen does enter.

Another issue is whether the plastic leaches compounds into the wine which could pose a health risk. The jury is still out on this.

Finally, there is the consumer image. Are we willing to purchase our night's wine in a plastic bottle? Certainly, some are, especially those already purchasing their meals in plastic. For the more traditional, the transition will take more time. However, as we get used to being served wine in the small plastic bottles while on board airplanes or at rugby matches, we might not be so hesitant when we see them on the supermarket shelves.

A few years ago, British supermarket chain Sainsbury launched two wines, a New Zealand white and an Australian Shiraz, in plastic PET bottles. To further reduce the total ecological footprint, they imported these wines in 24,000 litre bladders, and bottled them in the UK (Tipples, 2010). These wines are intended for a very short turn around on the market shelves. Nonetheless, a quick look at the wine shelves in any liquor store or supermarket, indicates that placing wine in plastic bottles has still yet to gain serious traction. An informal survey of wine shelves in shops and supermarkets in Australia, France, Portugal and the United States noted only at most two or three wines and wine-type products (Sangria being one) were being offered in plastic bottles.

FIGURE 7.2 Wine in individual serving plastic bottles and can
Glenn Cormier, Lisa Caron

EXPLORATIONS 7.3
MAILING WINE?

One innovative British company, Delivering Happiness, has radically changed wine packaging. Instead of glass bottles, their Bordeaux and Burgundy style containers are rigid, 750 ml size, very flat PET plastic bottles with plastic screw caps. They are designed to be mailed, and fit in the letterbox or be squeezed through the mail drop.

The idea for the design occurred when people complained about missing deliveries of their wine. With slim-line bottle, in a standard cardboard mailer, it can be pushed right in through a letter slot (Garcon Wines, 2017).

The bottles are recyclable, and won Best New Beverage Concept at the World Beverage International Awards, 2017.

FIGURE 7.3 Flat plastic wine bottle, ideal for sending through the mail
Intellectual property of Delivering Happiness, Ltd.

A look at the plastic itself

Besides PET, which is basically not biodegradable, there are two other
plastic options: PAL (Polylactide) which is made from corn and is biodegradable, and oxy-PET or OxSc-PET, which has an additive intended to
help scavenge oxygen from impacting the produce and may help to degrade
the package in 10 to 20 years (Shen, 2011).

Multi-layer PET bottles with oxygen scavengers have been tested against
the same Italian wines in glass bottles. For the red wines, this packaging was
found to offer more protection from oxygen than single layer PET containers. In another study, PAL containers were examined. After four
months, they showed greater quality loss than the same wine in glass or
PET packaging (Cravero, 2016).

In 2012, white and red Bordeaux wines were tested by comparing
changes in the wine contained in glass, bag-in-box, and single and multi-
layer PET containers. The glass and the multi-layer PET proved to be best
for the white wines, but none of the alternative materials provide for long-
term (12 month) preservation. The differences for the red wines were not
significant (Cravero, 2016).

A recent article about the use of plastic in the wine industry provides some sobering thoughts about wine or any product we consume in plastic. A number of ingredients are added to the basic materials of plastic in order to make them more useful for the particular application in which they are intended. Phthalates are one of the main additives; used to make plastic flexible. Unfortunately, Trela and Plank note that "As plasticizers, phthalates do not chemically bind to the plastics in which they are mixed, and plastic-bisphenol polymers can be hydrolyzed or may be incompletely polymerized, therefore, both types of chemicals can leach from the products into the environment" (2015). In other words, these phthalates can interact with the wine; seeping into the liquid over time. Some of these plastic compounds have been linked to human health problems (Trela and Plank, 2015).

But plastics are not just used in the bottles, they are incorporated into screwcaps, bag-in-box liners, and some synthetic corks, as well as some of the wine processing and handling machines, such as pump impellers, utilized in wineries. Grapes are now mostly harvested and placed in plastic bins to deliver to the wineries. "Plastics are used in the manufacture, transport and storage of wine. It has been estimated that synthetic closures have taken 19% of the world's closure market, with metal screwcaps making up 11% of the market of approximately 20 billion wine bottles per year" conclude Trela and Plank (2015).

Aluminium cans

To a much lesser extent, wine is packaged in cans for many of the same reasons as it is packaged in plastic bottles. Because the cans are often coated with plastics, they have many of the same issues as discussed above. However, while oxygen ingress is not usually a problem, the shelf life for these wines is not intended to be long.

Wine in cans must be ready to drink, that is because in an inert container there will be no interaction with oxygen, i.e. aging. This makes this wine intended for the 'on-the-go lifestyle' particularly that of the millennial generation. As a group, according to Wine Market Council report, in 2014 this generation drank 41% of their wine away from the home, as opposed to 35% of the Gen X group (Badenfort, 2017). Cans seem to fit with the individual serving, particularly in outdoor settings.

Bisphenols are another set of compounds added to plastics, in this case to help strengthen and harden them. Often, they are added to epoxy resins

FIGURE 7.4 'Milk carton' wine container
Glenn Cormier, Lisa Caron

and polycarbonates, which are in turn used as linings for the metal cans for wine. As Trela and Plank (2015) further note, their inclusion is also as an antioxidant in PVC production. Some of these are not acceptable for wine because the sulphites in wine can cause corrosion through the linings. However, recent improvements in the coatings are making offering wine in cans a more viable alternative (Reeves, 2010).

Laminated paperboard

One other type of newer packaging has found popularity in Latin America and Scandinavia, and other European countries. This wine is packaged in laminated paperboard (Reeves, 2010), packaging similar to milk containers.

Conclusion

Bag-in-box, plastic bottles, cans, and laminated paperboard containers are relatively new packaging options for wine vessels. They solve one of the big issues, the shipping weight of wine bottles, and to a lesser extent, breakage. However, with all of them employing plastic linings, they are designed for the ready-to-drink wine market.

Notes

1 US Patent number: 3977569
2 Australian Patent number: 2808261

References

Badenfort, K. (2017). What cans can do for wine. *Wine Industry Advisor*, [online] 16 February 2017.
Clark, O. (2004). *Australian Wine Companion: An Essential Guide for All Lovers of Australian Wine*. London: Time Warner/Websters.
Colman, T. (2009). Box wines that can be a hit. *Forbes*, [online] 16 July 2009.
Cravero, M. C. (2016). Alternatives to glass packaging. *Wines & Vines*, [online] 1 May 2016.
Fradique, S., Hogg, T., Perira, J. and Pocas, M. F. F. (2011). Performance of wine bag-in-box during storage: Loss of oxygen barrier. *Italian Journal of Food Science*, [online] 23, pp.11–16.
Lower, G. (2010). Thomas Angove, king of the cask, dead at 92. *The Australian*, [online] 31 March 2010.

Prestipino, D. (2015). 50 years of cask wine: the goon bag bangs on. *WAToday* (Australia), [online] 23 February 2015.

Reeves, M. J. (2010) Packaging and the shelf life of wine. In: Robertson, G. L., ed. *Food Packaging and Shelf Life: A Practical Guide*. Boca Raton, FL: CRC Press. pp. 232–252.

Shen, J. J. (2011). *Comparative Life Cycle Assessment of Polylactic Acid (PLA) and Polyethylene Terephthalate (PET)*. College of Natural Resources, University of California.

Specter, M. (2008). Big Foot. *The New Yorker*, [online] 25 February 2008, p. 44.

Standage, T. (2005). *A History of the World in Six Glasses*. New York: Walker and Co.

Steeman, A. (2015). The evolution of the bag-in-box. *Best in Packaging*, [online] 27 April 2015.

Tipples, R. (2010). Wine supply chain breaks: New Zealand wines from Cottesbrook, Canterbury. *International Journal of Wine Business Research*, 22(2), pp. 148–163.

Trela, B. and Plank, C. (2015). Plastic polymers in the wine industry. *Wine & Vines*, [online] 96(5), p. 70.

Websites

Routledge, G. (2016) 4 reasons to drink bag in box wine. The Food Rush, www.thefoodrush.com. 27 July 2016.

Angove Winery. (2018). www.angove.com.au.

AstraPouch North America. (2018). www.astrapouch-na.com.

Garcon Wines. (2017). Delivering Happiness Ltd. www.garconwines.com.

Funding Universe. (2017). Funding Universe – Liqui-box Corporation History. www.fundinguniverse.com.

Blog

Yeamans-Irwin, B. (2011). Alternatives to glass for wine packaging: Can plastic perform? *The Academic Wino*, www.academicwino.com.

8

WINE CONTAINER STOPPERS AND CLOSURES

Cork

Almost five hundred years ago, people were talking about corks. In his play, *As You Like It*, Shakespeare has Rosaline beg Celia to tell all about Orlando, "I prithee take the cork out of thy mouth so I may drink thy tidings" (Shakespeare, 1948).

One of the first recorded uses of a natural cork as a bottle stopper was in 1530 (Penzer, 1947). It was described as the seal on a bottle of wine which had been presented to an English king. Corks, however, most likely go much further back, having been used to seal amphorae, and possibly barrels, for hundreds, if not thousands, of years (Veseth, 2016). The evidence for this is difficult to pin down as the corks deteriorate, in much the same way that it is difficult to find the evidence of the first wooden barrels.

In 1750, a Spanish company was documented as the first to start producing commercial corks for wine bottles (Taber, 2007). This would have been well after the increased use of wine bottles had commenced within the European markets, so perhaps cork production for the early bottles was more a home industry, without official advertising or publicity. Portugal, with its extensive cork forests, soon took over as the primary commercial supplier. Now, while Portugal still maintains its position as the world's largest producer, smaller industries are ongoing in Spain and Italy, and to a lesser extent in Algeria, Morocco, France and Tunisia (Novacortica, 2017).

FIGURE 8.1 Clay stoppers for amphorae
Trustees of the British Museum

The cork comes from the bark of the cork oak (*Quercus suber*). The trees are well adapted to the Mediterranean climate of wet winters and dry summers. As with most oaks, they are a slow growing tree, typically taking up to 25 years for enough girth just to begin harvesting the bark. Another ten years are required before the cork bark can again regain the thickness to allow a subsequent cutting. With these extended time periods between harvests, generally only wealthy landowners can afford to grow them on large plantations, multi-hectare farms raising thousands of trees in orderly rows. However, some farmers are able grow them in modest, naturally cultivated groves of just a few hundred trees to supplement their income, while within Portugal's rural landscape, subsistence farmers continue to cultivate isolated plots with just a few trees.

I recently visited some cork forests in the Algarve of southern Portugal. There, the trees are found primarily in the hills rather than the flat valley floors. They are well spaced to minimize the competition for the scarce summer water. In one protected location, carob and olive trees were among the mix. Another site was high up (400 metres) in the hills, an area of mostly chaparral and brush. The small, detached groves held as few as two or three trees to perhaps ten. Despite the remoteness of these sites, someone had tended them, removing the grass and weeds from around their bases to maximize the water they could extract from the area and minimize the risk of a wild fire injuring the trees.

The methods of cork harvest have changed little throughout the centuries. Part of this has to do with the way the trees grow; the short main trunk is only a metre or two high before the large primary branches commence. Stripping the bark from these gnarly, diminutive divisions of the tree – the main trunk, the initial sections of the primary branches, and possibly gaining a few small pieces from further branches – necessitates hands-on labour.

Men, usually, wielding hand axes, chop horizontal and vertical breaks in the bark of mature trees, allowing sections to be peeled off. This work generally only takes place during the spring and summer months, as it is then when the warm weather expands the trees, enabling the bark to be peeled away relatively easily.

After harvesting, to reduce later shrinkage, the bark sections are dried, piled in its curved section just the way it was stripped off the tree. When needed for processing, these sections are placed into a hot water bath, using filtered, non-chlorinated water, to make them flexible enough to flatten for working (Novacortica, 2017).

The production of the cork then involves continual inspection, attempting to select the densest sections of the bark for the premium wine corks, while the remainder gets sorted into numerous subgrades for technical and alternative wine corks, and then for other products.

The high-quality sections are cut into strips from which the corks are punched out sideways through the thickness of the slice in order to stay with the grain of the cork, i.e. with the long dimension of the cork

FIGURE 8.2 Cork tree with bark cut away and number indicating the year it was last cut, in this case 2006

Henry H. Work

paralleling that of the tree. Building up that breadth – wider than the diameter of a cork – is why the trees need a decade between harvests. The punched-out cork cylinders are then again sorted for quality, branded, and in some cases, lubricants are applied to aid squeezing the cork *into* the bottle. The cases left over from the punching operations, as are all the other off-fall bits and pieces, are utilized for making composite corks, cork flooring, acoustical tiles, hand bags, wallets and shoe soles.

Cork taint has certainly been around, or at least since, chlorine or chlorine-type chemicals have come in contact with moulds in the cork or winemaking processes. It has only become a serious issue in the last 40 years as a number of disparate events came together. As in the gathering of a perfect storm, they became more than the sum of their parts.

George Taber, in his excellent book, *To Cork or Not to Cork; Tradition, Romance, Science, and the Battle for the Wine Bottle* (2007) provides a detailed account of the various mistakes and misfortunes which conspired to bring cork taint to the forefront. I offer here a summary.

The 1970s saw political and social upheaval in Portugal. After the 1974 revolution, socialist and communist factions started running the government; including taking over the management of the cork forests and the cork manufacturing. At the same time cork demand was rising due to more European *vin ordinaire* bottles being up-graded to cork-finished bottles, and new wineries, springing up around the world, were also requesting corks. Attempting to meet this growing demand, some of the nouveau cork plantation managers took shortcuts; planting oak trees in unsuitable areas and reintroducing chlorine as a quicker and cheaper method to clean the raw cork. As Taber has commented, this return to chlorine was "despite the warning from Switzerland's Hans Tanner [one of the first scientists to realize] that chlorine was the main cause of cork taint" (2007). To the consternation of those purchasing the corks, even into the 1980s these new managers seemed unaware of TCA (2,4,6-trichloroanisole); they were still pricing their corks based upon product appearance and rather than actual quality.

Taber maintains that "Cork-manufacturing is particularly susceptible to TCA. An Australian study published in 1987 found TCA in the bark of nearly half the cork oak trees in the forest" (2007). The cork producers used this as evidence to indicate that the resulting TCA was not their fault. Nonetheless, they failed to take immediate steps to remedy the TCA developing in their corks despite the mounting scientific evidence of the chlorine-mould connections. They clearly were part of the problem.

EXPLORATIONS 8.1
THE SCOURGE OF TCA 'CORK TAINT'

The 1980s were buoyant times for the French to sell wine. Wine critic Robert Parker was enthusiastic about several of the vintages, especially some from the Bordeaux top growth. Americans were buying like crazy, buoyed by a strong dollar. However, among themselves, the French vintners realized that something was amiss. The vintner's wives started to complain about the smells of 'cat pee' on their husband's clothing (Taber, 2007). A number of top wineries, including the champagne house of Roederer and Bordeaux's Chateau Latour, were having more than a few bottles returned. Rather than create a fuss, they willingly provided 'replacements' (Taber, 2007). This illusion that 'nothing was awry' lasted into the 1990s. As the grapevine gossip got more intense, however, almost everyone finally agreed that something had to be done.

During this period, as a budding academic, Pascal Chatonnet did his university thesis on the effect that oak had on wine quality. It won him several awards, and he quickly gained recognition as a specialist in the barrel-aging of fine wines. This allowed him to start working as a winery consultant. He continued his association with the faculty of the Oenology department of the University of Bordeaux doing food and wine research, and subsequently went on to obtain a doctorate.

The university's wine department had, at that period, received the equipment to run the technology for gas chromatography-mass spectrometry (GC-MS) analysis (Taber, 2007). Among other tests, this apparatus allowed for the detection of the chemicals causing 'cork taint'. As importantly, the machinery speeded up the testing time significantly; from weeks to days. Dr Chatonnet was able to utilize this equipment to start checking wines, including some coming from his own families' winery. His testing included samples not only from bottled wines, but those at various stages in the winemaking process as well. With some of the pre-bottled wine samples showing elevated levels of TCA, this was a serious wake up call to the extent of the problem.

The chemical compound of 'cork taint' is TCA (2,4,6-trichloroanisole). It was originally detected in natural corks. In the corks, TCA was caused by chlorinated water, used to clean the cork bark, mixing with the naturally occurring moulds in the corks to form the

TCA. But as researchers such as Dr Chatonnet continued to examine the sources they found many other places where TCA could and did occur.

Dr Chatonnet's family winery, like many others at the time, was upgrading. Part of the renovation included installing insulation in the walls and ceiling for improved temperature control. As he started investigating, Dr Chatonnet found that the new insulation contained chlorine compounds. These chemicals were released into the air, combining with the natural moulds in the winery. Whenever wine was exposed to these particles in the air, such as during filling or topping of the barrels, the taint commenced (Taber, 2007).

This was a revelation for the French. Not only were the corks causing the TCA in the wine, but within the wineries other sources of chlorine, which when combined with the air-borne mould, also caused TCA. Testing of the wines and checking at other wineries found further sources of chlorine. For instance, some wooden pallets upon which wine bottles were delivered and the cases of wine shipped out had been treated with chlorine-containing products. It was also found that paper used to make some cardboard cases had been bleached with chlorine. So even the cases of wine stored in the winery could potentially contaminate the yet to be bottled wine.

Dr Chatonnet realized that some serious investigation to identify the sources at each winery was needed. The University could provide long-term research, but it was not the best venue for the immediate testing of numerous wine samples. This 'rapid response' was what the wineries needed in order to determine the exact sources of their TCA contamination. Realizing an opportunity, he and his wife, also an oenologist, set up an oenology laboratory, Excell, in Merignac, just outside of Bordeaux. Investing heavily into the latest technology, they began to provide real-time testing services (Taber, 2007).

Finally, in the mid-1990s no one was dismissing the taint. Quietly, with Excell's help, wineries started cleaning up the sources causing the TCA taint. By 1998, French magazines *L'Express* and *Que Choisir* exposed the TCA problem, but by then the wineries had already been taking serious steps to eliminate most of the sources of chlorine in their wineries (Taber, 2007).

To continue with the upheaval in the Portuguese cork industry, improved testing equipment allowed scientists, such as Dr Chatonnet, to learn more about cork taint and where it was showing up. Their results were reaching both vintners and consumers, leading to a greater awareness of the problems. The cork companies were slow to respond to this emerging information. Stepping in to fill the void, the packaging companies and entrepreneurs, encouraged by a demand from the vintners, began offering alternatives: screw caps and the synthetic corks. The cork companies lagged behind with composite corks, but have recently come up with some innovations of their own, including a cork-lined screw cap.

To be fair, in the past 15 years, the natural cork companies have 'cleaned up their act'; they are now producing reliably taint free corks due to elimination of the chlorine chemicals from their production areas and supply chains (Veseth, 2016). The incidence of cork taint seems to be diminishing, as the results from the Wine Spectator's James Laube's tastings have documented (Laube, 2016), and a recent article stating that the 2016 cork exports broke all previous records at €937.5 million, beating 2015 by 4% (Anonymous, 2017).

During the past 50 years, with these revelations about TCA, there has been a significant shift away from the traditional corks used for wine bottles towards the use of screw caps, composite cork and cork alternative stoppers. Interestingly, to a large degree, these new closures have been seen more as a lifeline for vintners to overcome the possibility of their wines exhibiting 'cork taint', than new technology being forced down their throat. The dust from this shift is starting to settle, but it is still a hot button issue and has sent ripples through the wineries to make changes in areas where no one expected.

EXPLORATIONS 8.2
TCA ON THE OTHER SIDES OF THE WORLD

My wife, Karen, started our Work Vineyard wine brand just as concern about 'cork taint' was becoming finally understood. At that time, there were still somewhere between 5–8% of wine bottles experiencing 'cork taint'. While the percentages were bad enough themselves, it was the randomness – there was no easy way of knowing which bottles would be contaminated – which was most perplexing and frustrating to the winemakers, an annoyance to sommeliers, and a crap shoot for customers, especially those purchasing the costly bottles of wine. Naturally, she did not want to present bottles of her Sauvignon Blanc wine with flavours of 'wet horse blanket' to her customers. Despite purchasing the best corks in the market, she came to the realization that alternatives to the corks needed to be investigated.

With the help of our winemaking consultant, she trialled some wine with several brands of synthetic corks and screwcaps. After a year in the bottle with those various closures, they found that the cork alternatives decreased the sulphur which was added to the wine to help preserve it. The concern was that this would leave the wine vulnerable to degradation. When the wine that had been sealed with screw caps was tested no adverse changes could be detected. Subsequently, she started using screwcap closures on the bottles.

Certainly, another concern in this equation was whether our retail and online customers, and the sommeliers who served the restaurant patrons who ordered Work Vineyard wine, would accept the screwcaps on our bottles. This wine was retailing for US$25, and some restaurants were charging up to US$65 per bottle. Fortunately, by the early 2000s the general understanding of the reasons for cork taint and the acceptance of alternative closures was positive.

Unfortunately, ten years on, some wineries still have not got the message. In 2012, Karen and I were on a tour of the Hunter Valley wineries. The Hunter Valley, located about 150 kilometres north of Sydney, is renowned for its Chardonnay and Semillon as well as Shiraz and Cabernet Sauvignon. On that tour, extensive tastings at several wineries provided an excellent cross-section of the quality of the mix this region could produce.

At our second winery, we were offered their selection of white varieties. While not outstanding, they had no flaws. Then we were presented with their assortment of red wines. Several had a distinctive aroma of a smelly blanket. All the wines were using screw caps; corks could not be the culprit. Not expecting such a dramatic example of TCA, I did not relate my observation to our winery host, knowing that we were to have a tour of the winery after the tasting. It was my hope that some obvious cause would be revealed, and also that I might speak to him in private.

During the winery tour, we found that all the white wines were made solely in the wineries' stainless-steel tanks. There were no bottles of chlorine apparent, nor smell of its residue in the tanks or from the floors.

This did not seem to be the venue whence the TCA originated. The reds, on the other hand, were aged in barrels in a separate cellar room which also served for case storage. I suspected that the problem was here; in the damp cellar, the chlorine from the cases was getting into the air and mixing with the air-borne moulds creating the TCA in the wine when the barrels were opened for filling or topping.

We also learned that the owner/winemaker was generally off-site. From comments the guide made, I also sensed that the owner had an ego. His occasional visits apparently involved issuing instructions, and not wanting to hear feedback.

As our tour group was leaving, I pulled the guide aside and told him of my suspicion of the TCA in the red wines and their probable cause. He thanked me and told me he would pass on the information, but his response came with a sigh which I read to say there would not be any immediate changes.

Finally, corks are still used to stopper wine bottles because they have the ability to allow wines to 'age', that is to allow minute amounts of oxygen into the wine at the rate of about one milligram per year. At that rate most ageable wines should be oxidized within 20 years, due to that oxygen reducing the sulphites added to protect the wine. Recently, researchers at UC Davis theorized that the rate of oxygen flow through the cork decreases over time which would be why wines can last many years in the bottle (Grey, 2014). They have started a 100-year study to examine this.

Screwcaps – origins and use

Australia and New Zealand

In the 1990s, vintners in the 'land down under' and those from the islands of the 'long white cloud' were also seeing the impact of cork taint on their wines and customers. They felt, however, that they were getting a raw deal when it came to purchasing corks. Being small cork consumers, relative to their European and American counterparts, they did not have as much clout or recourse if they received inferior products. Therefore, after experiences with cork taint, and feeling that the cork suppliers were not taking their concerns seriously, with their 'can do spirit', they took matters into their own hands; instigating various screwcap initiatives.

Screwcaps, however, are not new. In fact, as New Zealand wine writer Sue Courtney notes, one of the earliest version was patented in the 1889 in the UK (2004). In 1933, researchers at Dow Chemical discovered poly-vinylidene chloride, the main material in the liner-seal that is in contact with wine, subsequently branded as 'Saran' and 'Saranex' (Saran sandwiched between layers of polyethylene or polyethylene-vinyl acetate). When a tin/saran liner is used, it is the tin layer that creates a barrier to oxygen ingress (Work, 2005). By the 1960s, threaded aluminium ROTE (Roll-on, tamper-evident) and ROPP (Roll-on, pilfer-proof) closures were intro-duced. Incorporating the cap and the liner, an early design specifically adapted to wine bottles was developed by French company La Bouchage Mécanique in the 1950s. It was branded the Stelvin screwcap (Courtney, 2004). From the 1970s through 1990s, various wineries introduced wines sealed with screwcaps, only to be rebuffed by the consumers as being 'untraditional'.

In practice, however, actually shifting to a different closure was more difficult than just getting consumer approval for the screwcap. A bottle specifically designed to accept the cap was required, as was special bottling equipment to install the caps. To absorb the initial costs, wineries either had

FIGURE 8.3 Screw cap and bottle
Glenn Cormier

to be very large, or a group of smaller wineries needed to band together. That the wineries in Australia and New Zealand were in the latter category, makes the story of their shift to screw caps all that much more impressive.

By the beginning of this century, once cork taint was clearly identified and the alternatives started to make positive reputations, winemakers in Australia's Clare Valley and a large group of regionally diverse New Zealand wineries, took the challenge; they made the drastic shift to screwcaps (Goode, 2004). This entailed more than just obtaining the bottles, caps and the machinery to install them. It was a radical departure into how consumers open their bottles. If the wait staff in restaurants could not make a big show of using a cork screw and smelling the cork, at least they could present the wine and deftly twist off the cap.

Besides a major swing in consumer acceptance, what has also changed for screwcaps is the 'wadding' or interior sealing layers. They are now available ranging from those that completely seal out all oxygen to those that allow some minute amounts in over time. Theoretically, this permits winemakers to tailor their caps to the expected shelf life of their wines.

A major concern for winemakers was, do the screwcaps present any detrimental characteristics to the wine? As my wife Karen and her consultant discovered, and several studies have reasonably confirmed, they do not; at least in the time frame that most wines are in the bottle. British wine writer, Jamie Goode, sums up the findings from the Australia Wine Research Institute (AWRI) study:

> First, screwcaps provide a seal that is better than that of cork. Second, that cork shows a wide variation in oxygen transfer characteristics. Third, that the synthetic corks included in the trial have the highest gas permeability and are only suitable for wines destined for early drinking (for the sake of fairness, I should add that newer, better synthetics are now available).
>
> *(2004)*

Further research in subsequent years has added immensely to our understanding of what exactly occurs with wine in the bottle, both with corks and the newer closures.

Scientists at AWRI commented in summary of the major ongoing study, "It must be clearly re-stated that screwcaps, or any other closure for that matter, do not cause reductive character [off flavours] in bottled wine, and also that the vast majority of wines sealed with screwcaps do not exhibit reductive characters [sulphury notes]" (Godden et al., 2005). However, as noted previously in the section on plastic wine bottles, certain compounds in the plastic seals of the screwcaps may react negatively with the wine. More long-term research is needed on the total impact of plastic packaging: plastic bottles, the plastics used in the liners in bag-in-box and aluminium cans, and the liners for screw caps.

Screw caps have been in general use for 15 years

Over the past 15 years, the world has seen a definite rise in the use of screw caps as wine bottle closures. Exactly how much is still a bit of a guess. In 2015 the wine trade magazine *Wines and Vines* conducted a survey of US wineries. Of the wineries responding, the results indicated that the use of corks was down approximately 20% from several years ago, while the use of screw caps has risen 20%. The use of synthetic corks had also risen, by about 10%.

Wine Spectator's Senior Editor James Laube, based in California's Napa Valley, noted the results of the tastings he and his staff conducted through-out 2015 (Laube, 2016). Of over 6,800 wine bottles, 23.9% were using screw-caps, up from 23.1% in 2014, and 22.4% in 2013. The majority, 72.1%, still had cork seals, while the balance were sealed with composite or synthetic corks. It should also be noted that typically the wines he is tasting tend towards the upper price ranges, and are from America's west coast wineries, Australia and New Zealand. Many of these wines are intended to be aged, thus have continued to utilize corks.

He also noted that the incidence of TCA was down 2.5% in the wines tasted, from highs of 7.5% to 9.5% in the 2005 to 2007 years. The cork companies are making improvements (Laube, 2016).

The majority of wines I have encountered while traveling through France, Spain, Portugal and Italy during the past several years are still using natural or composite cork stoppers, with only an occasional screw capped bottle; not anywhere near the 20 plus percentage mark for the alternatives noted for the US, Australian or New Zealand wines.

As with many other products where a range of types or styles is available, the winemakers are choosing what they think will be best for their product and its functions. Generally speaking, natural corks are being used for wines which are intended to age, with screw caps, composite and synthetic corks for wines that are expected to be drunk within a year or two.

Composite and synthetic corks

In response to the cork taint upheaval, in addition to the screwcaps, closure companies began offering various synthetic corks. The appeal was that they look and act like corks, but were chemically concocted and theoretically free of TCA.

An early concern with the synthetic corks was that of 'flavour scalping'. This is the absorption of certain 'aroma and flavour compounds' which can diminish the wine's flavours (Robinson, 2015). The initial iterations of the synthetic corks did some absorption. Additionally, the early synthetic closures allowed excessive oxygen ingress after about 18 months. However, in the past several years, the closure companies manufacturing those corks have done much to mitigate any negative impacts on the wine. Additionally, some companies now offer cork alternatives engineered to regulate the ingress of oxygen during a certain period of time, allowing winemakers the ability to specify the Oxygen Transmission Rate (OTR) when they order their corks (Robinson, 2015).

These look-alike corks are now available in many formats. They range from composites of natural cork (just bits of cork glued together to a similar style with a cork disc glued to one or both ends) to co-extruded synthetics to glass and plastic stoppers. Wineries are often utilizing more than one style, each adapted to a particular wine's potential shelf life, price point and target market (Firstenfeld, 2016).

Capsules

Regardless of the type of cork or cork alternative closure, almost all wine bottles cover the closures with a capsule. (The screw cap is its own capsule

FIGURE 8.4 A variety of cork alternatives
Glenn Cormier

cover.) Initially, made of lead or tin/lead because it was malleable, the capsules were used to hide the mould which occasionally developed when a tiny amount of seepage occurred in the cork as the bottles were laid on their sides. Gradually, the capsule material has shifted to aluminium and plastics as the dangerous health effects of lead became more understood.

Capsules have become part of the entire wine labelling package. They are colour coordinated with the paper label and bottle hue, and sometimes embellished with winery logo stamps on the top and/or logos or other details, such as the vintage. Some are perforated at the top to allow oxygen ingress for wines which are intended to be aged.

Shift to the new closures

While the rest of the world has moved more and more to the use of the screw caps and synthetic corks, France still remains somewhat hesitant. Jonathan Hesford, owner of Roussillon winery Domaine Treloar suggests that it is largely tradition, coupled with the perception among some consumers that screwcaps or the synthetic corks are associated with inexpensive wines (Hesford, 2017). Nonetheless, some French wineries are slowly starting to try screwcaps and other cork alternatives, while still demanding corks for their high-end, long aging wines; for which they have stepped up the standards from the cork suppliers by demanding certification for TCA-free corks.

Seals for other wine vessels

Large tanks and vats – wood or ceramic

The openings for the larger containers – be they wood, ceramic, cement, or now stainless steel – are normally large enough for someone to squeeze through in order to clean the inside. Thus, the seals are generally termed *doors* or *gates*, and the actual opening, or entrance, the *man-way*.

Historically, the seal on the dolia, was one or two pieces of wood, or a flat rock, which provided the base for a covering of clay. The wood or rock would often have a gasket of beeswax or clay (Barisashvili, 2011). This semi-permanent system of sealing the dolia would not work so well if the wine needed to be topped off or otherwise periodically checked.

Oak wooden tanks, vats and casks utilize a large wooden gate to plug their man-way. It is generally made of a moderately soft wood, such as fir.

The edges are tapered, narrowing towards the outside. The door is fitted from the inside out, so that the wine pushes against it to help the seal. A screw-type device is attached to a yoke to help pull the door tight from the outside. These too use a gasket of reed, beeswax, paraffin or cloth. Repeatedly used, they deform and must be periodically replaced.

The more modern versions of both dolia and wooden tanks are now incorporating doors and frames made of stainless steel with rubber gaskets for more reliable sealing and ease of opening.

Barrel bungs and the shift to silicone

Most wine barrels have but one small hole (about 50 mm diameter) which is used to both fill and empty the liquid. The term for this wine access point is the *bunghole*, and is sealed by a wooden, cork, or more likely now silicone *bung*. As a term, bunghole, has over the past 300 years, taken on other meanings. Some have found it a convenient term for anus, or as the MTV cartoon characters Bevis and Butt-head used it, a dolt or ass.

The bunghole is normally drilled in the widest stave at the bilge, usually reamed and cauterized to provide a smooth surface for better sealing.

The French, and Bordeaux vintners in particular, sometimes utilize a barrel with two additional holes in one end of the barrel. These are termed *esquive*. The bungs for these holes are usually wooden, with a small piece of muslin cloth to act as a gasket. If the barrel is resting on the bilge, with the bilge bunghole on the high side, one esquive is at the mid-point of the head and the other about a quarter of the way up. They are both used for racking, or emptying the barrel, in order to oxygenate heady wines.

After several months of settling, the highest esquive is opened first, allowing the clearest wine to pour out. This wine is caught in a large funnel-like trough. The swirling and frothing allows mixing with the air. This wine is sent to a clear barrel for further aging. When the wine drops to the second esquive, it is similarly opened and the wine allowed to pour into the trough. As this wine from the lower section of the barrel is cloudy with sediment, it will be added to similar wine from other barrels for further clarification. Wines from below this esquive are emptied by turning the barrel upside down over another trough. This wine usually has much sediment, the lees, which requires extended clarification, and is sometimes used as a second-tier wine.

For wines fermenting in barrels, the standard wooden or silicone bung cannot be used due to their tight seal. It would not allow the developing

FIGURE 8.5 Silicone bungs in use in a winery
Some are equipped with plastic fermentation locks.
Glenn Cormier

gases to escape. I have repaired more than a few barrels with the one head
blown out due the barrel being bunged prematurely, or when a bit of residual
fermentation is restarted by the cellar warming rapidly if the air-conditioning
malfunctions or a surprise late winter heat-wave sets in. The expanding wine
pushes on the largest surface area, which is the head not the bung.

Seals used during fermentation range from the very simple – a small sack
of sand placed over the bung hole – to the exquisite – a glass bung. In a

FIGURE 8.6 A glass fermentation bung
Glenn Cormier

candle lit barrel chai, these glass bungs provide a beautiful ambiance. Another fermentation lock format is a plastic 's' shaped tube filled with water which allows the gases out and keeps the air, and anything with it, from entering.

Further, the aging of wine in barrels has a different requirement than for those placed in the amphorae or dolia. Barrels need to be accessed for periodic topping as the water in the wine evaporates through the wood. A stopper which seals well but also can be conveniently removed is necessary. Initially this was served by wooden bungs. These 3- to 15-centimetre long, tapered pieces of wood were often pounded in with a hammer or rubber mallet to ensure a secure fit. Nonetheless, they have a few problems. If they were made of soft woods, such as pine, spruce, larch or redwood, they needed to be sealed with wax or other sealants so as to not wick or weep wine, nor impart any flavours into the wines from their wood resins. Once they were hammered in a few times they began to deform. Thereafter, if not placed in exactly the same way, they could leak – air into the barrel, or wine out. Some wineries use more temporary bungs, a short piece of soft wood with a square of clean, muslin or cotton cloth underneath it to help seal around the edges, but which also aids in the bung's removal.

Bungs made of oak or other hardwoods usually do not need to be sealed. However, they also deform, as well as deforming the bung stave itself, causing cracks at the bung hole which can allow air to enter the barrel. Again, I have repaired many broken bung staves due to overzealous pounding in of an oak bung.

In the 1980s, as food grade silicone became available, wineries began requesting, and closure companies began offering, bungs made of this malleable material. They were a god-send to the winemakers, sealing well, not deforming the bung stave or imparting any flavour into the wine, and they were cleanable. Fewer and fewer wineries are now using wooden bungs. Some of these silicone bungs have been adapted for fermentation.

Conclusion

The past 20 years have seen some significant changes in stoppers for wine bottles and barrels. The understanding of 'cork taint' led to the development of the screw cap and cork alternatives. Large tanks and vats are shifting to gates of stainless steel, while silicon bungs are being used more and more for wine barrels.

References

Anonymous. (2017). Cork exports break records. *The Portugal News*, [online] 4 March 2017.

Barisashvili, G. (2011). *Making Wine in Qvevri: A Unique Georgian Tradition*. Tbilisi, Georgia: Biological Farming Association "Elkana".

Firstenfeld, J. (2016). Multiple-choice: small to mid-size wineries don't limit themselves to just one style of capsule or closure. *Wine & Vines*, [online] August 2016.

Godden, P., Lattey, K., Francis, L., Gishen, M., Cowey, G., Holdstock, M., Robinson, E., Waters, E., Skouroumounis, G., Sefton, M., Capone, D., Kwiatkowski, M., Field, J., Coulter, A., D'Costa, N. and Bramley, B. (2005). Towards offering wine to the consumer in optimal condition – the wine, the closures, and other packing variables. *Infowine, Internet Journal of Viticulture and Enology*, [online] 2005, pp. 1–9.

Grey, T. (2014). Esdraela: The ceramic record from a settlement of Hellenistic and Roman times to Late Antiquity in Palestine. *Palestine Exploration Quarterly*, [online] 146(2), pp. 105–134.

Hesford, J. (2017). Why so few screwcaps in France? *Connexion France*, [online] 1 August 2016.

Laube, J. (2016). 2015 closure trends from California: twist-offs gain while cork taint subsides. *The Wine Spectator*, [online] 3 February 2016.

Penzer, N. M. (1947). *The Book of the Wine-Label*. London: Home & Van Thal.

Robinson, J. ed. (2015). *The Oxford Companion to Wine*. Oxford: Oxford University Press.

Shakespeare, W. (1948) *The Works of Shakespeare; As You Like It*. Quiller-Couch, A. and Wilson, J. D., eds. Cambridge: Cambridge University Press.

Taber, G. (2007). *To Cork or Not to Cork; Tradition, Romance, Science, and the Battle for the Wine Bottle*. New York: Scribner.

Veseth, M. (2016). Cork vs screwcap. *The Wine Economist*, [online] 14 July 2016.

Work, H. H. (2005). Bottling under screwcaps: quality control issues for premium wines. *Practical Winery & Vineyard Journal*, [online] July/August 2005.

Websites

Novacortica. (2017). Novacortiça. [online] www.novacortica.pt

Blogs

Courtney, S. (2004, December). The history and revival of screwcaps. *Wine of the Week*, www.wineoftheweek.com

Goode, J. (2004.) New Zealand screwcap initiative. *Wineanorak*. www.wineanorak.com

9

LABELS FOR WINE CONTAINERS

Historical wine container labelling

Labelling amphorae in ancient Egypt

In the late 1800s, as German archaeologists began uncovering some of the early Egyptian graves, they happened upon several rooms in the tomb of King Scorpion I, in Abydos. He ruled the First Dynasty in around 3150 BCE.

Packed within the King's chambers, were several hundred amphorae, which, in total, would have contained some 4,500 litres. Among them, a unique 'tiger-striped' jar, with a height of 40.8 cm, typical of the Levant, suggested that this was their origin (McGovern, 2009). Noted previously was the vast trading network in existence even in those early days, so this would not be unexpected. The jars were closed with clay and leather; with inscriptions and cylinder-seal designs on the outsides of the pots further pointing to the eastern Mediterraneans as the producers of the amphorae and most probably the wine.

Additionally, as well as marking the wine containers, pieces of marked bone and ivory were attached to the jars and boxes of food and other items the King *required* for the afterlife. The figures of plants and animals (jackals, scorpions, birds and bulls), some of the earliest hieroglyphic writings, are believed to signify the Egyptian origins where the food and other goods were produced (McGovern, 2009).

As noted, wine was transported to Egypt from other countries until around 3000 to 2700 BCE. The local demand for wine was increasing. In response, the Egyptian rulers, certainly with a thought of wanting more control in order to obtain taxes, had grapevines transplanted to grow in the raised lands along the Nile and around its Delta (McGovern, 2009)

Over time, the writing on the pots and amphorae, as well as systems for classifying and categorizing the wines, became more sophisticated (Lukacs, 2012). During the era of the pharaohs in the New Kingdom (1550 to 1070 BCE), they were denoting not only the vintage year, but the winemaker's name and a description of the quality. Lukacs relates that, "The famous tomb of Tutankhamen in the Valley of the Kings held twenty-six such [wine] jars, each inscribed in detail. One reads, 'Year Four. Wine of very good quality of the House-of-Aton of the Western River. Chief vintner Khay.' Another says, 'Sweet wine of the House-of-Aton – Life, Prosperity, Health! – of the Western River. Chief vintner Aperershop'" (2012).

As amphorae were being made, many of the amphorae potters stamped on the jars either their name, the name of the potential contents' producer (which could be one in the same as there is some evidence that large wineries and olive oil producing facilities also had their own ceramic factories and kilns), or the initial potential contents. For instance, in a first century BCE ship wreck off the Côte d'Azure, some of the wine amphorae were stamped with the name of *Lassius*, who apparently produced wine in Pompeii, Italy (Beard, 2008). Across the Mediterranean, in Carthage, amphorae have been discovered with the stamp of *L. Eumachius*, who was also from Pompeii. Unfortunately, it is not clear as to whether he was the potter for the jars or the producer of the wine. But his name has also been found on other amphorae as far afield as France and Spain, including one of his stamped amphorae being found in Stanmore, Middlesex, England (Beard, 2008).

Writing on Roman amphorae

As Dressel and subsequent archaeologists have unearthed millions of whole and partial amphorae, they have been aided in their understanding of what they possibly contained, where they originated and even occasionally the actual name of the ancient potter, by the stamped figures, symbols, characters and script on the outsides of those containers.

Akin to the finds of the amphorae in the wells and pits in the French town of Châteaumeillant (Chapter 1), amphorae and other pottery and kitchen utensils have also been discovered in ancient cisterns. Throughout history, it seems that if someone else had done the work of digging a hole in the ground – be it a well, pit, quarry, ditch or cistern – the rest of society was happy to fill it with their detritus.

Off the eastern coast of Spain, on the Mediterranean island of Ibiza, archaeologist Elise Marlière and her colleagues found an ancient cistern which was the repository for a number of amphorae from several Mediterranean regions, as well as other ceramic artefacts. The remains of various pieces, uncovered as her team dug down through the rubble, date mostly from the middle Roman era – roughly 100 BCE to 200 CE. Buried among the bits and pieces of the amphorae, were also a variety of jars, pitchers and tableware. From these accumulated finds, the researchers surmise that the cistern had been located near a tavern or kitchen, or at least a place where food and wine had been prepared and served (Marlière et al., 2016).

Of the hundreds of artefacts found and examined, there was special interest in the remains of three of the amphorae. For upon these had been written their contents, probably using an iron stylus, sometime *after* the amphorae were fired in the kiln. The researchers believe that given the location of the cistern – near or under a kitchen – and the fact that two of the amphorae were made locally and one had been shipped from Tarragona, just south of Barcelona on the Spanish coast, that the kitchen owner or one of his or her workers, wrote on these amphorae to note their contents (Marlière et al., 2016). Perhaps all these amphorae had originally been in a storeroom of the kitchen.

Upon one of the locally made amphorae was inscribed the Latin word, RVBRV, a reference to *vinum rubru(m),* for 'red wine'. It is believed that during that period Ibiza was an expanding community; growing the grapes for, and making and exporting both red and white wines. The notation of the wine's colour makes sense if a number of similar appearing amphorae containing different varietals were being stored in the same locale.

Upon another amphora was an indication that the liquid was some sort of a concoction of wine mixed with spices and perhaps honey; as we have seen, this was not an uncommon way to adulterate wine in the days when grape growing and the subsequent winemaking was still as much a miss, as a hit, type operation.

The third amphora, the one from Tarragona, indicated a family name, *SERVILA*. Most likely, this was the name of those who made the wine, or possibly from whose vineyard the grapes had been obtained (Marlière et al., 2016).

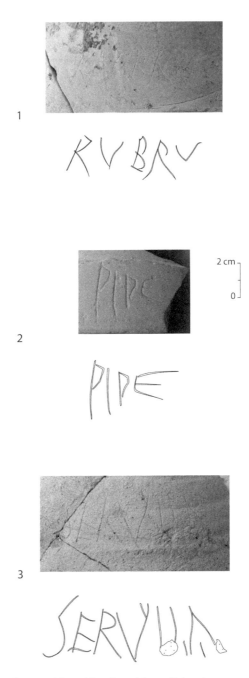

FIGURE 9.1 Amphorae with writing found in an Ibiza cistern
Elise Marlière, Josep Torres Costa, 2016

These finds all point to the fact that wine labelling is certainly not new. What is perhaps surprising is that the details which we now see on labels – alcohol, container amount, varietal, etc. – took so long to become required data.

Barrel labelling

Labelling, in some form or another, has always been evident on barrels. The initial signs were the cooper's name or mark, inscribed in or branded on the wood. Later, as with the amphorae, some marking as to what was in the barrel was inscribed. Towards the eighteenth century we start seeing stencils indicating the wine or other liquid, and occasionally the producer or where it was produced.

Other types of writing or branding, which could stand up to the weather when the barrels were left outside, must have been used as well, although these are not well documented. Like so many every day tools and activities, they were so common and/or intuitive that they failed to get the attention of the commentators of the day.

The individual staves of wine barrels and tanks were also labelled, or more specifically, numbered. Sometimes, the barrels were stored empty for some period prior to reuse. In order to conserve space, they were to be *broken down* or *knocked down*, with the 30 or so staves nested neatly together and the heads marked indicating to which end they should be fitted. In order to reassemble them precisely – that is so that the staves fit together exactly as they were originally built – they were sequentially numbered. Any slight extrusion on one stave fitted into the indentations on the stave next to it, thus minimizing any potential leakage when reassembling.

When I entered the cooperage business in the 1970s, the barrels were being shipped from France to California knocked down, with the staves, heads and hoops all numbered accordingly. By this method, the maximum number of barrels, weight-wise, were able to be shipped in a small, 20-foot container. In those days, the fee for shipping a container was charged according to its size. These numbering and knocking down processes were done in order to minimize the freight costs. One of our tasks as the recipient coopers of these shipments was to assemble all the pieces correctly.

Also, during this period, the barrels were branded or stencilled with the cooper's logo. Over the subsequent 20 years, notations about the wood source, toast levels and the date the barrel was fabricated have also been added, either as brands or stencils. Occasionally, for large orders, the wineries logo would be branded into the barrel head.

In the 1990s, the advent of the computer-controlled laser brander became a marketing advantage for the cooperages. It simplified imprinting the increasing amount of information and data they wanted to place on the head, or for some companies on both heads, as well as allowing the inscription of elaborate logos for wineries, which appealed to the egos of their owners. Like the use of oak in wine, it went overboard. It is now more common to see just the basic information, allowing the beautiful oak grain patterns to showcase the barrel.

Paper labels for bottles

Earliest formats

As we have seen, any time several similar containers, be they amphorae, barrels or glass, were clumped together, especially when the container was opaque and sealed, some indication of the contents was required.

In fourteenth and fifteenth century Europe, personalized jugs – those made of Turkish pottery, Chinese porcelain, or tin-enamelled pottery from Italy, or glass decanters – became popular. To identify the contents, rings or small identification plaques of bone, ivory, metals or wood, were hung around the container's neck with cords or small chains (Penzer, 1947). By the seventeenth century, parchment neck labels, stuck on with a gum, were being utilized.

To provide a label for those early bottles, and perhaps the cut–glass decanters, label designs could be etched in stone, inked and then produced on paper. By 1798, lithography had been invented. This allowed wine labels to be printed in mass quantities, encouraging vintners to advertise their wine via the label (Novin, 2012). Robinson notes that it was not until the 1860s that strong glues allowed the common use of these paper labels (2015).

One of the oldest surviving paper-type labels is from the 1775 vintage of a German winery near the Rüdesheimer mountain: a simple tag denoting the date, an appellation (that the area is in the land of the Duke Herzog) and name of the winery company (Novin, 2012; Muthmann, 2017). It included no bar codes, clichéd or flowery language (except some flowery script), alcohol level, volume or varietal of wine (one was expected to know that this was a Riesling).

In America, the oldest winery was Brotherhood, established in upstate New York in 1839. This early label, noted below, is similar to the one from Germany; simple and to the point for a knowledgeable clientele, or at least with little apparent attempt at marketing the wine.

FIGURE 9.2 1874 label from New York's Brotherhood Winery
Brotherhood Winery

The growing amount of information on the labels

Labelling regulations have been enacted only after labels began appearing. The rules came about as a government response from irate consumers about what they did or did not receive when they purchased their wine. Historically, the dispute was typically about the size of the container; an amphora or barrel that was smaller than specified or glass bottles with too much capacity variation. More recently, the regulations resulted from fraudulent statements on the labels: stating that such-and-such wine was in the bottle when it was not; alluding to grapes originating in a famous area when they were actually grown elsewhere; hedging the alcohol levels – too high or too low – to counter taxes which might reduce sales; or stating that more wine was in the bottle than there truly was. Additionally, warnings about the side-effects of alcohol or the additives to wine, such as sulphites, have been deemed important enough to require prominent inclusion on the labels.

The French initiated regulations towards wine quality in 1935 and by extension, what could be noted on the bottle. Germany did not get serious with labelling until 1971. America lagged, and did not commence defining viticultural areas until 1980, surprisingly with Augusta, Missouri being the first designation, and then slowly enacted regulations as to what could or could not be denoted on the labels.

Now a myriad of information is required. British wine writer Janice Robinson relates some of the information required in various countries: varietal; country of origin and geographical reference; vintage year; name and address of importer, producer, or bottler; volume of wine; alcoholic strength; (percentage of alcohol by volume); lot marking; fining materials; health warnings; bottling data; environmental labelling – organic, biodynamic, sustainable; sweetness; fizziness; and acidity (2015).

In the United States, the information basis was raised to a new level in 1988 by the adoption of the Surgeon General's health warning statement. First proposed in the late 1970s, it only finally got traction in the 1980s and by 1988 congress passed The Alcoholic Beverage Labeling Act which went into effect for all beverages with 0.5 per cent alcohol or more in 1990 (Golden, 1999). The 41 words are in two phrases; warning that drinking alcohol can place pregnant women at risk of birth defects and the potential impairment to operators when driving vehicles or using equipment. If nothing else, the words certainly takes up space on what is becoming an overcrowded label. Many wineries resorted to adding a back label to provide the additional space to such supplementary information as bar codes, export or import data, to say nothing of the information about the actual wine – winemaking processes, nuances, flavours, suggested paring, etc. – all of which further fill up the limited label space.

The European countries have also subsequently issued requirements for the posting of health warnings, although varying by country, for their wine labels. For example, France felt alcoholic beverages were most damaging to pregnant women and chose to require a warning about the damage to the foetus during pregnancy. This could be in the form or a pictogram or a phrase to the effect: "Consumption of alcoholic beverages during pregnancy, even in small amounts, may have serious consequences on child's health" (Farke and Veillard, 2012). Other countries followed suit with various warnings and suggested drinking limits.

New trends in label information

To squeeze in the information about the actual wine, some wineries are resorting to placing a QR code [Quick Response Code], the square matrix barcode, on their back labels. Smartphones with an app are able to read this diagram to bring up information about the wine and the winemaking processes. It is the modern-day equivalent of a figure stamped or inscribed on a Roman amphora to enable the dock and warehouse workers to move it to its correct destination.

Technology is also used to help avert future wine fraud. Wineries can now embed microchips, equipped with code and sensors, in their labels which document the wine's travels through the entire supply chain – winery, warehouse, transportation, and final distribution – in order to ensure that the wine's provenance can be tracked (Fitzgerald, 2016). Furthering this, researchers at the Australian Wine Research Institute have an on-going project to identify exactly were the grapes for a particular wine were grown. By analysing the minerals and elements that have formed the grapes from the ground, water and air of where they are raised, a unique signature is generated which can then be utilized if the domain of a wine is in question (Sedghi, 2018).

Not all the new innovations concern paper labels. Certainly, embossing bottles is not new. Now, however, bottle makers and packaging companies are taking labelling to new heights, or at least new textural feelings. One bottle company has added a rose pattern to the bottom punt which can be seen when white wines are in the bottle (McCrone, 2017). Others are adding veneers of velvet, wood, leather or resins, or even pewter medallions to the outsides of the bottle. The whole intent is to 'engage' the customer, encourage an emotional experience, to have them purchase the wine (McCrone, 2017).

Today's labels

With thousands of bottles on the shelves, from the vintners' and their marketers' perspective, the primary focus of labelling and wine bottle design has been to catch the consumer's eye; and more and more consumers are women (Franson, 2006). The range of designs of the labels goes from minimalist to flowery, black and white to garish colour, etched, and even embossed glass symbols. The colourful caps and foils add an element of style, often embellished with gold thread, or even the use of a burlap cloth sack for one Spanish winery.

EXPLORATIONS 9.1
THE RHONE RANGER RIDES AGAIN

One of the first winemakers to break out of the staid, 'facts, just the facts, ma'am', information-only type paper labels was Randall Grahm, owner/ winemaker of Bonny Doon, a Santa Cruz, CA winery. His formative years, sweeping floors in a Los Angeles wine shop, had allowed him to taste numerous excellent French wines. He became obsessed with the Pinot Noirs (Bonny Doon Vineyard, 2017). Upon establishment of his winery, but after difficulty growing the Pinot Noir cultivars in the cool, wet coastal hills, he gravitated toward the Rhône varietals such as Syrah, Marsanne, Roussanne and Viognier. He became a tireless promoter of those varieties, in a time well before most modern California winemakers had started looking for alternatives to the basic Cabernet Sauvignon and Chardonnay.

He is a larger-than-life figure. Commenting upon Randall Grahm's nature and incredible brilliance and humour in his labels, Andrew Jones writes that "Grahm, a major extrovert in a state full of extroverts, has set the US wine stores alive with laughter as the uninitiated read his labels for the first time" (1994).

When it came to making and promoting his wines, he was totally an out-of-the-box thinker and innovator. In the 1980s, I was privileged to observe this first-hand while engaged as a cooper, erecting some wooden tanks in his winery. At the end of the day, I and my tank-building colleagues were invited to join him and his winemaking staff for dinner at a local restaurant. There were ten of us. His extraordinary imagination was shown when, instead of each of us placing our own orders, he ordered ten different dishes for the table. As the restaurant was BYOB, he brought at least a case.

When the wait staff served the dishes, we each tried a fork full from the plate set in front of us. We then passed it on to the person on our left, receiving one from the person on our right. On and on this went until all the food was consumed. My memory gets a bit fuzzy here, but I think we stayed until all the wine was gone as well. Truly, a memorable evening.

Grahm's creations for the Bonny Doon labels included word plays – *Il Fiasco Ca'del Solo* (a play on 'the house of the solitary man' in reference to an outlying vineyard, and perhaps initiated at the time when Grahm was a bachelor) (Perry, 1990); puns on local or French lore – *Clos de Gilroy* (a nearby town not particularly well known for wine) and *Le Cigare Volant* (in reference to some supposed UFO sighting in Châteauneuf-du-Pape); and down-right goofy – *Big House Red* (a nod to the local Soledad prison).

If you have not had a chance to enjoy the Bonny Doon wines, do try some the next time you find them in a wine shop. And do not be embarrassed when people look at you a bit funny as you stand there wincing at the wine names, and laughing at the back labels.

For the winery or proprietary wine names, the subjects are just as varied. They range from animals, generally termed 'critters' – *Yellowtail*, for the Australian marsupial, to puns on famous wine regions – *Frog's Leap* for Stag's Leap. Others note celebrities (dead or alive) such as *Marilyn Merlot*, cartoons, homonyms such as *Stu Pedasso*, to blatant sex appeal, such as *Sexy* (Franson, 2006). If some winemaker or wine marketer thought they had a clever idea, or could get away with a risqué phrase, word or image, it has been put on, or at least it has been attempted to put it on a label.

EXPLORATIONS 9.2
NEW ZEALAND WINE LABELS

When we moved to New Zealand, Karen and I advised some winery clients about developing the labels for their wines which they wanted to export to the United States. Our initial exercise was to take the wineries' marketing people to a local wine shop. There we asked them to look at all the bottles on one shelf, say all the Chardonnay bottles or all the Cabernet bottles. The purpose was for them to see which brands stood out because of labelling or bottles, and why.

Certainly, the colour labels were more prominent. But colour adds to the label printing cost. One of the simple, but subtle, ideas which we tried to drive home was to utilize a white background instead of black. (Perhaps the New Zealand love for the black colour stems from their justified admiration of the All Blacks rugby team.) If you do this exercise, you will see that those bottles with the darker colour labels do tend to disappear when looking at a row of bottles.

Although a new trend, now, thankfully that the 'critter' labels seem to be passé, is back to black. It is perceived as classier – the wine more expensive but of better quality – although it does not necessarily stand out on the shelf. Referring to other liquor labels where black seems to work, *Wines & Vines* Managing Editor Kate Lavin notes, "Black label Johnny Walker Scotch is more expensive than the red label, and Jack Daniel's whiskey has long been identified by its black label" (2016).

In the early 1900s, the champagne house of Perrier-Jouët embraced the Art Nouveau style on their bottles. Artists produced swirls of anemones wreathed in gold for the Perrier-Jouët bottles. In the New World, and much more recently, Jordan Winery did something similar, however, in a far more minimalist style. Tom Jordan and his daughter Judy produced a sparkling wine from Pinot Noir and Chardonnay which they placed in an elegant bottle, etched only with a simple gold 'J' on the front (Jones, 1994).

EXPLORATIONS 9.3
DEVELOPING AND DESIGNING THE WORK VINEYARD LABEL

In between the humour of the Bonny Doon labels and the elegance of Jordan's etched motif, Karen designed a simpler label for our Work Vineyard Sauvignon Blanc and late harvest sweet wine.

First, we had to choose a name for the wine. With our vineyard at the base of Mount St Helena, the imposing ancient volcanic plug guarding the northeast corner of the Napa Valley, the logical choice was something associated with the mountain. The obvious ones, such as Chateau Montelena, however, were already taken. Continuing the search, we realized our own family name, Work, might be appropriate, but needed a logo that could connect the wine with the labour of growing and harvesting the grapes, and the wine's production.

Together with her graphic designer, Karen brainstormed for ideas. She found it by looking at something we saw daily; highway roadwork warning signs. In California, as well as other areas, road maintenance or construction caution signs are usually diamond-shaped placards, coloured in bright orange with black lettering. Inside, the words 'Caution' or 'Men at Work' are often noted.

Karen and the designer incorporated those fundamental elements – the orange colour and the diamond sign – with a stylized person pruning a grape vine. This distinct logo was then superimposed on the various bottle labels, along with the required information about each wine and vintage we produced.

Another interesting story about how a brand name was developed for a wine comes from a Chilean winery, Concha y Toro. Its owner, Marqués de Casa Concha had his personal stock of wine stored in one of the winery's cellars. It seems that some employees got into it on a regular basis. Rather than moving the wine to another cellar, he developed a protection system based upon the worker's superstitions. For several nights he rattled around the cellar throwing bottles and making eerie noises, pretending to be the devil in the cellar. From this experience, a reserve wine evolved named, *Casillero del Diablo* 'the cellar where the devil lives' (Jones, 1994)

FIGURE 9.3 Original logo of Work Vineyard, Napa Valley, California Karen Work

The consumer's take on labels

Most of us look at labels from the point of view of a consumer. Fortunately, or unfortunately, this is becoming more and more difficult, even for seasoned professionals. The array of origins, brands and varietals, not to mention the choices between red, white and rose, or even dry or sweet, are almost staggering.

Recently I experienced, or re-experienced, what the novice wine drinker must feel, while shopping for Portuguese wine in a Portuguese supermarket. For not only are the winery names a bit difficult, but for a small country Portugal has an incredible number of wine regions. They each have their own unique mix of varietals, many unfamiliar to those of us from outside of the country. It was perplexing and a bit overwhelming.

There was no 'expert', nor the typical 'shelf talkers', to make suggestions. I could only narrow the options. I started by choosing red wine from the Alentejano region (a large region in southern part of the country), then, over the course of several weeks, worked my way through a few different brands by trying their offerings with our meals.

As Puckette proposes: "The process usually involves starting with what you know, followed by a comparison of prices and discounts, and then label gawking until you find something… and then you're still not sure if it will be good!" (2017). Although, I must say, I had no bad wines in Portugal.

In choosing the wines, I utilized the strategy that we were advising our winery clients to use; among the bewildering array of bottles, my eyes could focus only on those bearing clear, readable labels, with white backgrounds.

While wine labels certainly have a subtle influence, Wine Folly further suggests that to get past the brands, one should look at the wine's 'provenance', that is, the location of the actual vineyards. If the specific winery or brand is unknown, a region is often more indicative of quality. For instance, a pinot noir from Oregon is, in general, going to be better than one from a warmer climate.

Do wine labels influence our buying decision? Generally, no, or very little if you have a particular brand and variety you are going after. Yes, if you are unsure of what type of wine you want.

Australian researchers found recently that regular wine drinkers sought descriptors such as 'smooth' and 'easy-drinking' as well as 'full-bodied' and 'rich', with women preferring the former while men the later. They seemed to value these descriptions in their decisions on which wine to purchase above those of the suggestions of the wine shop staff (Pittaway, 2017). As a group, the millennials are more adventurous than older consumers. They are willing to try wines which noted more exotic flavours such as 'pepper' and 'leather'.

However, while the researchers were able to isolate certain descriptors that help to key the purchaser's decision, they were just one part of the total package which influences the consumer. The price, the front label, and the overall design of the bottle and label must present some appeal which makes the potential buyer at least pick up the bottle to read the descriptors.

Wine label fraud

Wine label fraud has been around since people started writing on amphorae. It ranges from the very simple – that of using ill-defined words – to actually putting inferior wine in bottles labelled with prominent, high-end producers.

Unfortunately, as marketing people get involved in creating a label, they often tend to introduce many of the same terms; which by now have become overused. The meanings of those words are vague, and often adjectives are employed without evidence, such as 'boutique', 'reserve', or 'grand estate'. Back labels often read like they have been developed by committee, the original meaning and sincerity totally lost. It takes someone of the calibre of Randall Grahm to write witty and amusing back label stories, which few seem to achieve.

The use of oak alternatives – the chips and pieces of toasted wood which are utilized to provide oak flavour without the need to place a wine in oak barrels – have grown dramatically in use over the past 30 years. Yet their descriptions have occasionally become misleading. Quickly read, 'aged with oak', or, 'French oak was used to process this wine', might lead one to believe that the wine was placed in oak barrels, when only oak alternatives were utilized.

Another fraudulent practice is the allusion in the terminology on the label that the wine in the bottle was grown in a famous wine area, when it was not. In the Napa Valley, one winery brought in grapes from California's Central Valley and produced wine under its Napa Valley label. Another winery bottled its wine in the Napa Valley so it could state on the label 'Bottled in the Napa Valley' but the wine was made outside the Valley. Both these practices were stopped when, in 1981, the Appellation of Origin laws were enacted (Napa Vintners, 2017). Now, in the United States, states or county names can be used only if 75% of the wine is sourced from those areas. American viticultural area names may be used if 85% of the grapes are from those areas, and the notation of a vineyard designation on the label requires 95% of the grapes to be from the said vineyard. California law took things one step further by requiring 100% of the grapes to come from California if that name is stated on the label.

Wine fraud was raised to a new level in the 2000s by one Rudy Kurniawan (Cumming, 2016). Specializing primarily in Burgundian reds, he allegedly faked many Romanée-Conti wines, passing off good Pinot Noir in bottles with labels from brands that were even more expensive and rare. In a 2006 auction, he sold US$24.7 million worth of wine. In another event he out did himself by selling vintage bottles, ranging from 1945 to 1971, of Burgundian winery Domaine Ponsot; the winery had not been started until 1982 (Cumming, 2016).

It was this revelation to the Domaine Ponsot owner, Laurent Ponsot, as well as a suspicion from wine collector Bill Koch, one of the Kochs of the gas and oil industry, which started people looking into Mr Kurniawan's activities.

Initially, some saw, Mr Kurniawan, also known as 'Dr Conti', as someone who could play the game with the big boys, relieving them of some of their money due to their gullibility and lack of effort at investigating the provenance of the wine they were purchasing. However, as private and government investigators, and even several movie directors who made the film *Sour Grapes* about Kurniawan's misdeeds, began to realize, the extent of his fraud was serious. Even if some of the wine collecting investors made mistakes, at stake was the reputation of Burgundian wines, to say nothing of the huge amounts of money fraudulently taken from wine investors.

As the investigations proceeded, damaging evidence was found in Mr Kurniawan's house; old style bottles and equipment to fabricate what appeared to be antique labels. He was subsequently convicted and imprisoned for ten years.

Mr Kurniawan's tale does not stop there. More recently a lawsuit has been filed alleging that some other well-known wine auctioneers, dealers and storage operators were acting in collusion with Mr Kurniawan when he sold US$2.45 million worth of Domaine de la Romanée-Conti wines in 2011 (Hellman, 2016).

Labelling for biodynamic and organic wines

In the late 1980s, Amigo Bob (aka Bob Cantisano) was starting to make a name for himself in the Napa Valley. He was one of the first to provide consulting services on how to grow grapes organically. The gossip through the local *grapevine* disclosed only bits and pieces of his emphasis and techniques; all we heard was that he planted cow horns in the vineyards. Obviously, there was more to his activities.

With magazines the likes of *Mother Jones News* encouraging a shift to organics during the Age of Aquarius, by the 1980s the Napa Valley wine-growing scene had matured enough for some far-thinking winemakers to start examining how to grow and make organic wines on a commercial scale. Thus, Amigo Bob started to have a following, doing more than just planting cow horns. While a few wine operations did turn to making organic wines, most at least examined all the chemicals that they were putting on the vineyards and being used in the winery. Subsequently a number of vineyards have shifted to growing biodynamic wines, a more encompassing regime than just growing organic grapes.

One of the early disciples was John Williams, the owner of Frog's Leap Winery:

> We know that healthy, vibrant, microbial-dense soil will better absorb the winter rains and provide for the nutritional and water needs of the plant all year long. We've learned that if we maintain biodiversity through cover crops and insectary borders that the vine will be able to communicate with other plants and bugs in a meaningful way.
>
> *(Frog's Leap Winery, 2017)*

The designation for organic wines is now on some wine labels, and there are even sections in the wine shops for organic wines. The organic/biodynamic/sustainable mind-set has slowly melded into all of our foods – meats, fruits and vegetables, dairy products and grains (Locke et al., 2014).

Sulphur has come under scrutiny as some people are sensitive to it, and it has some restrictions for growing and making organic wine. The US Food and Drug Administration (FDA) in 1985 required that the addition of sulphites to wine be stated, and that wines containing more than 10 ppm, and intended to be sold throughout the US, include a warning statement on the label (Briones-Labarca et. al., 2017). According to the Organic Consumers Association, an American based group:

> For a wine to be labelled 'Organic' and bear the USDA organic seal, it must be made from organically grown grapes and give information about who the certifying agency is. A wine in this category cannot have any added sulfites. It may have naturally occurring sulfites, but the total sulfite level must be less than 20 parts per million.
>
> *(Organic Consumers Organization, 2017)*

European Union rules for organic labels are similar, citing low levels of sulphur and sorbic acid (European Commission, 2012). In both cases, the wine must be grown with certified organic grapes under the existing rules regarding the limits of use of pesticides, fungicides, herbicides and fertilizers (McEvoy, 2013).

Conclusion

The labelling of wine vessels has occurred almost as long as people have been making wine. The sophistication we see in today's wine bottle labels has been a long time coming. Some are extremely helpful, while others are just marketing jargon.

References

Beard, M. (2008). *Pompeii: The Life of a Roman Town*. London: Profile Books.

Briones-Labarca, V., Perez-Wom, M., Habib, G., Giovagnoli-Vicuña, C., Cañas-Sarazua, R., Tabilo-Munizaga, G. and Salazar, F. N. (2017). Oenological and quality characteristic on young white wines (Sauvignon Blanc): effects of high hydrostatic pressure processing. *Hindawi Journal of Food Quality*, [online] p. 12.

Cumming, E. (2016). The great wine fraud. *The Guardian*, [online] 11 September 2016.

Fitzgerald, B. (2016). Microchip label and smart phone app protects products against counterfeit scams. *ABC* (Australia), [online] 24 February 2016.

Franson, P. (2006). Labels gone wild. *The Wine Enthusiast*, [online] 1 February 2006.

Golden, J. (1999). "An argument that goes back to the womb": the demedicalization of Fetal Alcohol Syndrome, 1973–1992. *Journal of Social History*, [online] 33(2), pp. 269–298.

Hellman, P. (2016). Firm alleges Rudy Kurniawan sold it $2.45 million in fake Burgundy, and wine merchants helped. *The Wine Spectator*, [online] 24 May 2016.

Jones, A. (1994). *The Stories Behind the Labels: The History, Romance & Characters of the World of Wine and Drink*. Bathurst, NSW, AU: Crawford House Publishing.

Lavin, K. (2016). Shedding light on dark labels. *Wine & Vines*, [online] October 2016.

Locke, S., McAloon, C., McHugh, B. and Barbour, L. (2014). The facts behind the labels: the truth of organic, biodynamic, free-range and grass-fed food labelling. *ABC News* (Australia), [online] 8 September 2014.

Lukacs, P. (2012). *Inventing Wine: A New History of One of the World's Most Ancient Pleasures*. New York: W. W. Norton & Co.

Marlière, E., Parrilla, A. M., Torres Costa, J. (2016). Rubrum, piperatum et servilianum. Algunos vinos y preparados vinarios consumidos en Ebusus. In Járrega, R.

and Berni, P. (eds) *Amphorae ex Hispania: paisajes de producción y consume*. Tarragona: Instituto Catalán de Arqueología Clásica (ICAC). pp. 407–422.

McCrone, E. H. (2017). It's what's in the bottle that counts … or is it? The role of texture in wine packaging. *Wine Industry Advisor*, [online] May 24, 2017.

McGovern, P. E. (2009). *Uncorking the Past: The Quest for Wine, Beer, and Other Alcoholic Beverages*. Berkeley: University of California Press.

Muthmann, H. (2017). Question [email].

Penzer, N. M. (1947). *The Book of the Wine-Label*. London: Home & Van Thal.

Pittaway, I. (2017). Wine label descriptions influence consumers more than shop staff, awards: report. *ABC News* (Australia), [online] 18 April 2017.

Perry, C. (1990). The Woody Allen of wine making. *Los Angeles Times*, [online] 23 November 1990.

Robinson, J. ed. (2015). *The Oxford Companion to Wine*. Oxford: Oxford University Press.

Sedghi, S. (2018). New project to help prevent wine fraud. *ABC News* (Australia), [online] 2 January 2018.

Websites

Bonny Doon Vineyard. (2017). www.bonnydoonvineyard.com

European Commission (2012). *Organic Farming: Organic Wine*. European Commission, Agriculture and Rural Development. [online] www.ec.europa.eu

Farke, W. and Veillard, P. (2012). *PROTECT Factsheet – Health Warning Labels on Alcoholic Beverages*. Eurocare. www.eurocare.org

Frog's Leap Winery. (2017). www.frogsleap.com

McEvoy, M. (2013). *Organic 101: Organic Wine*. United States Department of Agriculture. www.usda.gov. 8 January 2013.

Napa Vintners. (2017). Napa Valley Vintners. www.napavintners.com

Organic Consumers Organization. (2017). www.organicconsumers.org

Blogs

Novin, G. (2012). A history of wine labels, Chapter 61. *Guity Novin's A History of Graphic Design*. www.guity-novin.blogspot.com

Puckette, M. (2017). Are we overly influenced by wine labels? *Wine Folly*. www.winefolly.com. 29 March 2017.

10

MOVING WINE AROUND THE WORLD

Moving wine on land – amphorae and dolia

Bordeaux developed as an important city due largely to its proximity to the Garonne River, which in turn provided access to both the Atlantic and a large area in southwestern France. Via the rivers, wine could be received and shipped for export. But what of other towns, such as Châteaumeillant, without significant river or sea approaches?

What did it take to transport amphorae from the vineyards of Italy to Roman administrators the middle of France, or to the religious leaders in rural German wanting wine for ceremonies? How were the barrels moved? And what modes bring our bottles to the supermarket or wine shops?

Celtic transportation

An increasing understanding of the historical trade indicates that it was still very much weather dependent. Cart and wagons could have operated when the primitive roads were solid, not when full of mud or the creeks so high as to be unpassable. But the evidence is emerging that the Celts used carts – in her tomb, the Lady of Vix was lying in a substantial one. If they utilized carts, then most likely the Celts were also building all-weather roads. Again, new evidence has shown that they built corrugated roads – those in which a series of gutter pipe-sized logs were laid parallel to each other. Several of these primitive roads have been found *under* the Roman-built roads (Baillie and Brown, 2002; Robb, 2013; Salač, 2010). Additionally, the rivers could have only been navigated and crossed when they were not in flood. Although, again, research is now finding the remains of extremely ancient wooden bridges – the remnants of pilings and metal fasteners. All this shows an overland network was more advanced, and travel perhaps more efficient and easier than historians have originally proposed.

For the overland transportation of amphorae, at many sites along the northern European rivers, significant piles of broken amphorae have been found. Archaeologists believe that these are points at which wine and oil was shifted from the amphorae, which were used to transport the products via boats and barges, to animal hide sacks in order to be loaded on to pack animals or wagons for overland journeys (Morris, 2010). Removing the wine from the amphorae would reduce the total cargo weight by almost half. Additionally, as well as enabling the horses or donkeys, and possibly carts, to carry more product and less container, it also minimized amphorae breakage as the animals jostled their way along the rudimentary paths and tracks. Yet, as finds at Châteaumeillant and Bibracte indicate, amphorae did make their way in large numbers to sites well away from the navigable rivers. Perhaps carts, with some sort of suspension, and well-made roads were more numerous than currently believed.

As the historical record keeps unfolding, we are learning that much trade did take place. André Tchernia, a French archaeologist who has long studied the evolution and movements of the wine, has estimated that just for one type of amphorae, the Dressel 1 style, some 55 to 65 million of them were imported into Gaul (Tchernia, 1986). These are huge numbers, especially considering that each amphora was laboriously moved by hand at every change of transportation mode along the journey – from the pottery factory to the winery to be filled, to the sea-going ship to river barge to be transported, and then overland to the nobility or well-to-do clients in an oppidum or village for consumption. Roughly, these numbers equate to about 2 million litres of wine per year going into northern Europe. For comparison, in one recent year, 2012, France consumed about 31 million litres (European Commission, 2017). Nonetheless, the historical Celts were imbibing a significant amount of wine.

Further in Bibracte, from the over 500,000 amphorae sherds uncovered, it is estimated that, over several hundred years, over 1 million amphorae were imported to site (Loughton, 2014). At say 20 litres per amphora, that is 20 million litres of liquid – wine, olive oil or garum. Republican wine trade into Gaul is believed to have started about 120 BCE, after the conquests by Romans in southern Gaul, with a sudden decline about 50 BCE (Loughton, 2014) due to the final mopping up operations, then picking up again as the Roman administrators reorganized the trade and life returned to a more normalized routine.

EXPLORATIONS 10.1
BORDEAUX ROMAN VILLA

Imagine a classic Mediterranean villa; small gardens surrounded by portico-covered hallways leading to the various rooms. Say 1,000 or 2,000 square metres. Now, expand it to be 6,000 square metres. This would be the size of some of the Roman emperor's villas on the Palatine Hill in Rome. This one is not in Rome. It is northwest of Bordeaux, in the town of Plassac, overlooking the Gironde Estuary.

This particular villa had not one garden but two; expansive ones surrounded by column-supported covered porticos. Recent excavations have revealed that several of the large rooms had mosaic floors, some of the motifs incorporating elaborate images of vines; this leads the archaeologists studying the site to believe the owner was involved in the wine trade. Research on the villa has revealed that the pieces of marble making up the designs were sourced from the far corners of the Mediterranean, which, in itself, signals an extensive trading system in place. Other rooms had under-floor heating; whereby heat from a central fire was circulated in tiled ducts. That would have been a real luxury when in the middle of a Bordeaux winter the temperatures can drop below freezing. Within the villa, it is believed that many of the walls were painted in a faux-marble motif. A room, thought to be the dining room, looks south, out over the Gironde Estuary, to what is now Bordeaux's famous Medoc wine region on the opposite shore.

This villa was the home of a well-to-do Roman. Archaeologists believe that he was a man by the name of Blattius, whose wealth was derived from wine, either as a négociant and/or wine grower (Plassac villa Gallo-Romaine, 2016). He had the villa built about 20 CE, in what was then considered the "Wild West" of the Aquitaine. Given the size of the villa and the work that went into preparing the site and building it, Mr Blattius must have done quite well in the wine business.

With the Romans having subdued the Gauls some 70 years earlier, the period in which Blattius was constructing his villa was known as the Imperial Era. Bordeaux at that time traded extensively with Britain and northern Europe, sending hundreds of ships north with wine and returning with tin (Aubin et al., 1996) and possibly wool and cheese. While Plassac may have seemed like an 'out-post' to one sitting on a curule in Rome, it was most certainly not. It was a region thriving from the trade, and now coming into its own with the planting of grapes and making wine (Brun and Laubenheimer, 2001), rather than just trans-shipping it from eastern France and Italy on to the Atlantic seaboard communities.

To build such a villa, many skilled workmen must have either been about or drawn to the area for significant wages. Built into the hill below the villa was a large building. It was possibly used for wine storage. With the research still ongoing, we do not know how much vineyard was owned by this villa or what its production was. Nor is it apparent as to whether the money used to build the villa came from wine sales or whether its owner made the money elsewhere, such as a payment for being in the Roman military. But its size, and the extensive wine motifs, do indicate that at that time wine was already a critical commodity for the region.

Moving wine on the sea

Amphorae in shipwrecks

An increasingly important source of information about the wine trade in amphorae has been the ancient ships which sank. A number of the wrecks have been located carrying 5,000 amphorae, and a few have had up to 10,000 (although some may have been empty, simply being transported for later filling). Regardless of the number of amphorae, which individually are of course a treasure trove for the marine archaeologists, their preponderance points to the fact that the traders and merchants were sending forth huge cargo manifests.

Not only are more and more wrecks being located in the Mediterranean, but some also have been found in the Indian Ocean coastal waters between the Red Sea and India (Frankopan 2016), as well as within the rivers of Europe. Let us look at a couple which have been found in the Mediterranean.

The Minoans were a third and second millennium BCE civilization located on the island of Crete (Bonn-Muller, 2010). They preceded both the Mycenaean's and the Ancient Greeks. Minoan sailors plied the eastern Mediterranean, moving goods via their ships back and forth from Anatolia (Turkey), the Levant (Israel, Lebanon and Syria) and as far south as Egypt.

In 2003, Greek diver and archaeologist Elpida Hadjidaki was exploring around some of the small outlying islands at Crete's northwest corner searching for wrecks of these ancient boats. She and her team discovered the remains of a ship which apparently had capsized off the island of Pseira (Bonn-Muller, 2010). During their mapping of the wreck site they identified over 200 whole and partial amphorae and jars. The amphorae were most likely carrying wine and olive oil, although no remains of those liquids have been found. By 2009, further finds of more amphorae, and subsequent studies dated the wreck to between 1800 and 1675 BCE.

Hadjidaki and other marine archaeologists believe that the ship which had been carrying the amphorae was roughly 12 to 14 metres long. Typically, larger ships criss-cross the Mediterranean and out into the Atlantic or Indian oceans, so the size of this vessel, with its particular type of pottery, suggest that it was engaged in coastal trade (Bonn-Muller, 2010). Based upon the orientation of the amphorae, when the ship sunk it overturned, possibly as a result of a storm and/or from overloading. The upturned wooden hull was thus exposed to the eroding effects of the sea and subsequently disintegrated. The more durable ceramic amphorae and jars remained on the sea floor.

What is important about this find is that it indicates that amphorae were a standard container for a good portion of the traded commodities at least 4,000 years ago.

The Kyrenia wreck – loading amphorae

Another find in the Aegean was not only amphorae but the actual ship in which they were being ferried. Off the Cypriote town of Kyrenia, a Greek ship with its cargo went down in the fourth century BCE. It was located in 1968 and found to be 11.4 metres long by 4.8 metres in width. In this case, the wooden ship sunk into the muddy ocean floor, and was thereby preserved. By 1974 it was raised, the wood conserved, and the ship reassembled and named the *Kyrenia*; it is protected in the town's museum (Katzev, 2008). Some informative research has since ensued.

Susan Katzev was one of the original people assisting in extracting the ship from the sea bottom. More recently, along with colleague Laina Wylde Swiny, the pair engaged in a hands-on research mission based upon the findings from the original wreck. They wanted to find out how, in actual practice, a ship like the *Kyrenia* was loaded and the amphorae stowed.

The first problem was obtaining replicas of the amphorae. Katzev and Swiny found a family of potters who could reproduce all the amphorae from some 384 pieces in a variety of shapes and styles. These models were based upon the underwater photos that Katzev and the original team had made. Next, Katzev and Swiny were able to enlist the services of a replica ship, the *Kyrenia* II built in 2003. Finally, with the reproduced amphorae and ship, they loaded and sailed, experimenting with various methods of hoisting the amphorae aboard and finding the correct buoyancy and balance requirements to haul a full load yet keep the ship safe from capsizing.

Loading was the initial issue. First, they tried hand loading – two men handing off each full amphora to another two-man team on the ship. Of the amphorae, the largest type, a style from Rhodes, weighted 49 kilograms when full of wine. Even for two men, these heavy amphorae would have been awkward, especially trying to stow them on a swaying ship. Additionally, part of the original load also included some yet-to-be-shaped millstones, weighing 57 kilograms each. Hand-to-hand loading of these proved to be slow, and also risked breaking the amphorae if they were dropped (Katzev, 2008).

Block and tackle, albeit primitive, were known to exist in the era of the *Kyrenia*. Some pulleys were simple blocks of hard wood through which the ropes could be pulled. Others, such as a pulley found with the *Kyrenia* wreck, actually had a rotating wheel – a solid piece of wood with two protrusions to act as an axel (Katzev, 1969). For the experiment, a system of ropes and pulleys attached to the horizontal boom of the ship's mast was utilized. In this manner, a metal hook, identical to the one found in the excavation, hung from the rope. It was used to grab a simple rope sling fitted in the two handles of the amphora. The amphora could then be raised, the boom swung back over the ship, and the amphora lowered into the hold, placing it exactly where the load master directed. This operation took 20 seconds for each amphora (Katzev, 2008).

The total weight of the original *Kyrenia's* load was 17 metric tons. Using the block and tackle, loading all the replica amphorae took the four-man crew 2.5 hours, and probably saved a lot of back problems.

As the team proceeded with the loading exercise, they began to realize that the original *Kyrenia* ship must have been modified from when it was first constructed. It is believed that the initial ship was built to hold 10 tons (Katzev, 2008). Then, at some point, side boards were added, upping the capacity to 12 tons. Yet the total weight of the cargo found was 14 tons. Was this why the ship sank or were there further modifications?

It was determined that there were later modifications to not only raise the sides, but to reorganize the interior in order to accommodate more amphorae. The team accomplished these modifications to the *Kyrenia II*, thus being able to stow all the 14 tons of replica amphorae without endangering the ship.

Another problem bothering researchers has been the stoppering of the amphorae. Where amphorae have been discovered in ruins on land, stoppers of various types have been found – clay, wood, cork and animal skin. In the underwater remains, however, all or any natural materials were long gone. In the case of the *Kyrenia*, no clay stoppers were found. So, most probably the ones used on the *Kyrenia* amphorae were organic in nature.

Again, the crew tried a number of possible options (Katzev, 2008). Most likely in this case, the amphorae were covered with wetted goat skin which was tied over the rim of the amphorae. It became tight when it dried. Years under the sea would have dissolved the skin and their securing cords, permitting the contents to disperse.

Katzev and her teams have provided some extremely practical aspects of moving and shipping amphorae.

Phoenician ship wrecks

Most wrecks have been located in relatively shallow water, enabling the reconnaissance and research using SCUBA gear. Two wrecks of the early first millennium BCE Phoenician ships carrying wine in amphorae have been found in 400 metres of water off the coast of Ashkelon, Israel. At that depth, they required an underwater submersible for both the discovery and subsequent exploration (Ballard et al., 2002; McGovern, 2009).

Nicknamed the *Tanit* and *Elissa*, these ships lay on a transit line between the Levant and Egypt. It is believed that they were caught in a storm and overturned on their way to Egypt (McGovern, 2009) or possibly Carthage (Ballard et al., 2002). From what can be seen, they were transporting almost 400 amphorae apiece.

Using a deep-submergence vehicle, the wrecks were mapped and then some of the Israel/Lebanon-style amphorae were recovered using the vehicle's grasping arm. Dr McGovern has subsequently analysed scrapings from the interior of these amphorae. He dated the torpedo-shaped amphorae to around 725 BCE. There were traces of tartaric acid, indicating that at least some of the amphorae contained wine.

Supporting this, an elaborate jug for pouring wine was found on the *Elissa*. McGovern describes it as a "beautifully red-slipped and highly burnished jug with a flaring mushroom like lip … a distinctive calling card of the Phoenicians…. Part of the Phoenician 'wine set', the decanter was used to serve wine with an ostentatious flourish" (2009). On this decanter was the inscription *yyn khl*, which indicates a type of wine (Ballard et al., 2002).

Additionally, McGovern observed that the amphorae were lined with pine pitch to minimize seepage, another good indicator that the amphorae contained wine. Ballard and his fellow researchers suggest that these would be some of the oldest amphorae found to be pitch lined (2002).

Ballard and his colleagues also noted that the size of amphorae (which averaged 17.8 litres) was extremely uniform, possibly as "purpose built maritime containers" (2002). Their identical size would have facilitated nesting of the amphorae in the ships.

Dolia on ships

At the end of the first millennium BCE, the Roman Empire started moving significant quantities of wine and olive oil around the Mediterranean between Italy, Spain and north into the territories of the Celts. Their ships carried amphorae, but some also had large dolia placed within the ship's framing as they were built. Basically the 'tankers' of their day, these ships have been termed *cistern-boats*. They were in service for about 300 years, being phased out after 200 CE (Marlier and Sibella, 2002). It is likely that, as Elise Marlière suggests, they were used to provide the vast amounts of wine and oil provisions needed by the Roman troops as the Empire moved to conquer the north and west (Marlière, 2001).

Around the Mediterranean, some ten wrecks of the *cistern-boats* have been located, each containing 8 to 15 of the large ceramic pots. (Perhaps this large number of wrecks indicates that the ships with dolia on board were not particularly seaworthy.)

One wreck, found just off coast from Marseille, has been named the *Petite-Congloué*. It had 15 dolia, averaging 130 litres each (Corsi-Sciallano and Liou, 1985). The dolia were made by Italian potters, probably from Minturna, a coastal community about half way between Rome and Naples and where the ship was built. This is evident from the stamped names in their shoulders which could be clearly photographed by the divers. Additionally, the wear and tear from rocking and rolling on the ship was apparent with a number of lead sutures, used to seal over and across cracks, preventing them from widening. If a dolia did separate, a rapid leak of several hundred kilograms of wine spilling into the ship's bilge would have seriously endangered its sea-going ability (Marlier and Sibella, 2002).

With the dolia built into the ship there comes an obvious question: How was the wine loaded and subsequently removed once the ship got to its designation? Researchers Corsi-Sciallano and Liou (1985) suggest that it was siphoned or pumped out. In the wreck of a similar ship, named *La Giraglia*,

FIGURE 10.1 Barrels on a Roman-era cart
Courtesy of the Kunstsammlungen und Museen der Stadt Augsburg, Römisches Museum; by Andreas Brücklmai

lead pipes and some brass fittings were found. The archaeologists presume this was for bilge pump. These early pumps were of a *Ktesibian* style; that is those with a piston which sucked the liquid in through the intake pipe on the up-swing and forced it out through a separate pipe as the piston descended (de Camp, 1963). Another pump style, suggested from parts found in the *Asterix* ship wreck, was a *chapelet* style (Dean, 2004; Marlier and Sibella, 2002). This type of extraction system consisted of many small buckets attached to a chain. It would have been hand or foot operated to turn the chain enabling the buckets to scoop the liquid out of the dolia, dumping it into a receiving bin or pipe and then into awaiting receptacles on a pier, riverbank or beach.

By 200 CE, the dolia-containing cistern-boats appear to have been phased out. Several possible explanations exist for this: the demand by the Roman army for large quantities of wine was decreasing; the function of the dolia was being better fulfilled by barrels; vineyard expansion had increased production in the further reaches of the Empire so that wine from Italy was no longer needed or could not be shipped economically; and/or the cistern-boats themselves were just too unsteady on rough seas with the merchants losing too much cargo. Further research is needed to narrow the reasons.

Moving large quantities of wine on land – barrels and glass bottles

With the evidence from the inland oppidum and other sites, we know that wine moved beyond the rivers and seas. Besides moving it in dolia, amphorae and animal skin sacks, we get a glimpse of another large, bulk vessel from a wall painting on a Pompeii bar wall. Preserved these thousands of years by the ash from the eruption of Vesuvius in 79 CE, the mural depicts a wagon with a huge animal-hide sack lying atop its bed (Beard, 2008). The capacity of this bag appears to be somewhere between several hundred to perhaps a thousand litres. In the mural, two men are filling several amphorae with wine from a hose at the end of the sack. Nearby, stand several horses or mules, which presumably draw the wagon.

How common were these bulk-wine delivery systems? Few large sacks have been found, and their images are unusual, so how often these horse-drawn tankers were utilized around the Roman towns is not clearly known. Viewed from today's perspective, however, utilizing a large sack to haul wine seems practical in terms of logistics, if not particularly beneficial to the wine's taste. It would have been an excellent method to deliver large volumes of wine to a city's inns and taverns from a winery on the outskirts.

Shift from amphorae to barrels

At the end of the first millennium BCE and the beginning of the first CE, there was a shift in the shipping containers used for wine – from amphorae to barrels. How instrumental the city of Bordeaux was in this change is not totally clear, but certainly its wine merchants and shipping operators must have been some of the key players as it occurred.

I noted earlier that Bordeaux was an important shipper of wine to Britain and northern Europe. Initially this involved transhipping it in amphorae from Italy through Narbonne. Later, once vineyards were planted and wine made, Bordeaux became a producer in its own right. Moving wine, in amphorae, across from Italy and around the Mediterranean or up the European rivers seemed to work well in the relatively shallow keeled barges and ships developed for those water ways. However, once out on the rougher Atlantic, a ship with a deeper keel was required to slice through the heavier seas. Packaging professor Diana Twede suggests that the barrels nested better within the deeper 'V' shaped hold of those ships, hence some of the momentum for the shift (Twede, 2005). Another possibility was that more and more wine was being shipped. The vintners and traders knew that amphorae were inefficient in terms of both space and extra packaging weight. With the larger holds of these Atlantic-going ships, the evidence points to a relatively quick shift to barrels by the Bordeaux traders as those containers came into the supply system.

One example of those early coastal Atlantic ships has been found in the mud in the Port of St Peter, on the Isle of Guernsey (Work, 2014). It has subsequently been restored for viewing and examination. Denoted as the *Asterix*, for the iconic French adventurer comic book character, it has been dated to about the second or third century CE. It was rigged for sail, 25 metres in length and 6 metres wide. Built with thick oak planks and fully decked, both its bow and stern were curved. It plied the eastern Atlantic seaboard, ranging possibly as far north as the Baltic and south into the Mediterranean.

In those days of the Roman Empire, the standard shipping unit for the wine barrels was the *tun*, a large barrel of 900 litres. A ship was rated by how many tuns it could carry. (We use the similar word today, ton, for the capacity of ships; for example, 'the ship has a rated tonnage of xxx'. Today, we would call this type of large barrel a *puncheon*, yet those ancient tuns were still almost twice as large as today's standard 500 litre puncheons.

The literature from Roman writers described these barrels being used; several were placed on a more permanent basis in the middle of the ship's hold, in a manner similar to the bulk ceramic dolia in the Mediterranean cistern-boats. It has been suggested, however, that many more barrels of the 225-litre size, as well as various boxes and sacks for other commodities, were the more typical cargo stowed on board these Atlantic-going ships (Aubin et al., 1996).

However, for the purpose of examining one of the influences that pushed vintners and merchants to shift from utilizing amphorae to barrels, let us assume that the *Asterix* carried a full load of only the 900 litre *tuns*. Based upon the measurements of its cargo hold, at 200 cubic metres (Dean, 2004), it could conservatively load 100 such barrels. And the capacity of the ship could be conservatively 100 metric tons. Table 10.1 compares an equivalent loading of amphorae versus barrels in the ship.[1] Suffice it to say, almost twice the wine could be shipped in barrels as in amphorae, due largely to the extra weight of the amphorae themselves.

The captains of the ships like the *Asterix*, and the merchants who utilized their services, certainly must have understood that shipping wine, and not the weight of amphorae themselves, was far more cost efficient, and probably much safer in the Atlantic waters. Thus, as barrels became more available within the trading systems, their capacity to weight ratio must have been a factor, if not the most significant factor, in pushing the shift from amphorae to barrels.

TABLE 10.1 Comparison of barrel versus amphora cargo on *Asterix* (102 metric tons)

	Weight (in kilograms)		Estimated amount		
	Empty	*Full*	*Numbers*	*Litres*	*Total weight (kilograms)*
Amphora (20 litres)	20	40	2,550 amphorae	51,000	102,000
Barrel (900 litres)	120	1,020	100 *tun* barrels	90,000	102,000

Transporting wine barrels

Wine in barrels can be transported equally well on ships and barges as on carts or drays on land. This is due to their design; their ability to be easily rolled and directed while loading or unloading. Additionally, barrels have 'handles'. These are the extension of the ends of the staves beyond the heads. This is termed the *chime*. This protrusion allows a labourer to manipulate the direction and speed of the barrels by grabbing the chimes on both sides of the barrels as he rolls the barrel up or down a loading ramp, or across the ground. For loading on aboard a ship, hooks can be used to grab the chime of the barrel in order to lift it over the rail and lower it into the hold, much the same way Katzev and her colleagues found they could load the amphorae.

Even if the roads were rough, or the wagon had little or no suspension, another advantage of the barrels over amphorae is that they have a bit of flexibility. If the wine barrel is gently jostled, the staves can move slightly without leaking the wine. Without cushioning of straw, on a wagon, or a wooden frame in holds of ships, amphorae, while strong, are brittle and could crack or break, leaking the wine.

Once on board a cart or wagon, the barrels would be held in position by ropes, assisted by small chocks (triangular pieces of wood). On ships, they

FIGURE 10.2 Peters Cement barrels being loaded on board ship at Blue Boar
Wharf, Rochester, Kent
Courtesy of Mark Peters

were stored wherever there was space, but usually towards the bottom of the ship; their weight providing ballast to lower the ship's centre of gravity. While some barrels – such as those containing grain, salted meat or water – might be stored upright, on their heads – wine barrels would be laid on their sides. Then to make sure they did not move during the rocking of the ship, all manner of dunnage – extra sails, ropes, firewood, repair wood, smaller barrels, etc. – would be stuffed in and around them. Having a full, heavy barrel rolling around would be as dangerous as a loose cannonball.

Aside from shipping on the seas, the building of the canals throughout Britain, France, the Netherlands and Germany, and later in the eastern states of America, vastly improved the inland transportation, of which barrels on barges became the standard mode.

EXPLORATIONS 10.2
PARIS, ENTREPÔT OF BERCY

In the early 1980s, Karen and I saw barrels still being delivered to the Paris wine entrepôt of Bercy, a river port on the Seine just east of the city. At these docks, wine barrels, having been shipped from vineyards throughout France, were received from the river and canal barges. Along the quay, the barrels were arranged in lines to be tallied and taxed. Those barrels were then placed within the warren of cellars and warehouses for further aging. At some point, the wine was removed from the barrels to be bottled for distribution to the restaurants and shops within the Paris region. At the time of our visit, we observed some barrels with wine lining the wharf, while others were placed outside the aging cellars and bottling plants.

However, by the late 1990s, a return trip revealed an entirely different story – the passing of what now seems like a nostalgic history. No longer were any full barrels lying around. Any wine paraphernalia thereabouts was solely for decoration. The cellars and bottling plants had been replaced by cafés, boutique shops, hotels and a large park. Wine was no longer shipped to Bercy in barrels; it was bottled at the regional wineries, or in nearby wine distribution warehouses. The few reminders that Bercy was once a wine entrepôt were a restaurant by the name of Chai 33, and two streets with names reminiscent of the Bordeaux region – Cour Saint-Emillion and Rue de Libourne.

> Nor of course is wine still shipped in barrels overseas. If it is not in glass bottles, it is sometimes sent in rubber or plastic bladders – bulk shipments – with the wine then bottled much closer to the end user, thus reducing the shipment weight and increasing the amount of wine actually transported.

Shift from barrels to glass bottles

By the twentieth century, just shy of having lasted for 2,000 years as a container for shipping wine, wooden barrels too succumbed to the same fate as the amphorae; their use as primary vessels to ship wine overtaken by other containers. As the bottles morphed into the shapes we are familiar with today – basically thinner and straighter, and easily packed in wooden boxes and now primarily cardboard cases – wine merchants, particularly in the UK, did not want to deal with the labour of topping and repairing barrels (Pitte, 2008). Additionally, they did not want the expense of sitting on wine for years waiting for it to age; they wanted it aged in the wineries' cellars, delivered ready to sell.

Other modern-day wine movements

Historically, barrels in wine cellars were moved around, stacked and unstacked in long straight stacks, all by hand; this was laborious and time-consuming and in many situations added to the wine's costs. Laid horizontally, as they are in the stacks, they nest but only with their bilges touching. Small chocks, fitted between them, or long timbers placed at the ends, must be utilized to keep them stable.

A revolution in this cellar activity came about in the 1970s and 1980s with the advent and incorporation of forkliftable pallets upon which to store the barrels. Instead of many hands shifting the barrels around, one man (or a woman) driving a forklift can now easily move large numbers of barrels, removing and replacing them in and out of the stacks for filling, topping, emptying and cleaning. Today, these pallets are configurations of stainless steel, galvanized or enamelled metal holding two, or occasionally four, barrels. This shift to the use of forklifts and pallets often took the barrels out of traditional cellars, and placed them in huge, temperature-controlled warehouses where they can be stacked six high when full and eight high when empty. It has increased the number of barrel-aged wines which can economically be made by dramatically lowering the cost of labour.

Glass in cases, packed on pallets, shipped in trucks, and containers

Shipping wine in glass bottles necessitated a need for protection against bottle damage. Wooden boxes initially filled the requirements, with straw adding the cushioning until wooden dividers and bottle uniformity could be established. As cardboard came into the market place in the early 1900s, slowly wineries shifted, largely for economic reasons; a cardboard case is less expensive than a wooden one. To a certain degree, protection was also needed from bottle theft, especially in the days when each case was loaded by hand onto carts, trucks or ships.

As forklifts become available, wineries incorporated them in the 1970s and 1980s, both for moving cases of wine on pallets, and also barrels on pallets. Soon all wine was shipped on pallets. Various formats of shrink wrap, plastic wrap, and just simple string was utilized to hold the cases together. But pallets themselves do take up space. A further refinement

FIGURE 10.3 Cardboard cases of wine displayed in a supermarket
Henry H. Work

placed the cases on *slips* of cardboard, or with the forklift using side arms to squeeze the stack of cases, eliminating the need for a pallet altogether.

Today's wine, in its bottles and cases, usually moves via trucks around a country or in multi-modal, sea-going containers between continents. Like many foods and liquors, they are often delivered first to distributors or distribution centres. There the cases are divided, when necessary to ship less than whole-pallet orders. In a manner similar to that in the large wineries, the big supermarket chains have their own storage and shipping facilities and can ship full trucks or containers to the market place. Smaller wineries need consolidation. Thus, many warehouses have sprung up in wine regions around the world to accommodate the less-than-truckload lots by consolidating the small shipments of numerous wineries.

Sustainability: individualized vs bulk packaging

Finally, there is the question of whether all this individualized containerization − be it the standard 750 millilitre bottles or even individual servings of wine − is sustainable. Which container has the best ecological footprint − glass, cardboard, barrel, or bladder? And if we really could pinpoint the very best, would the world move towards it? We will discuss this in the next chapter.

Conclusion

The desire to move wine had to go hand-in-hand with the transportation systems of the day. Because of their weight and fragility, amphorae were transported largely on river boats and sea-going ships. Barrels worked equally well on both land (wagons and drays) and water (barges and ships). These modes of transportation were well developed by the time wine was placed in bottles for shipping. As wineries and transporters continue to seek more and more efficient methods to move wine, the improvements tend to be modern versions of historical methods − plastic bladders instead of animal skin sacs, or light-weight glass bottles instead of amphorae.

Note

1 The ship is estimated to have had 200 cubic metres of cargo space. At 1.5 cubic metres per *tun*, the ship could load 133 tuns (200/1.5), so let us conservatively call

it 100 *tuns*. A full *tun* weighs 1,020 kilograms (1.02 metric tons). This cargo would then weigh 102,000 kilograms or 102 tons, totalling 90,000 litres of wine.

A convenience when using metric measure is that one litre of water weighs one kilogram. While wine does not have the same specific gravity as water, for the purposes of our rough calculations, it is close enough. We can say that one litre of wine also weighs one kilogram. Another convenient rough conversion is that for the 20 litre-containing size amphorae, the weight of the amphorae itself is approximately equal to the weight of the wine within it. Therefore, an amphora filled with 20 litres of wine would weight approximately 40 kilograms (20 for the wine and 20 for the amphorae).

The theoretical 102 metric tons would equate to 2,550 amphorae. At 20 litres per amphorae, these could contain only 51,000 litres, roughly half the capacity of the wooden *tuns*. Again, this is only a rough approximation, but it does provide an idea of the capacity to weigh differences between the amphorae and wooden barrels.

References

Aubin, G., Lavaud, S. and Roudié, P. (1996). *Bordeaux vignoble millénaire*. Bordeaux: L'Horizon Chimérique.

Baillie, M. G. L. and Brown, D. M. (2002). Oak dendrochronology: some recent archaeological developments from an Irish perspective. *Antiquity*, [online] 76 (292), pp. 497–505.

Ballard, R. D., Stager, L. E., Master, D., Yoerger, D., Mindell, D., Whitcomb, L. L., Singh, H. and Piechota, D. (2002). Iron Age shipwrecks in deep water off Ashkelon, Israel. *American Journal of Archaeology*, [online] 106(2), pp. 151–168.

Beard, M. (2008). *Pompeii: The Life of a Roman Town*. London: Profile Books.

Bonn-Muller, E. (2010). First Minoan shipwreck. *Archaeology*, [online] 63(1), p. 44.

Brun, J.-P. and Laubenheimer, F. (2001). La viticulture en Gaul. *Gallia*, [online] 58 (1), pp. 5–11.

Corsi-Sciallano, M., and Liou, B. (1985). Les épaves de Tarraconaise à chargement d'amphores Dressel 2–4. *Archaeonautica*, 5.

Dean, B. (2004). *A 3rd Century AD Gallo-Roman Trading Vessel from Guernsey aka The St. Peter Port Wreck or "The Asterix Ship"*. Swansea University [online].

de Camp, L. S. (1963). *The Ancient Engineers*. New York: Doubleday.

Frankopan, P. (2016). *The Silk Roads: A New History of the World*. New York: Alfred A. Knopf.

Katzev, M. L. (1969). The Kyrenia shipwreck. *Expedition Magazine*, [online] 11(2), pp. 55–59.

Katzev, S. (2008). The Kyrenia ship: her recent journey. *Near Eastern Archaeology*, 71 (1–2), pp. 76–81.

Loughton, M. (2014). *The Arverni and Roman Wine: Roman Amphorae from Late Iron Age Sites in the Auvergne (Central France): Chronology, Fabrics and Stamps*. Oxford: Archaeopress.

Marlière, E. (2001). Le tonneau en Gaule romaine. *Gallia*, 58, pp.181–201.

Marlier, S. and Sibella, P. (2002). La Giraglia, a dolia wreck of the 1st century BC from Corsica, France: study of its hull remains. *The International Journal of Nautical Archaeology*, 31(2), pp. 161–171.

McGovern, P. E. (2009). *Uncorking the Past: The Quest for Wine, Beer, and Other Alcoholic Beverages*. Berkeley: University of California Press.

Morris, I. (2010). *Why the West Rules – for Now*. London: Viva.

Pitte, J.-R. (2008). *Bordeaux/Burgundy: A Vintage Rivalry*. Berkeley: University of California Press.

Robb, G. (2013). *The Ancient Paths; Discovering the Lost Map of Celtic Europe*. Picador: London.

Salač, V. (2010). De la vitesse des transports à l'âge du Fer (Translated from Czech to French by G. Pierrevelcin) *Celtes et Germains au 1er s. a.C. en Bohême et en Europe centrale* (n°405/11/0603), la Grantová agentura de République tchèque (GAČR).

Tchernia, A. (1986). Le vin de l'Italie romaine. *Essai d'histoire économique d'après les amphores*. Rome: École française.

Twede, D. (2005). The Cask Age: the technology and history of wooden barrels. *Packaging Technology and Science*, 189(5), pp. 253–264.

Work, H. H. (2014). *Wood, Whiskey and Wine: A History of Barrels*. London: Reaktion.

Websites

European Commission (2017). *EuroStat*. European Commission, Agriculture and Rural Development. www.ec.europa.eu

Plassac villa Gallo-Romaine. (2016). Gironde le département – la villa Gallo-Romaine. www.plassac.gironde.fr

11

WINE PACKAGING SUSTAINABILITY

Recycling and waste

Sustainability

Wine, with its 8,000 year history, "is generally considered by the consumer as a natural, handcrafted product and its historical reputation as a 'green' beverage (in terms of the environmental impact) provided an advantage over most other food products" (Pierpaolo, 2016).

But is it? At the level of the home winemaker or artisanal winery it is probably as close as one can get. However, the largest wineries have become factories, turning out thousands of litres of wine which is being shipped around the world. Are these facilities still 'green', and with large carbon footprints, are they sustainable?

Around the world, regional winery groups are setting standards for their members to reduce their carbon footprints, achieve sustainability and live up to the 'clean, green' image which many customers believe. Typical of the statements towards sustainability, the New Zealand sustainability initiative states, "sustainability means delivering excellent wine to consumers in a way that enables the natural environment, the businesses and the communities involved, to thrive" (New Zealand Wine, 2016). The New Zealand and other regional initiatives cover all aspects of the growing, making and selling processes. Let us briefly examine three to see how they apply directly to the wine vessels; the barrels, tanks, and the packaging for the wine.

California Sustainable Winegrowing Alliance

The mission of the California Sustainable Winegrowing Alliance (CSWA) is for all wineries to achieve the highest standards of sustainable practices by working with each other, their neighbours, their communities and their consumers (California Sustainable Winegrowing Alliance, 2017). Through the setting of performance metrics, and offering workbooks and workshops, the initiative encourages the wineries to produce quality wine while protecting the environment and their people. It encourages the wineries to reach out to the general community, and to continue to support and implement improvements (California Sustainable Winegrowing Alliance, 2017).

Related to the wine vessels, some specific areas towards which the mission statement recommends action are:

- Improving water efficiency, as regards to washing tanks, barrels and winery equipment.
- Conducting a solid waste audit, including the quantity amassed and what is done with the used or damaged barrels, glass bottles, cardboard, paper, capsules, cork, plastic, wood pallets, and other miscellaneous packaging.
- Conducting an energy audit for the winery as well as for the environmental freight costs and logistics of transporting the products to the marketplace, whether it is next door or around the world.
- Based upon the results of the above, making the changes necessary to incorporate the best practices which lead to a more sustainable future.
  (California Sustainable Winegrowing Alliance, 2017)

Conseil Interprofessionnel du Vin de Bordeaux

In 2008, after an exhaustive audit of regional grape farmers and wineries, the Conseil Interprofessionnel du Vin de Bordeaux (CIVB) set a standard to reduce the carbon emissions for all winery activities by 75% by 2050 (Goinere, 2008). An interim progress assessment, carried out in 2013, found that overall the wine sector had achieved a 9% reduction in its greenhouse gas (GHG) emissions (Etcheburu, 2014).

In the audit, and as related to the wine containers, it was found that a significant decrease had been made by reducing the weight of the glass wine bottles – improvements, as noted in Chapter 5 made by the glass manufacturers, towards making the bottles 20% lighter, yet just as durable – and a slight decrease in the use of bottles towards other eco-packaging such as bag-in-box. Nonetheless, the survey found an overall increase in CO_2 emissions in the freight sector, due largely to growth in exports – good for the Bordeaux vintner's pocketbooks but not necessarily for the environment. Within this sector, the trucking industry had made improvements in reducing emissions, however, freight haulage by air and water had not achieved the same advances. Based upon these 2014 findings, the Bordeaux vintners renewed their efforts by setting a five-year goal of reductions of 20% in GHG emissions for energy, renewable energy, and saving water (Etcheburu, 2014).

Sustainable Winegrowing New Zealand

The New Zealand wine industry was one of the first to get on board with sustainable standards for its wineries, developing a plan in 1997 and adopting standards in 2002 (New Zealand Wine, 2016). The vintners who were instrumental in organizing the initiative wanted to satisfy their customers' concerns that the impact on the environment from producing their wines would be minimal, provide a guarantee of quality control, and that the best possible practices would be utilized from the vineyard all the way through to shipping the product to the consumer (New Zealand Wine, 2016).

Recycling various wine containers

Recycling glass

Many towns now have recycling, and programmes to encourage its use for disposing of wine bottles, cardboard from bag-in-box, and plastic and aluminium wine containers. Sadly, still roughly 70% of all waste ends in the landfills (Penn, 2009). Some also ends up on the grounds of our towns, cities and byways as litter from that portion of our population who still do not get the message that litter mars not only the visual landscape, but is destroying some ecosystems in the environment as well. In the United States, for 2013, only 34% of all glass was recovered, and of that total, wine bottles made up 34.5% (Glass Packaging Institute, 2018). The Institute calculates that recycling this total amount of glass is the equivalent of taking 210,000 cars off the road annually. Great, but what happens to the other 2/3 of all the glass used? On the other hand, by 2012, the European Union had achieved a 70% recycling rate, about 25 billion bottles and jars (Morton, 2014).

EXPLORATIONS 11.1
MOUNTAINS OF GLASS

While on a bicycle ride in 2016, west of Melbourne, Australia, I passed through an industrial park. On one side of the cycle track was a huge steel mill. Its furnaces were at one end of the property. At the other end were the piles of scrap metal – wrecked cars, bent pipes and twisted pieces of rebar – all apparently destined as the raw materials, in whole or in part, awaiting to be ground up and melted in the kilns for the company's products. On the other side of the track was a mountain of broken glass. It reminded me of a newer version of the mountain of ancient, broken amphorae I had seen previously in Rome – Mount Testaccio – only not so overgrown.

As I pedalled further along, I began to wonder why, with Melbourne's yellow recycling bins dutifully out on the streets once a week for pickup, was all this glass mounded on this lot, starting to grow weeds? I presumed it was recycled glass from the bins, and thought it was supposed to be sold on to the glass manufacturers to be made into new bottles.

Apparently, I was not the only one questioning this mass of accumulated glass. Reporters for one of Australia's investigative TV shows, *Four Corners*, were also wondering why. Their investigation revealed that the money needed to subsidize the freight costs to ship it to the glass manufacturers were not available (Meldrum-Hanna et al., 2017). The communities pay to get the glass picked up in the recycling bins, but once sorted, there are additional costs to transport it to the glass bottle plants. This money normally comes from the fees which are collected at the general waste sites. Those fees were apparently being diverted to other projects. Thus, the waste companies, who were locked into contracts with the communities, continued to pick up the recycle materials, but were forced to stock pile it as they were not being paid to send the glass on to the kilns (Meldrum-Hanna et al., 2017).

Most of that stockpiled glass was stored in bags under cover from the weather so as not to leech any residuals into the ground (Meldrum-Hanna et al., 2017). This exterior mound that I witnessed was apparently in violation.

The majority of today's wine containers for consumers are glass bottles – about 3.6 billion bottles each year (Penn, 2009). These have a great potential for recycling; glass can be continually reheated with no loss of quality (Bragg, 2016). The used, furnace-ready glass is termed *cullet*. Typically, the amount of cullet utilized in new bottles varies from roughly 33% (Bragg, 2016) to up to 95% (Glass Packing Institute, 2018). Utilizing this cullet, the glass manufacturer reduces the need and costs of obtaining the raw materials – the sand, limestone and soda ash – and the emissions from obtaining, and the energy to melt, those unprocessed items (Glass Packing Institute, 2018). The best cullet comes from those communities in which the glass is recycled separately, such as in much of Germany were glass goes into one of five colour-coded bins – the others being packaging, paper, compost, and trash (McCarthy, 2016) – and especially those where it is delineated by colour – green, brown, or clear.

There are some downsides to using recycled glass, particularly where it is picked up in mixed bins. It is this system that the paper, cardboard, metals and plastics are co-mingled with the glass. During the handling and subsequent sorting, some of the glass gets broken, making colour separation difficult for the smaller pieces. Some of these other materials become mixed in with the glass – such as bits of metal, ceramics, and plastics – leading to impurities in the glass. Additionally, certain types of glass, such as Pyrex baking containers, mirrors, windows and light bulbs, are manufactured using different processes than that used to make wine, beer and food bottles. Mixed in with the cullet, these dissimilar glass materials can create defects in future bottles (Glass Packaging Institute, 2018).

Glass recycling creates other problems for the recyclers. Its weight, as compared to the other recycled products such as cardboard and plastic, adds to increased handling and haulage costs (Flower, 2015). Bits of glass are hard on the sorting equipment, and the infiltration of broken pieces lower the value of the other recycled products. While other products can be formed from recycled glass, such as fibreglass and road-building material, it is often not cost effective for the sorting and subsequent freight to the glass companies which make these products (Flower, 2015)

Plastic containers

It is estimated that Americans use 2.5 million plastic bottles every hour (Brigham Young University-Idaho, 2017), and that 480 billion plastic bottles were sold worldwide in 2016 (Laville and Taylor, 2017). By 2014, unfortunately, only 34% of plastic bottles were recycled, according to the American Chemistry Council (2017). Europe did considerably better: in 2014, 57% were reported being recycled (Petcore Europe, 2015). The data is not broken down by the types of bottles, either for the products they contained nor the type of plastic. Nonetheless, in a manner similar to the recycling of glass, recycling of the PET (polyethylene terephthalate) plastics can reduce the energy use in new plastic production by up to 84% (Brigham Young University-Idaho, 2017).

One of the larger users of wine in plastic bottles are the airlines, primarily the 187-millilitre bottles often provided as wine service in economy class. In 2016, it was estimated that airlines generate in total 5.2 million tonnes of total waste each year (Boyd, 2017), which included those mini bottles. If you have watched the flight attendants pick up the remains of your meal, you may have noticed that little if any gets separated. This is due to a combination of factors: there is little incentive for airlines to recycle, despite dealing with the waste costing them an estimated US $500 million per year (Boyd, 2017). Even for those airlines which separate the items, many airports have yet to organize for recycling; all the waste gets dumped together when the plane is cleaned, as most airports were not designed to provide separate facilities (Farley, 2009). Fortunately, this seems to be changing with London's Gatwick and Heathrow, Madrid's Barajas (Boyd, 2017), Fort Lauderdale/Hollywood's International, Seattle-Tacoma's International and Portland's International among the leaders (Farley, 2009).

Other rationale for the limited amount of airline recycling concerns the spread of infectious diseases from one country to another (Boyd, 2017). However, that might hold for the people who have to sort the items, but not for the end user of the recycled produces as both PET plastic bottles and glass bottles are melted during the re-manufacturing process.

Aluminium cans

Aluminium cans have a 67% recycle rate – higher than other beverage containers (Badenfort, 2017), due in part because companies will pay by weight for the aluminium. In 2015, Australians recycled over two billion aluminium cans (Planet Ark, 2017), while the United States, which consumes some 88 billion cans per year recycled at 64% or 1.6 billion pounds, which equates to approximately 56 billion cans (Aluminum Association, 2015).

For comparison of the three main alternative wine containers, the Owens-Illinois glass company analysed the carbon footprint of 355 millilitre size glass, aluminium and PET plastic containers, in both North America and Europe (Owens-Illinois, 2009).

What jumps out from Table 11.1 below is that the percentage of energy requirements for glass and aluminium are relatively similar for obtaining the raw materials and making the products. The plastic products, however, require significantly more energy to obtain the materials and considerably less for product manufacturing. Nonetheless, as shown in Table 11.2, further down, it is more efficient to recycle plastic bottles. While this is a positive point, as discussed in Chapter 7, the plastic bottle's usefulness as a vessel to contain wine for long periods is still under examination.

The lower figures for the CO_2 in Europe are due to a greater use of refillable bottles and containers, which helps to decrease the overall CO_2 requirements.

Bag-in-box

The cardboard structures which surround the bags can be recycled. The interior bag with its combination of plastics and metal film, has yet to reach the quantity nexus which 1) finds an economical procedure for its recycling, and 2) an end use for the recycled material.

TABLE 11.1 Carbon footprint of glass, aluminium and PET containers by percentage

	North America			Europe		
	Glass	Aluminium	PET	Glass	Aluminium	PET
Raw material extraction & processing	15	32	52	27	29	65
Raw material transport	5	2	2	2	4	1
Production process	75	66	46	67	66	33
Transport of finished goods	5			4	1	

Owens-Illinois, 2009

TABLE 11.2 Carbon footprint by kg/CO_2 for glass, aluminium and PET containers

	North America			Europe		
	Glass	*Aluminium*	*PET*	*Glass*	*Aluminium*	*PET*
Kg/CO_2/ container	0.171	0.401	0.214	0.110	0.122	0.152
Post-consumer content (%)	25	43	2	47	52	2

Owens-Illinois, 2009

The future of recycling

In December 2017, a major shift in recycling occurred. China which had been importing up to half the recyclables from the US and other major countries, announced it will be discontinuing this flow. This change is due in part to the country's own growing rate of trash and recyclables (Profita and Burns, 2017). Without China as an important market for recyclables, significant modifications are expected in how countries process their glass, aluminium, plastic and cardboard. Unfortunately, much will initially become 'trash', added to the landfills, at least in the short term until other onshore or offshore sites can be found to process the glass, plastics and cardboards.

If we are lucky, this major shift could produce some innovations. It is expected that, to help lower the cost and make recycling more efficient, robots will become more common for the sorting processes (Profita and Burns, 2017). Perhaps, this might lead to more capable glass sorting, encouraging increased use of the cullet for the wine bottle manufactures. Hopefully, the cost of adding material to the landfills will encourage more recyclable and refillable containers, and at the very least push countries to be more efficient in collecting, sorting, and then actually processing their recyclables 'in country', rather than shipping overseas (Lasker et al., 2017). As an example, currently in my home town in New Zealand, glass is sorted by colour right at the curb, enabling New Zealand's glass manufacturer to include more cullet because there is less colour mixing.

Wine barrels

There is no formal accounting of all the new wine barrels sold annually by the world's cooperages and barrel suppliers. Nonetheless, based upon adding some estimates to the available statistics (Dekker, 2017), a rough figure of

800,000 each year can be realized. For the used barrel market, accounting for the yearly variations and some deductions for limited market expansion and damaged barrels, roughly this same number are sold, or at least are for sale, each year.

There is now a good market for the used wine barrels; many wineries around the world want to age their wine in barrels, but cannot afford the expense of the new barrels. Previously, most of these barrels were sold winery to winery. Now, as wineries have improved their programmes for maintaining their barrels, a number of négociants-type companies have become involved, leasing the new barrels to wineries, then retrieving the barrels after several years, and reselling the used barrels to other wineries. At the end of the barrels' life, however, they become planters, tables or other furniture. The remainder get burnt or tossed in a landfill.

For the metal hoops, where significant numbers can be salvaged, they are taken to metal recyclers. Most, unfortunately, probably end up in landfill as well. At one point in history, the rare metal hoop was given to, or taken by, indigenous peoples to be made into tools: scrapers, knives, diggers, and the like. The wood, especially of the barrels made from hard woods, would have been burned for cooking or heating fires.

Additional steps wineries are taking to be more sustainable

Over the past ten years, one of the most important achievements towards lowering the overall carbon footprint of packaging wine in 750 ml glass bottles has been the introduction of lightweight bottles. From an average of 500 grams per bottle, the wine bottle manufacturers have developed techniques to lower the weight 18 to 28 per cent; to roughly 300 to 400 grams per bottle style (Waste & Resources Action Programme, 2017). This, subsequently, has saved many hundreds of tons in shipping, with a subsequent carbon reduction.

For example, by 2015 Owens Illinois Australia was offering 21 of its wine bottle products in the lighter format. According to their estimates, this resulted in 5,895 tons less glass being used to manufacture some 502 million wine bottles. By other estimates, in 2013–14, some 256,571 tonnes of glass packaging were diverted from landfill and used to produce new containers (Planet Ark, 2017). Accompanying these product changes is the Returnable Packaging Program, which encourages wholesale and retail customers to return composite and plastic dividers, pallets, and the top frames used to ship the pallets of wine bottles. These items are returned via the existing distribution network (Planet Ark, 2017).

The wineries are also taking specific steps to reduce waste, and ultimately their carbon footprint. Wineries generate waste with their packaging processes and daily operations. The plastic wrap which secures the empty bottles and cardboard, pallets, the wrapping of new barrels, broken bottles from the bottling lines and empty bottles from the tasting rooms, all accumulate, especially in the largest wineries where millions of litres of wine are processed. Encouraged by the sustainable goals for the various wine regions around the world, and the costs of dealing with waste, most have instituted recycling procedures.

Take, for instance, the global wine company, Pernod Ricard Australia, which has enacted operations that have reduced its landfill waste material. By incorporating a Sustainability Packaging Toolkit, all the company's packaging material is to be recyclable (Planet Ark, 2017). To accomplish this goal entails a constant series of staff trainings, and meetings with industry suppliers about how to improve the entire supply chain. Grove Mill Wines, in New Zealand's Marlborough wine region, has switched to lighter bottles (Grove Mill Wines, 2017). This has enabled them to place more wine in each ocean-going container for export, lowering the carbon footprint per case. In 2015, Frog's Leap Wines in California's Napa Valley started placing some of its Cabernet Sauvignon in stainless steel wine kegs for distribution to restaurants and pubs (Frog's Leap Winery, 2017). However, despite these positive actions, as already noted with the European surveys, further effort will be required to meet the various regional sustainability goals.

Individualized containers versus bulk?

As we have seen, recycling is not always the answer. The drink and food industries account for nearly half of all consumer packaging. Elgaaïed-Gambier suggests that consumers "can change their consumption patterns in order to extend products' lifetime, and they can also change their purchasing habits to buy in bulk or to avoid excessively packaged products" (2016).

Applying Elgaaïed-Gambier's proposals towards wine purchases, buying wine in larger containers (1.5 litre bottles), large plastic jugs, or bag-in-box would satisfy the purchase in bulk. There are also systems in some countries – for example *en vrac* in France, or *sfuso* in Italy – in which the consumer brings his or her own container to be filled directly from a tank. The individuals typically arrive with containers in the range of one litre to five

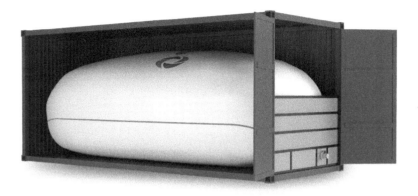

FIGURE 11.1 Wine in bladder in container
Courtesy of Bulk Liquid Solutions, Pvt. Ltd.

litres, small and light enough to transport easily. These containers are re-used over and over, adding to sustainability. Alternatively, as Frog's Leap is doing, wine is being sold in stainless steel kegs by companies to restaurants and bars to be offered on tap; a method that is similar to draft beer. One California company offers wine from a selection of 150 wineries.

Certainly, some of the labelling and adornment on wine vessels could be classified as excessive: a large foil when a small cap atop the cork would do; front and back labels and/or neck labels; and the ultra-heavy, wine bottles in which high-end Chardonnay, Cabernet Sauvignon, or Bordeaux blends. All of these could be reduced or eliminated.

Ideally, we could all have a barrel of wine in our cellar, from which we would fill a pitcher for our evening meal. This, of course, is almost impossible with today's lifestyles, nor practical as we downsize to smaller homes and apartments. What is reasonable, however, is to encourage wineries to place higher quality wine in their bag-in-box offerings. And for the wine industry to embrace some of the bulk distribution systems already noted.

Conclusion

Where are we in the evolution of the various vessels used for wine? It is difficult to tell as the oldest styles of ceramic pots to the most modern stainless steel and glass containers are all, to one degree or another, still in use.

As Tim Flannery notes in his book on the evolutionary changes in North America, "Without the benefit of time as a yardstick it is difficult to

FIGURE 11.2 Stainless steel wine kegs awaiting filling at the headquarters of Free
Flow Wines, Napa, California
Courtesy of Free Flow Wines

distinguish dead-ends-to-be from enduring strategies" (2001), or in our case, the vessels which will ultimately come to be utilized to store, age, and transport wine.

What factors need to be changed to discourage individualized packaging and encourage more bulk, biodegradable packaging? What environmental factors of shipping wine in heavy, individualized containers will come into play? With so many regions and countries now growing their own grapes and producing their own wine, how much wine will continue to be shipped across the globe? Will barrels, or some similar bulk container, make a comeback? And finally, will we improve our recycling, up to 90 or 100%?

What could a future ideal container encompass? Could it be a combination of all the previous ones? Could it contain a large quantity of wine as does a barrel, be completely inert and recyclable as is glass, be relatively easy on the environment to manufacture as are the ceramic vessels, and be light weight for ease of shipping and pouring? Hopefully, the packaging developers are attempting to incorporate some of the advantages of the historic containers as they look for new materials and styles. This is all food, or perhaps a liquid to accompany the food, for thought.

References

Boyd, O. (2017). The ridiculous story of airline food and why so much ends up in landfills. *The Guardian*, [online] 1 April 2017.

Badenfort, K. (2017). What cans can do for wine. *Wine Industry Advisor*, [online] 16 February 2017.

Bragg, L. (2016). Industry leaders join forces to strengthen glass recycling. *Ceramic Industry*, [online] August 2016, p. 25.

Dekker, A. (2017). Moderate growth in 2016 for French cooperages. *Fédération des Tonneliers de France*, [online] 30 June 2017.

Elgaaïed-Gambier, L. (2016). Who buys overpackaged grocery products and why? Understanding consumers' reactions to overpackaging in the food sector. *Journal of Business Ethics*, [online] 135(4) pp. 683–698.

Etcheburu, A. (2014). Bilan carbone de la filière des vins de Bordeaux. *Aquitaine Online*, [online] 29 January 2014.

Farley, D. (2009). Airlines and recycling: The not-so-green skies. *Scientific America*, [online] 1 September 2009.

Flannery, T. (2001). *The Eternal Frontier: An Ecological History of North America and its People*. New York: Atlantic Monthly Press.

Flower, W. (2015). Focusing on the economics of glass recycling. *Waste360*, [online] 1 October 2015.

Goinere, C. (2008). La filière des vins de Bordeaux fait son bilan carbone. *L'Usine Nouvelle*, [online] 20 November 2008.

Lasker, P., Goloubeva, J. and Birtles, B. (2017). China's ban on foreign rubbish leaves Australian recycling industry eyeing opportunities. *ABC News* (Australia), [online] 10 December 2017.

Laville, S. and Taylor, M. (2017). A million bottles a minute: World's plastic binge 'as dangerous as climate change'. *The Guardian*, [online] 28 June 2017.

McCarthy, N. (2016). The countries winning the recycling race [Infographic]. *Forbes*, [online] 4 March 2016.

Meldrum-Hanna, C., Davies, A., and Richards, D. (2017). Recycling companies stockpiling thousands of tonnes of glass as cheap imports leave market in crisis. *ABC (Australia) Four Corners*, [online] 5 September 2017.

Morton, A. (2014). EUROPE: EU ramps up glass recycling rate – figures. *Just Drinks*, [online] 4 April 2014.

Penn, C. (2009). Packaging: wine bottle recycling to wash and reuse bottles in California. *Wine Business Monthly*, [online] August 2009.

Pierpaolo, P. (2016). *Sustainability, Environment, Innovation and Marketing: The Wine Industry Challenge*. Trieste: MIB Trieste School of Management, [online] pp. 1–28.

Profita, C. and Burns, J. (2017). Recycling chaos in U.S. as China bans 'foreign waste'. *NPR Radio*, [online] 9 December 2017.

Websites

AluminumAssociation. (2015). The Aluminum Association. www.aluminum.org

American Chemistry Council. (2017). Plastics recycling: two and a half decades of growth and momentum. www.plastics.americanchemistry.com

Brigham Young University-Idaho. (2017). University operations, sustainability. https://www.byui.edu/university-operations/facilities-management/recycling-and-sustainability/recycling-statistics

California Sustainable Winegrowing Alliance. (2017). www.sustainablewinegrowing.org

Frog' Leap Winery. (2017). www.frogsleap.com

Glass Packaging Institute. (2018). www.gpi.org

Grove Mill Wines. (2017). www.grovemill.co.nz

New Zealand Wine. (2016). www.nzwine.com

Owens-Illinois. (2009). Owens-Illinois Glass Company, Life Cycle Assessment (carbon footprint) of glass, aluminum and plastic containers. www.o-i.com

PetcoreEurope. (2015). European PET (polyethylene terephthalate) industry association. www.petcore-europe.org.

Planet Ark. (2017). www.recyclingweek.planetark.org

Waste & Resources Action Programme. (2017). Case study. Lightweight wine bottles: less is more. www.wrap.org.uk/retail

INDEX